面向"十三五"高等职业教育精品规划教材

汽车商务英语

主　编　孟思聪　陆红宏　马天博
副主编　杨　娜　孙丽敏　王　扬
参　编　闫冬梅　李楠舟　毕　然
　　　　朱艳丽　姜吉光
主　审　姜吉光

北京理工大学出版社
BEIJING INSTITUTE OF TECHNOLOGY PRESS

版权专有 侵权必究

图书在版编目（CIP）数据

汽车商务英语/孟思聪，陆红宏，马天博主编. —北京：北京理工大学出版社，2016.6（2020.1重印）

ISBN 978-7-5682-2470-3

Ⅰ. ①汽…　Ⅱ. ①孟…②陆…③马…　Ⅲ. ①汽车–商务–英语–教材　Ⅳ. ①H31

中国版本图书馆 CIP 数据核字（2016）第 139656 号

出版发行 /	北京理工大学出版社有限责任公司
社　　址 /	北京市海淀区中关村南大街 5 号
邮　　编 /	100081
电　　话 /	（010）68914775（总编室）
	（010）82562903（教材售后服务热线）
	（010）68948351（其他图书服务热线）
网　　址 /	http://www.bitpress.com.cn
经　　销 /	全国各地新华书店
印　　刷 /	三河市天利华印刷装订有限公司
开　　本 /	787 毫米×1092 毫米　1/16
印　　张 /	15.5
字　　数 /	306 千字
版　　次 /	2016 年 6 月第 1 版　2020 年 1 月第 3 次印刷
定　　价 /	37.00 元

责任编辑 / 梁铜华
文案编辑 / 梁铜华
责任校对 / 周瑞红
责任印制 / 马振武

图书出现印装质量问题，请拨打售后服务热线，本社负责调换

前 言
PREFACE

结合当今汽车前、后市场对高技能型人才的需求，依据国家高等职业院校培养汽车前、后市场人才的新型培养方案，长春职业技术学院汽车专业英语组与长春理工大学联合推出一本适合新型汽车市场人才的商务英语教材。

本教材共设6个单元，分别是汽车文化、汽车英文配置单的认知、最新车型的产品知识介绍、汽车使用说明书的解读、汽车销售流程用语及礼仪方面的英文讲解、汽车后市场以二手车及汽车保险为主的衍生业务。

这本书全部使用最新国外资料，涉及的车型都是最新款车型。我们通过文化长廊让学习者了解汽车发展史及世界著名的汽车品牌，通过官网上的最新车型向学习者呈现英文配置单的应用，通过销售技巧中的FAB原则向学习者展示营销人员的基本岗位技能及新款车的相关产品知识，通过路虎揽胜运动版客户使用手册教会学习者如何应用英语知识解读全英版资料，通过了解汽车4S店销售人员的岗位技能学习如何用流利的英语及标准的礼仪接待外籍购车客户，通过学习衍生业务让学习者了解国内外二手车市场现状及汽车保险业务的区别。

本教材的编写离不开长春职业技术学院汽车学院专业英语课程组的努力，同时感谢长春理工大学姜吉光老师为此次编写提供了大量的原版资料，并承担本教材的主审。本教材主编有孟思聪、陆红宏、马天博；副主编有杨娜、孙丽敏、王扬；参编人员有闫冬梅、李楠舟、毕然、朱艳丽、姜吉光。本教材在编写过程中，参考引用了大量的原版资料，在此对文献的原作者表示诚挚的感谢。

限于编者水平限制，书中的缺点及不足在所难免，恳请广大师生和读者批评指正。

目录
CONTENTS

Unit 1
Automobile Culture

Learning Objectives ········· 1
Warm Up ········· 1
New Lesson ········· 3
Exercises ········· 36

Unit 2
Automobile Specifications Reading

Learning Objectives ········· 42
Warm Up ········· 42
New Lesson ········· 44
Exercises ········· 52

Unit 3
Automobile Product Introduction

Learning Objectives ········· 58
Warm Up ········· 58
FAB Statements ········· 59
New Lesson ········· 59
Exercises ········· 66

Unit 4
Automobile Manual Reading

Learning Objectives ··· 70
Warm Up ··· 70
New Lesson ··· 71
Exercises ··· 83

Unit 5
Sales Procedure

Learning Objectives ··· 88
Warm Up ··· 88
New Lesson ··· 89
Exercises ··· 104

Unit 6
Derived Businesses

Learning Objectives ··· 111
Warm Up ··· 111
New Lesson ··· 112
Exercises ··· 118

Notes

Translations

Answers

Words

Phrases

References

Unit 1

Automobile Culture

 Learning Objectives

After learning this unit, you should be able to:
- grasp the variable classifications of vehicles.
- know the famous automobile brands of different countries, the meanings of logos and classic models.

 Warm Up

There are countless predecessors that are full of intelligence and ideals on the way to the automobile birth. They witnessed the birth of the first automobile in the world by their own inventions. Please guess the following persons who made significant contributions to the birth of the automobile and the important inventions according to the pictures.

In 1765, British inventor (　　　　　) (See Fig. 1-1) successfully designed and developed the innovative (　　　　　) (See Fig. 1-2).

Fig. 1-1　James Watt

Fig. 1-2　A Steam Engine

In 1769, Nicholas Cournot, a French army engineer, developed the first wholly self-propelled (　　　　　) (See Fig. 1-3). This was a milestone in the history of the automobile and the start of the era of mechanically driven vehicles.

Fig. 1-3　The First Wholly Self-Propelled Steam Vehicle

In 1866, (　　　　　), a German engineer, successfully created a (　　　　　), known as the Otto internal combustion engine (See Fig. 1-4). Later, people named the four-stroke cycle "Otto cycle."

Fig. 1-4　Nikolaus Otto and His Four-Stroke Gasoline Internal Combustion Engine

In 1897, (　　　　　) (See Fig. 1-5) successfully produced the first diesel engine (See Fig. 1-6).

Fig. 1-5　Rudolf Diesel　　　　Fig. 1-6　The First Diesel Engine

On January 29, 1886, German engineer (   ) (See Fig. 1-7) trailed out the first three-wheeled automobile (See Fig. 1-8), granted with a certificate of Automobile Patent. That date was remembered as **the birthday of automobiles**. Carl Benz was dubbed as the **"father of the automobile."**

 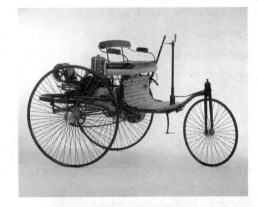

Fig. 1-7　Carl Benz　　　　　　　Fig. 1-8　Benz Patent-Motorwagen

In August 1885, (   ) (See Fig. 1-9) developed a "two-wheeled riding car." This was the first motorcycle in the world. That's why Daimler was known as the "father of motorcycles." In August 1886, Daimler produced the first four-wheel automobile in the world (See Fig. 1-10).

 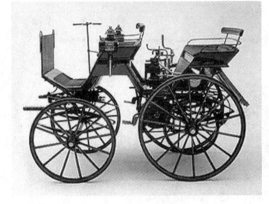

Fig. 1-9　Gottlieb Daimler　　　　Fig. 1-10　The First Four-Wheel Automobile

New Lesson

Part One　Automobiles Classification

In 1886, the first gasoline powered automobile was invented by Carl Benz, announcing the end of the era of horse-drawn vehicles and ushering in the era of automobiles. The invention of the automobile was a milestone in the history of human transportation. Cars have not only changed people's way of transportation and concept of time and space, but also affected their way of life and work, carrying forward the modern civilization of the human society.

Nowadays, automobiles have been an integral part of life. First of all, let's talk about the different classifications of automobiles to know them thoroughly.

I. Classification by Vehicle Uses

(1) Passenger Cars: manufactured for the transportation of passengers, baggage and goods, mainly including three types—the sedan, limousine and station wagon (See Fig. 1-11 to Fig. 1-13).

Fig. 1-11　A Benz Passenger Car　　　　　Fig. 1-12　A Volvo Passenger Car

(2) Roadster: light-weight and high-speed, designed for sports and entertainment (See Fig. 1-14).

Fig. 1-13　A Ford Passenger Car　　　　　Fig. 1-14　A Lamborghini Sports Car

(3) Multipurpose Passenger Cars: designed with a box-type and open (or can be opened) body, for the convenience of goods transportation (See Fig. 1-15 and Fig. 1-16).

Fig. 1-15　A Mazda Multipurpose Passenger Car　　　Fig. 1-16　A Ford Multipurpose Passenger Car

(4) Motor Trucks: primarily designed and manufactured for the transportation of goods (See Fig. 1-17 and Fig. 1-18).

Fig. 1-17　A Motor Truck (I)　　　　　　Fig. 1-18　A Motor Truck (II)

(5) Buses: primarily designed and manufactured for the transportation of passengers and baggage, each equipped with over 10 seats including the driver's seat (See Fig. 1-19 and Fig. 1-20).

Fig. 1-19　A Bus (I)　　　　　　Fig. 1-20　A Bus (II)

(6) Special Purpose Vehicles: an ordinary car installed with a special car body in the chassis for a particular purpose　(See Fig. 1-21 and Fig. 1-22).

Fig. 1-21　A Special Purpose Vehicle (I)　　　　　　Fig. 1-22　A Special Purpose Vehicle (II)

(7) Special Vehicles: equipped with special devices for particular purposes, including sweepers, medical vehicles, fire trucks, and concrete mixers, as well as agricultural work vehicles, sports cars and racing cars (See Fig. 1-23 to Fig. 1-28).

Fig. 1-23　A Police Car

Fig. 1-24　A Fire Truck

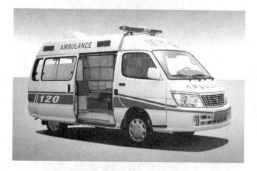

Fig. 1-25　An Ambulance

Fig. 1-26　A Concrete Mixer

Fig. 1-27　A Sweeper

Fig. 1-28　A Tractor

II. Classification by Design Concept

(1) SUVs (Sport Utility Vehicles): The SUV has high ground clearance and combines the comfortable space of a sedan and the off-road capacity of a station wagon (See Fig. 1-29 and Fig. 1-30).

Fig. 1-29　A BMW X6

Fig. 1-30　A Porsche Cayenne

(2) CRVs (City Recreation Vehicles): The CRV is a series of Honda, known as Dongfeng Honda CRVs in China (See Fig. 1-31).

(3) SRVs (Small Recreation Vehicles): SRVs are mostly two-door models, such as Geely Haoqing SRVs (See Fig. 1-32).

Fig. 1-31　A Honda CRV　　　　　　　　Fig. 1-32　A Geely Haoqing SRV

(4) The RAV derives from a small sports car model of Toyota RAV4. As explained by Toyota, RAV represents "Recreation" "Activity" and "Vehicle," while "4" indicates the four-wheel drive (See Fig. 1-33).

(5) The HRV derives from the Excelle HRV model of Shanghai General Model, an innovative car design concept that embodies "Healthy" "Recreation" and "Vigorous." (See Fig. 1-34)

Fig. 1-33　A Toyota RAV4　　　　　　　　Fig. 1-34　A Buick Excelle HRV

(6) MPVs (Multi-Purpose Vehicles or Mini Passenger Vans) integrate the capacities of sedans, wagons and vans. Every seat in the car is adjustable, making it possible for a variety of combinations. With the recent trend toward smaller MPVs, there emerges the S-MPV (Small MPV) characterized by a compact body with 5-7 seats (See Fig. 1-35 and Fig. 1-36).

Fig. 1-35　A Dongfeng Honda Elysion　　　　　　　　Fig. 1-36　A Buick GL8

(7) CUVs (Car-Based Utility Vehicles) are car-based utility vehicles that combine the characteristics of the sedan, MPV and SUV, also known as Crossover (See Fig. 1-37 and Fig. 1-38).

Fig. 1-37　A Changcheng Haval CUV

Fig. 1-38　A Mitsubishi Outlander

(8) NCVs (New Concept Vehicles) are chassis-based vehicles that integrate the comfortable space of sedans and the off-road capacity of SUVs (See Fig. 1-39).

Fig. 1-39　A Chery Tiggo 5

(9) RVs (Recreation Vehicles) are vehicles for entertainment, leisure and travelling. The RV concept was first raised in Japan. In addition to sedans and sports cars, RVs include all lightweight passenger cars, such as MPVs, SUVs, CUVs, etc.

The New National Standards for Automobile Classification has taken into effect since March 2002. According to vehicle uses, the New Standards establishes the concept of passenger cars and commercial vehicles, and makes huge changes in the classification of cars, solving the conflicts between management and classification and making itself closer to national standards.

A. Cars
(a) Passenger Cars
(b) Commercial Vehicles
B. Trailer

Part Two　The Evolution of Automobile Appearance

Since they were developed over a century ago, automobiles have had earth-shaking changes in the aspects of body modeling, power, chassis and electronic equipment. And the evolution of automotive appearance is the most characteristic and visual (See Fig. 1-40).

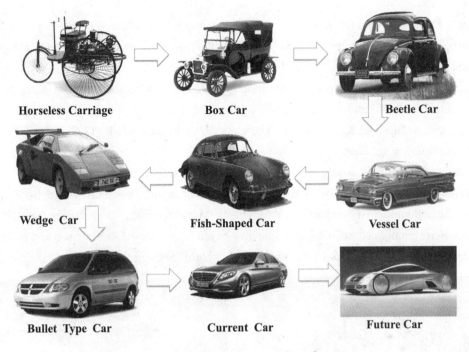

Fig. 1-40 Automobile Appearance Evolution Chart

Part Three Introduction of Automobile Companies and Brands

I. German Automobile Companies and Brands

1. Mercedes-Benz

The German automobile company Mercedes-Benz is among the top ten biggest automobile companies and the most famous bus and heavy truck manufacturer in the world.

Mercedes-Benz was founded in 1926 upon the merger of two automobile companies Benz & Cie and Daimler Motoren Gesellschaft and is now headquartered in Stuttgart, Germany. Benz & Cie was founded by Carl Benz in 1883, and Daimler Motoren Gesellschaft by Gottlieb Daimler in 1890.

After the merger of Benz and Daimler in 1926, car logos of both companies became integrated. The following chart shows the evolution of Benz's logo (See Fig. 1-41).

Fig. 1-41 Mercedes-Benz Logo Evolution

The logo of Benz cars resembles a simplified steering wheel, a three-pointed star encompassed by an annular ring. The three-pointed star stands for the all-round development of the company for the armed services.

Daimler-Benz cars are classified by four grades. A-Class represents mini cars, "C-Class" compact cars, "E-Class" mid-size cars, and "S-Class" limousines. There are a wide range of sports car series, such as SLK, CLK, SL and CL. There are SUVs which include "G-Class"and "M-Class," and "V-Class" utility vehicles.

Daimler-Benz brands mainly include Mercedes-Benz, Maybach, Smart and the like.

Maybach logo (See Fig. 1-42) consists of two intersecting "M" surrounded by a spherical triangle. The double "M" represents "Maybach Manufacturing." On November 19, 2014, Mercedes-Benz announced in Guangzhou the new brand Mercedes-Benz Maybach and unveiled the first Mercedes-Benz Maybach S-Class vehicle to the world (See Fig. 1-43).

Fig. 1-42　Maybach Logo

Fig. 1-43　Maybach 62 S

Smart is the cooperation outcome of the German car manufacturer Mercedes-Benz and the Swiss watch giant Swatch. In SMART, S represents Swatch, M Mercedes-Benz, ART the literal meaning of "art" (See Fig. 1-44). This car line represents the art of cooperation between Swatch and Mercedes-Benz, while "smart" in English also indicates intelligence and quick wit, in line with the design concept of Smart Company. The compact shape, together with smart and user-friendly control design, makes the model of "smart" series look like a clever big toy (See Fig. 1-45).

Fig. 1-44　Smart Logo　　　　　　　　　　Fig. 1-45　2015 Smart Fortwo 1.0 L

2. Audi

Audi, a developer and manufacturer of international high-quality automobiles, is now a subsidiary of Volkswagen.

In 1932, Audi began to use four interlinked rings that make up the Audi badge today, representing the four brands of the Audi Union AG-Audi, DKW, Horch and Wanderer. Every ring represents a company of the Union. The four rings share the same size and interlink in parallel, signifying the equal position among the four brand companies and the unshakable alliance among them.

Now the product lines of Audi mainly include Q3, Q5, Q7 (SUV), R series, convertibles, sporty cars, etc. The A series are the leading models of Audi, among which A3, A4, A6 and A8 are the most sought-after models and are classified by A-, B-, C- and D-class, rivaled by BMW 1,3,5,7 series and Mercedes-Benz B-, C-, E-, S-class. Audi sedans and MPV models all begin with the first letter of Audi-A. The larger the number behind A, the higher the price (See Fig. 1-46 to Fig. 1-49).

Fig. 1-46   An Audi Q3

Fig. 1-47   An Audi Q5

Fig. 1-48   An Audi Q7

Fig. 1-49   An Audi R8

A1 is a compact hatchback car (including the five-door sportback model, three-door model and convertible model) (See Fig. 1-50).

A2 is a compact MPV-styled supermini car (See Fig. 1-51).

Fig. 1-50　An Audi A1

Fig. 1-51　An Audi A2

A3 is also a compact MPV-styled supermini car (See Fig. 1-52).

A4 is a sporty car (See Fig. 1-53).

Fig. 1-52　An Audi A3

Fig. 1-53　An Audi A4

A5 is a coupe model (See Fig. 1-54).

A6 (A6 L) is an executive car (See Fig. 1-55).

Fig. 1-54　An Audi A5

Fig. 1-55　An Audi A6

A7 is a large luxury sports car (See Fig. 1-56).

A8 (A8 L) is a large executive car (See Fig. 1-57).

Fig. 1-56 An Audi A7   Fig. 1-57 An Audi A8

S lines are based on high performance of A series model (See Fig. 1-58), rivaled by BMW 135i, 335i, 550i and other top low-emission BMW models.

RS lines are based on the top-notch car performance of A series (See Fig. 1-59).

Fig. 1-58 A 2015 Audi S8 Plus   Fig. 1-59 A 2016 RS7 Sportback Gain

3. BMW

BMW, an automobile company founded in March 1916 by an aircraft engine manufacturer and formerly known as Rapp Motorenwerke but later changed to Bayerische Motoren Werke. In 1918, the company was renamed as BMW.

BMW is the acronym of Bayerische Motoren Werke. BMW produces sports cars, sedans, motorcycles and other products, famously known as one of the best-selling automakers in the world.

BMW adopts the prototype of double circles (inside and outside) for its logo badge and print "BMW" in between the inside and outside rings (See Fig. 1-60). Within the inner circle are the blue and white panels, representing a blue sky, white cloud and a rotating propeller and indicating the long history of BMW AG. This trademark logo signifies the prominent role of BMW AG in aero-engine technology in the past and embodies the company's consistent goal and its ever changing new look.

BMW owns three brands, namely BMW, MINI and Rolls-Royce.

Fig. 1-60 BMW Logo

With a wide range from mini cars to top-notch luxury cars, these brands share a big slice in different car segments, making BMW the whole's sole manufacturer exclusively specializing in luxury cars and motorcycles (See Fig. 1-61 to Fig. 1-64).

Fig. 1-61   MINI Logo   Fig. 1-62   Rolls Royce Logo

Fig. 1-63   A Mini Countryman   Fig. 1-64   A Rolls-Royce Phantom 6.7 Standard

BMW product lines include 1, 2, 3, 4, 5, 6, 7, 8 (discontinued), i, M, X, and Z series. Among them, 1 Series is a mini sedan, 2 Series is the sports wagon and sports car, 3 Series is a sedan or wagon, 4 Series is a mid-size sedan (including convertible), 5 Series is a mid- or large-sized cars, 6 Series is a mid- or large-sized sedan (including convertible), 7 Series is a luxury Class-D car, i Series is a BMW concept car without mass production, M Series is a high-performance sports car version, X Series is a specific BMW SUV model, and Z Series is an entry-level sports car (See Fig. 1-65 to Fig. 1-76).

Fig. 1-65   A BMW 1 Sery   Fig. 1-66   A BMW 2 Sery Sports Car

Fig. 1-67   A BMW 3 Sery

Fig. 1-68   A BMW 4 Sery

Fig. 1-69   A BMW 5 Sery

Fig. 1-70   A BMW 6 Sery

Fig. 1-71   A BMW 7 Sery

Fig. 1-72   A BMW X6

Fig. 1-73   A BMW i8

Fig. 1-74   A BMW Z4

Fig. 1-75　A BMW M6

Fig. 1-76　A BMW 1 Sery Sports Wagon

4. Volkswagen

On March 28, 1937, Ferdinand Porsche (See Fig. 1-77) founded the Volkswagen company with the support of Mercedes-Benz and renamed it as "Volkswagenwerk GmbH." Volks Wagenwerk (VW) is the largest and youngest German automaker and an international corporation group, as one of the world's leading car manufacturers and the largest European car producer (See Fig. 1-78).

Fig. 1-77　Ferdinand Porsche

Fig. 1-78　Volkswagen Logo

Volks Wagenwerk means "people's car" in German. Its trademark logo is formed by the superimposition of initial letters of "Volks Wagenwerk"—V and W, signifying the "win-win-win" goal of the company and its products.

There is a wide range of Volkswagen models, such as Beetle, Golf, Jetta, Passat, Magotan, CC, Phaeton, Santana, Polo, Vento, Caravelle and so on. Volks Wagenwerk Limited is a member of Volkswagen Group. Other group members include: Audi, Neoplan, Seat, Skoda, Bentley, Bugatti, Lamborghini, Porsche, Ducati Motorcycle and Man Truck (See Fig. 1-79 to Fig. 1-90).

Fig. 1-79　A Bettle

Fig. 1-80　A Passat

Fig. 1-81　A Magotan

Fig. 1-82　A Phaeton

Fig. 1-83　Seat Logo

Fig. 1-84　Skoda Logo

Fig. 1-85　A Seat IBE Electrical Concept Vehicle

Fig. 1-86　A Skoda Scout

Fig. 1-87　Bentley Logo

Fig. 1-88　Bugatti Logo

Fig. 1-89　A Bentley Bentayga

Fig. 1-90　A Bugatti Veyron

II. American Automobile Companies and Brands

1. Ford Motor Company

Ford Motor Company, one of the world's largest automakers, was founded in 1903 by Henry Ford (See Fig. 1-91). The logo of Ford cars is printed with the "Ford" script, white letters on a blue background. Since the founder Henry Ford was a lover of small animals, logo designers shaped the Ford script into a rabbit-like pattern. In 1908, Ford Motor Company produced the world's first car for ordinary people—Ford T-shape Car (See Fig. 1-92), kicking off the automobile industry revolution throughout the world. In 1913, Ford Motor Company developed the world's first assembly line. Mr. Henry Ford is known as the man who "put the world on wheels."

At present, Ford Motor Company owns brands including Ford, Lincoln, Mercury, Aston Martin, Jaguar, Mazda, Volvo and Land Rover. Among them, Jaguar and Land Rover have been sold to the Indian Tata Group; Mazda shares belonging to Ford have declined; Volvo has been sold to Geely Group; Aston Martin has also been sold. Mercury series have been ceased as well (See Fig. 1-93 to Fig. 1-98).

> You can't build a reputation on what you're going to do.
>
> —Henry Ford

Fig. 1-91　Henry Ford

Fig. 1-92　Henry Ford and the First T-shape Car

Fig. 1-93　Ford Logo　　　　Fig. 1-94　Lincoln Logo

Fig. 1-95　A Ford Kuga　　　　Fig. 1-96　A Lincoln MKX

Fig. 1-97　A Ford Mondeo　　　　Fig. 1-98　A Lincoln MKZ

2. General Motors Company

General Motors Company, originally the Buick Motor Company, was founded by David Buick (See Fig. 1-99) in 1907, which was later acquired by the largest American manufacturer of horse-drawn vehicles Durant-Dort Carriage Company in 1908. William C. Durant (See Fig. 1-100) became the general manager of Buick and introduced the C-model car (See Fig. 1-101).

Fig. 1-99　David Buick　　　　Fig. 1-100　William C. Durant

Fig. 1-101 A Buick C-Model Car

In 1908, Buick Motor Company became a leading auto manufacturer in the United States. Durant founded an auto holding company General Motors upon Buick and Olds and merged another two auto companies, Oakland Motor Company and the Cadillac Automobile Company, in 1909.

The GM logo (See Fig. 1-102) consists of the initial letters of the first two words of "General Motors Corporation."

The company has been producing and selling Chevrolet, Buick, GMC, Cadillac, Bao Chun, Houghton, Isuzu, Jiefang, Opel, Vauxhall and Wuling series and relevant services (See Fig. 1-103 to Fig. 1-110). Currently, a full range of models under GM brands are sold in more than 120 countries and regions, including electric cars, mini cars, heavy-duty full-size trucks, compact cars and convertibles.

Fig. 1-102 General Motor Logo

Fig. 1-103 Chevrolet Logo

Fig. 1-104 Buick Logo

Fig. 1-105 A Chevrolet Camaro

Fig. 1-106 A Buick Envision

Fig. 1-107　GMC Logo

Fig. 1-108　Cadillac Logo

Fig. 1-109　A GMC SAVANA

Fig. 1-110　A Cadillac Escalade

3. Chrysler Corporation

The Chrysler Corporation, as the third largest American automotive corporation, was founded in 1925 by Walter Chrysler (See Fig. 1-111). Headquartered in Detroit, the company is a multinational corporation that owns subsidiaries in many countries overseas.

Chrysler's logo (See Fig. 1-112) is a pentastar, like an honored pentastar medal, a symbolic representation of Chrysler workers' ambition. This five-point star within a pentagon has five angles with each "slice" representing Asia, Africa, Europe, America and Australia respectively, and also means that Chrysler has its vehicles sold throughout five continents.

Fig. 1-111　Walter Chrysler

Fig. 1-112　Chrysler Corporation Logo

The Chrysler Corporation has the Dodge Sedan Division, Downwind Sedan Division, Chrysler Sedan Division, Dodge Truck Division and Spare Parts Division and so on (See Fig. 1-113 to Fig. 1-116). In 1998, Chrysler and Mercedes-Bens announced a cooperation merger, forming the world's another largest automobile group. Now, Chrysler and Mercedes-Benz co-own brands such as Mercedes-Benz, Chrysler, Jeep, Mitsubishi, Maybach and so on.

Fig. 1-113 Chrysler Logo

Fig. 1-114 Dodge Logo

Fig. 1-115 A Chrysler 300 C

Fig. 1-116 A Dodge JCUV

III. Japanese Automobile Companies and Brands

1. Toyota Motor Corporation

Toyota was started in 1933 by Kiichiro Toyota (See Fig. 1-117) as a division of Toyota Automatic Loom Works devoted to the production of automobiles. On August 28, 1937, Toyota Motor Company was officially established as an independent company. On July 1, 1982, Toyota Motor Company and Toyota Motor Sales merged into one company, Toyota Motor Corporation, headquartered in Toyota, Aichi, Japan.

In the late 1980 s, the logo of Toyota Motor Corporation was changed into a three-oval pattern (See Fig.1-118). The three ovals are craftily combined to symbolize the close link and mutual trust between users and Toyota. The big oval in the logo represents the earth, within which another two ovals are vertically combined to form a T-shape, the initial of TOYOTA, which represents the Toyota Motor Corporation. The logo means that Toyota Motor Corporation is looking forward to the future with confidence and that Toyota places a great importance on technology and innovation.

Fig. 1-117 Kiichiro Toyota

Fig. 1-118 Toyota Logo

Toyota brand models include Crown, Corolla, Reiz, Prisu, Prado, RAV 4, Previa, Land Cruiser, Vios, Coaster, FJ Cruiser, Highlander, Yaris and so on (See Fig. 1-119 to Fig. 1-126).

Fig. 1-119　A Toyota Crown

Fig. 1-120　A Toyota Corolla

Fig. 1-121　A Toyota Reiz

Fig. 1-122　A Toyota Prisu

Fig. 1-123　A Toyota Prado

Fig. 1-124　A Toyota RAV 4

Fig. 1-125　A Toyota Highlander

Fig. 1-126　A Toyota Landcruiser

Lexus: Initially translated as Lingzhi in Chinese, Lexus was a division branched out of Toyota Motor Corporation in 1989 for luxury car sales abroad. Lexus sounds like the English word "luxury" and inspires a strong association with luxury cars.

The Lexus logo consists of graphics and words. The initial L of "Lexus" is embedded in an oval. The oval represents the earth and indicates the worldwide penetration of Lexus (See Fig. 1-127 and Fig. 1-128).

Fig. 1-127　Lexus Logo　　　　　　　　　　Fig. 1-128　A Lexus LX570

2. Honda Motor Company

Honda Motor Company, formally known as Honda Technical Research Institute, was established by Soichiro Honda (See Fig. 1-129) in 1948. As the world's largest motorcycle manufacturer, the company began to produce automobiles in 1962. Its production and scale was among the top 10 list in the world. Headquartered in Tokyo, Japan, the company has established branch companies in the United States, Asian countries and the United Kingdom.

"H" in the logo is the first letter of "Honda" (See Fig. 1-130). The logo represents for the youth, developed technology and original design of Honda Motor Company.

Honda Motor Company possesses two major brands, Honda and Acura (See Fig. 1-131 to Fig. 1-136).

Fig. 1-129　Soichiro Honda　　　　　　　　Fig. 1-130　Honda Logo

Fig. 1-131　A Honda Accord

Fig. 1-132　A Honda Civic

Fig. 1-133　A Honda CR-V

Fig. 1-134　A Honda Odyssey

Fig. 1-135　Acura Logo

Fig. 1-136　An Acura MDX

Honda models mainly include Accord, Civic, City, Odyssey, Fit, CR-V and so on.

3. Nissan Motor Company

Nissan Motor Company was developed from Kwaishinsha Motorcar Works and Tobata Casting. In 1933, Tobata Casting and Nihon Sangyo established an automobile manufacturer that was renamed as Nissan Motor Company in 1934. NISSAN is the abbreviation for Nihon Sangyo.

The circle on the logo (See Fig. 1-137) represents the Sun, while the "Nissan" script lies across the circle. The whole pattern signifies the pursuit for "the tomorrow of human beings and cars."

Fig. 1-137　Nissan Logo

Nissan models mainly include Versa, SUNNY, Livina, Qashqai, TEANA, CEFIRO, and CEDRIC, etc (See Fig. 1-138 and Fig. 1-139).

Fig. 1-138 A Nissan TEANA

Fig. 1-139 A Nissan Qashqai

Infiniti: "Nissan technology and Toyota sales" are leading in the auto industry. Infiniti is the luxury brand of Japanese cars. The logo of Infiniti is a "road leading to infinity." The elliptical curve is a symbol of endless expansion and an emblem of the "whole world." The two straight lines represent the road leading to infinity, a symbol of endless development and an emblem of relentless pursuit of Infiniti people (See Fig. 1-140 and Fig. 1-141).

Fig. 1-140 Infiniti Logo

Fig. 1-141 An Infiniti QX70

IV. South Korean Automobile Companies and Brands

1. Kia Motors Corporation

Kia Motors Corporation (KMC) is South Korea's oldest manufacturer of motor vehicles. Founded in December 1944, it was in the name of Kyungsung Precision Industry. In March 1952, the company produced the first bicycle in South Korea and changed its name to Kia Motors Corporation.

The name "Kia" derives from the Sino-Korean words *ki* (to come out) and *a* (stands for Asia), so it is literally translated as "arising or coming up out of Asia," which reflects the great ambition of Kia to arise out of Asia and advance to the world.

The old logo of Kia Motors Corporation consists of a white oval, a red background and "KIA" in black, while the new logo is comprised of a red oval, a white background and "KIA" in red, giving people a refreshing feeling. The English words "KIA" in the logo resemble a flying eagle, signifying the company stretching its wings like an eagle (See Fig. 1-142).

Peter Schreyer (See Fig. 1-143) is the man that changes and overturns the image of brands. Before joining Kia Motors Corporation, he had already been among the three most leading car designers in Europe. He had designed the Volkswagen New Beetle, Audi TT, Audi A6 and other classic models. What Schreyer brings to Kia is not only the change of Kia vehicles' appearance design but also the innovation of Kia's overall design concept, leading car design of Kia toward a trend full of young and energetic elements.

Fig. 1-142 Kia Logo

Fig. 1-143 Peter Schreyer

The main models: Quoris/K9 (the first rear-engine model, poised for the market launch), K4 (poised for the market launch), K3, K2, Picanto/Morning, Rio/Pride, Venga, Cee'd, Soul, Shuma, Forte/Cerato, Oprius/K5, Cadenza/K7, Sorento, Sportage, Sportage R, Borrego/Mohave/Borrego, Carens/Rondo, Carnvial/Sedona/VQ, OPIRUS (discontinued) and the like (See Fig. 1-144 to Fig. 1-147).

Fig. 1-144 A Kia K5

Fig. 1-145 A Kia K9

Fig. 1-146 A Kia Sportage

Fig. 1-147 A Kia Sportage R

2. Hyundai Motor Company

Founded in December 1967 by Chung Ju-yung (See Fig. 1-148), Hyundai Motor Company is the largest automaker in South Korea, and one of the world's 20 largest automobile companies. The company is headquartered in Seoul, South Korea, with an annual auto output of over one million vehicles. Now Hyundai Motor Company has grown into Hyundai Group, whose businesses are expanded from the automotive industry to the fields of architecture, shipbuilding and machinery, etc.

On October 18, 2002, Hyundai Motor Company teamed up with Beijing Automotive Group to build a joint venture named Beijing Hyundai Motor.

The logo of Hyundai Motor Company is formed by an italic H circled by an oval (See Fig. 1-149). H is the initial of HYUNDAI, while the oval represents either the steering wheel of vehicles or the earth planet, which in combination indicates that Hyundai vehicles will spread across the whole world.

Fig. 1-148   Chung Ju-yung

Fig. 1-149   Hyundai Logo

The business philosophy of Hyundai is to create a colorful auto lifestyle in the spirit of innovation and challenges and to balance the interests among shareholders, customers, employees and the car industry.

The typical car models of Hyundai include Elantra, Accent, VERNA, Sonata, Mistra, ix35, Santa Fe, Tucson and so on (See Fig. 1-150 to Fig. 1-153).

Fig. 1-150   A Hyundai Elantra

Fig. 1-151   A Hyundai Mistra

Fig. 1-152　A Hyundai ix35

Fig. 1-153　A Hyundai Tucson

V. French Automobile Companies and Brands

The automobile derives from Germany but thrives in France. After the Germans invented the automobile, the predecessors of the French automobile industry quickly launched on manufacturing cars, improving car structure and building car companies. In 1890, Armand Peugeot (See Fig. 1-154) manufactured the first automobile in France and carved out a path for the French automobile industry.

PSA Peugeot Citroën

In 1903, Peugeot launched its motorcycle and continued to use the Peugeot brand since then. In 1929, Peugeot 201 was released, the product first named by digital numbers (a three-digital number with "0" in the middle). This continues as the traditional name-making approach of Peugeot.

Fig. 1-154　Armand Peugeot

In 1976, the Peugeot Company acquired Citroën and became the Peugeot-Citroën Motor Company. In 1980, the company was renamed as PSA—Peugeot Societe Anonyme, including Peugeot Motor Company, Citroën Motor Company and TALBOT Motor Company. PSA Group produces and sells automobiles and motorcycles under the two main brands of Peugeot and Citroën.

The Peugeot logo is a standing lion. The lion serves as the badge of the Peugeot family and then becomes the emblem of Montbéliard. The lion was initially used for saw blades and evolved into the unique trademark of Peugeot in 1880. From 1850 to 2003, the Peugeot lion went through transformations for nine times (See Fig. 1-155). Now, the lion is a standing lion with front paws stretched out. The lion trademark highlights the strength of Peugeot and emphasizes the stress and rhythm, full of modernity. The badge suggests that Peugeot keeps its forever vitality like a mighty and agile lion.

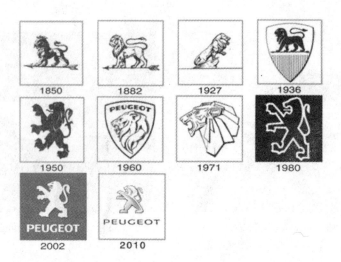

Fig. 1-155   Peugeot Logo Evolution Chart

Main Peugeot models include 206, 207, 307, 308, 408, 508, 3008, RCZ series and the like (See Fig. 1-156 to Fig. 1-159).

Fig. 1-156   A Peugeot 408

Fig. 1-157   A Peugeot 508

Fig. 1-158   A Peugeot 3008

Fig. 1-159   A Peugeot RCZ

The logo of Citroën (See Fig. 1-160) is a pair of herringbone gears, a graphic representation of close cooperation, concerted effort and advancement. This logo also indicates the leading technology of Citroën Automobile Company.

Main Citroën models include Elysee, C2, C3-XR, C4, C4 L, C5, C-Quatre series and the like (See Fig. 1-161 to Fig. 1-163).

Fig. 1-160   Citroën Logo

Fig. 1-161   A Citroën C4 L

Fig. 1-162   A Citroën Elysee

Fig. 1-163   A Citroën C3-XR

VI. Italian Automobile Companies and Brands

1. FIAT Automobiles

FIAT (See Fig. 1-164) is the acronym of Fabbrica Italiana Automobile Torino in Italian (Italian Automobile Factory of Turin). Through the development over the last century, FIAT Group has already become the largest automobile manufacturer in Italy. With its auto production accounting for 90% of Italy's total automobile output, the company controls many brands such as Alfa Romeo, Maserati, Lancia, Ferrari and so on. For the convenience of business operation, FIAT Automobiles became an independent subsidiary of the FIAT Group in 1979.

Fig. 1-164   Fiat Logo

Well-known automotive marques under FIAT include Fiat, Lancia, Alfa Romeo and Maserati. Ferrari is also an independently-run subsidiary of FIAT, while Iveco is the engineering vehicle company of FIAT.

Main models under FIAT brands include Panda, Palio, Siena, Viaggio, Freemont, and Uno, etc. (See Fig. 1-165 and Fig. 1-166), all of which are designed by the famous Italian designer Giorgetto Giugiaro (See Fig. 1-167).

Fig. 1-165　A Fiat Viaggio

Fig. 1-166　A Fiat Freemont

2. Alfa Romeo Automobiles S.p.A.

Alfa Romeo Automobiles S.p.A., established in 1910 and headquartered in Milan, Italy, is an Italian car manufacturer involving limousines, sports cars and racing cars.

In 1911, Alfa Romeo Automobiles S.p.A. places "ALFA ROMEO" on the upper part of the circular emblem of Milan city to form its badge (See Fig. 1-168). The badge is to commemorate Visconti and his family, founders of Milan city. The red cross is a part from the emblem of Milan city to commemorate ancient crusaders at the Crusade, while the crowned viper swallowing a Moor derives from the badge of an ancient family and tells the legend of the House of Visconti in the Middle Ages repelling the "Dragon Snake" that inflicted people in the city.

The classic models of Alfa Romeo include Alfa, Spider, Alfetta, Guilietta, and Alfasud, etc. (See Fig. 1-169).

Fig. 1-167　Giorgetto Giugiaro

Fig. 1-168　Alfa Romeo Logo

Fig. 1-169　An Alfa C4

3. Ferrari S.p.A.

Ferrari S.p.A. is an Italian luxury sports car manufacturer. Enzo Ferrari (See Fig. 1-170), a world champion of car racing, established the Scuderia Ferrari (Team Ferrari) in 1929 in Modena, Italy. Ferrari S.p.A. is now a subsidiary of FIAT. FIAT Group took a 50% stake in Ferrari S.p.A.

The company operates independently from Fiat.

The badge of Ferrari S.p.A. is a prancing horse (See Fig. 1-171). During the World War I, there was an outstanding pilot. His plane had a prancing horse that brought him good luck, and helped him repeatedly shoot down enemy fighters. After the pilot won in the Ferrari tryout, the pilot's parents, an Earl couple, suggested that Ferrari should print such a good-luck horse on its racing cars. Ferrari took the advice with pleasure and made the prancing horse the mascot of the Ferrari Race Contest. Afterwards, the pilot died, so the color of the horse turned to black. The logo background is the color of the canary in Modena, the headquarter of the company. Red is the dominant color for Ferrari racing cars, hence the name of Red Prancing Horse or Red Devil.

Fig. 1-170   Enzo Ferrari

Fig. 1-171   Ferrari Logo

Classic Ferrari models include F355 Spider, F50 Ferrari, 458, LaFerrari, Ferrari FF, F12 berlinetta, etc. (See Fig. 1-172 to Fig. 1-175).

Fig. 1-172   458

Fig. 1-173   LaFerrari

Fig. 1-174   Ferrari FF

Fig. 1-175   F12 berlinetta

4. Maserati S.p.A.

In 1914, Maserati brothers (See Fig. 1-176) created the Maserati automobile company headquartered in Bologna, manufacturing sedans and sports cars and enjoying a high population in Europe. Now Maserati is a subsidiary of FIAT.

Italy is the kingdom of sports cars. The particular unrestrained personality of Apennine people is blended into their beloved racing cars, full of passion. When mentioning Italian cars, Ferrari is well-known among Chinese people but Maserati is rarely heard of among them. Indeed, Maserati has a longer history than Ferrari and had achieved brilliance earlier than Ferrari in the car-racing arena.

The logo of Maserati is a trident placed on a leaf-shaped pedestal, which is also an emblem of the Italian city Bologna (See Fig. 1-177). It is the weapon of Neptune in Roman mythology (known as Poseidon in Greek mythology) that displays an enormous power of the sea god. The logo of Maserati and its vehicles looks like a roaring, vast sea, suggesting the potential of fast speed of Maserati cars.

Fig. 1-176　Maserati Brothers

Fig. 1-177　Maserati Logo

The main models of Maserati include Maserati GT, Ghibli, MC 12, GTS and so on (See Fig. 1-178 to Fig. 1-181).

Fig. 1-178　Maserati Ghibli

Fig. 1-179　Maserati GTS

Fig. 1-180　Maserati GT

Fig. 1-181　MC 12

5. Automobili Lamborghini S.p.A.

Automobili Lamborghini S.p.A. was established in 1961 by Ferruccio Lamborghini (See Fig. 1-182) and headquartered in Sant's Agata Bolognese, Italy, producing sports cars and racing cars.

Lamborghini was born with a domineering charm that has helped him establish a prominent position in the automotive industry.

In 1998, Lamborghini was sold to Volkswagen Group where it was placed under the control of the Group's Audi division.

The logo of Lamborghini (See Fig. 1-183) is an energetic, provoked and poised bull, which suggests the high power capacity, fast speed and invincibility of Lamborghini cars. It is rumored that the bull shows the obstinate character of Lamborghini himself and reflects the features of Lamborghini products.

Fig. 1-182　Ferruccio Lamborghini

Fig. 1-183　Lamborghini Logo

The main models of Lamborghini include Aventador, Murcielago, Gallardo, Miura, Diablo, Reventon, and etc. (See Fig. 1-184 to Fig. 1-189).

Fig. 1-184　A Lamborghini Aventador

Fig. 1-185　A Lamborghini Diablo

Fig. 1-186　A Lamborghini Miura

Fig. 1-187　A Lamborghini Gallardo

Fig. 1-188　A Lamborghini Murcielago

Fig. 1-189　A Lamborghini Reventon

Exercises

I. Choose the correct answer according to the knowledge. (10')

1. (　　) is the "father of the automobile."
   A. James Watt　　　B. Henry Ford　　　C. Carl Benz　　　D. Rudolf Diesel
2. (　　) produced the first four-wheel automobile in the world.
   A. Gottlieb Daimler　　　　　　　　B. Nikolaus Otto
   C. William Maybach　　　　　　　　D. David Buick

3. Fire trucks and ambulances belong to (   ).
   A. sports cars   B. passenger cars   C. business cars   D. special vehicles
4. Audi Q7 belongs to (   ).
   A. MPVs   B. SUVs   C. CRVs   D. SRVs
5. Daimler-Benz brands mainly include Mercedes-Benz, Maybach, (   ) and the like.
   A. Audi   B. Lincoln   C. Ford   D. Smart
6. (   ) is the largest European car producer.
   A. Volks Wagenwerk   B. BMW   C. Chrysler   D. Buick
7. (   ) is one of the world's largest automakers that produced T-shape cars for ordinary people.
   A. General Motors Company   B. Ford Motor Company
   C. The Chrysler Corporation   D. Toyota Motor Corporation
8. The full-time four-wheel drive system and (   ) are the two features of Subaru.
   A. In-line Engine   B. V Engine   C. Boxer Engine   D. W Engine
9. (   ) is the designer who changes and overturns the brand of Kia.
   A. Peter Schreyer   B. Jujiro Matsuda   C. Enzo Ferrari   D. Maserati
10. (   ) has already become the largest automobile manufacturer in Italy.
    A. Ferrari   B. Alfa Romeo   C. FIAT Group   D. Lamborghini

II. Match the following English phrases with the correct Chinese meaning. (10')

(   ) 1. 通用汽车公司
(   ) 2. 旅行车
(   ) 3. 外观
(   ) 4. 铰接客车
(   ) 5. 多功能车
(   ) 6. 克莱斯勒
(   ) 7. 楔形车
(   ) 8. 油耗
(   ) 9. 人字形齿轮
(   ) 10. 自动变速器

a. MPV
b. Station Wagon
c. Articulated Bus
d. Wedge Car
e. Fuel Consumption
f. appearance
g. Automatic Transmission
h. herringbone gear
i. General Motors Company
j. Chrysler

III. Decide whether the following statements are true (√) or false (×) according to the professional knowledge. (10')

( ) 1. Nikolaus Otto created a four-stroke gasoline internal combustion engine, known as the Otto internal combustion engine.

( ) 2. In 1998, Lamborghini was sold to the FIAT Group.

( ) 3. Ferrari S.p.A. is an American luxury sports car manufacturer founded by Enzo Ferrari.

( ) 4. Well-known automotive marques under FIAT include Fiat, Lancia, Alfa Romeo and Maserati.

( ) 5. PSA Group produces and sells automobiles and motorcycles under the two main brands of Peugeot and Renault.

( ) 6. Hyundai Motor Company is the largest automaker in South Korea, and one of the world's 20 largest automobile companies.

( ) 7. FHI and Ferrari are the only two companies capable of boxer engine technology in the world.

( ) 8. William C. Durant is known as the man "put the world on wheels".

( ) 9. CRV is a series of Honda, known as Dongfeng Honda CRV in China.

( ) 10. Daimler was known as the "father of automobile."

IV. Fill in the blanks according to the text. (10')

1. _____: manufactured for the transportation of passengers, baggage and goods, mainly including three types—the sedan, limousine and station wagon.

2. _____: light-weight and high-speed, designed for sports and entertainment.

3. _____: equipped with special devices for particular purposes, including sweepers, medical vehicles, fire trucks, and concrete mixers, as well as agricultural work vehicles, sports cars and racing cars.

4. The German automobile company _____ is among the top ten biggest automobile companies and the most famous bus and heavy truck manufacturer in the world.

5. A1 Series are _____ cars (including the five-door sportback model, three-door model and convertible model).

6. BMW owns three brands, namely BMW, MINI and _____.

7. _____ is the largest and youngest German automaker and an international corporation group, as one of the world's leading car manufacturers and the largest European car producer.

8. _____ is the world's largest automaker, which was founded in 1903 by Henry Ford.

9. _____ is the cooperation outcome of the Mercedes-Benz and the Swiss watch giant Swatch.

10. _____ is now a subsidiary of FIAT. FIAT Group took a 50% stake in the company, but it operates independently from FIAT.

V. Translate the following sentences into Chinese. (15')

1. Multipurpose Passenger Cars: designed with a box-type and open (or can be opened) body, for the convenience of goods transportation.

2. Special Vehicles: equipped with special devices for particular purposes, including sweepers, medical vehicles, fire trucks, and concrete mixers, as well as agricultural work vehicles, sports cars and racing cars.
3. In 1932, Audi began to use four interlinked rings that make up the Audi badge today, representing the four brands of the Audi Union AG—Audi, DKW, Horch and Wanderer. Every ring represents a company of the Union.
4. Volks Wagenwerk means "people's car" in German. Its trademark logo is formed by the superimposition of initial letters of "Volks Wagenwerk"—V and W, signifying the "win-win-win" goal of the company and its products.
5. On January 29, 1886, German engineer Carl Benz trailed out the first three-wheeled automobile, granted with a certificate of Automobile Patent. That date was remembered as the birthday of automobiles. Carl Benz was dubbed as the "father of the automobile."

VI. Recognize the classification of the following models and fill in the blanks. (15')

1. _____

2. _____

3. _____

4. _____

5. _____

6. _____

7. _____

8. _____

9. _____

10. _____

11. _____

12. _____

13. _____

14. _____

15. _____

SUV	Passenger Car	Multipurpose Passenger Car	Motor Truck	SRV Bus
Roadster	MPV	Special Purpose Vehicle	NCV	CUV

VII. Fill in the blanks according to the given models and your automobile knowledge. (30')

Beetle, the model of ____(1)____ company, was designed by ____(2)____ who is also the founder of Volks Wagenwerk and Porsche. Volks Wagenwerk means "____(3)____" in German. Its trademark logo is formed by the superimposition of initial letters of "Volks Wagenwerk"—V and W, signifying the "____(4)____" goal of the company and its products.

CR—V, its full form is ____(5)____ ____(6)____ ____(7)____, whose Chinese meaning is ____(8)____. It belongs to ____(9)____. The logo represents for the ____(10)____, ____(11)____ and original design of the company. ____(12)____ is the high-end brand of Honda.

BMW X6 is an model. SUV represents for ____(13)____ ____(14)____ ____(15)____, which means ____(16)____ in Chinese. BMW stands for Bayerische Motoren Werke, whose Chinese meaning is ____(17)____. BMW produces sports cars, sedans, ____(18)____ and other products. BMW owns three brands, namely BMW, ____(19)____ and Rolls-Royce.

RAV 4 is the model of ____(20)____. As explained by the company, RAV represents for ____(21)____, ____(22)____ and ____(23)____, while "4" indicates the ____(24)____.

Audi A3 is a ____(25)____ ____(26)____ ____(27)____ car. The logo represents for the four brands of the Audi Union AG-Audi, ____(28)____, DWK and ____(29)____. And Audi is the largest ____(30)____ of Volkswagen.

Unit 2

Automobile Specifications Reading

Learning Objectives

After learning this unit, you should be able to:
- identify the basic interior and exterior equipment in some English edition, such as Automotive Specifications.
- read technical data and interpret some advanced technical terms in the modern auto model's manual.

Warm Up

Situation: Most often we are puzzled by interpreting English automotive specifications, which have no figures to match with these strange terms. In that case, should we get a good knowledge of its basic structure or read some English specifications of automotive models at first?

I. An outlook structure chart shows us the related vocabulary and terms in the English automotive specification (See Fig. 2-1).

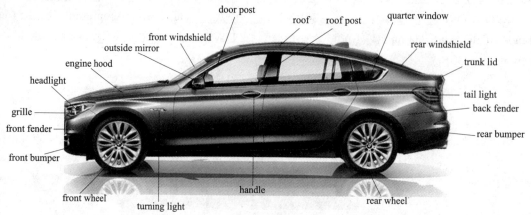

Fig. 2-1 Outlook Structure Chart

Try to give the proper English expression according to your understanding.

前保险杠（　　）　　　　　　　发动机舱盖（　　）
与车身同色系车门（　　）　　　门把手（　　）
前大灯（　　）　　　　　　　　进气格栅（　　）
后轮（　　）　　　　　　　　　三角窗（　　）
后翼子板（　　）　　　　　　　车顶（　　）
尾灯（　　）　　　　　　　　　后视镜（　　）
前风挡（　　）　　　　　　　　门柱（　　）

II. The dimensions of an Audi Q5 show us the related technical data in the English automotive specification (See Fig. 2-2).

Fig. 2-2　Dimensions of An Audi Q5

Try to tell what the dimensions stand for.
Key words: overall length　　overall width　　overall height　　wheel base...

_____

_____

_____

New Lesson

BMW 5 Series GT 528i Vantage

Panoramic views and the versatility of powerful performance make the BMW 5 Series Gran Turismo 528i Vantage (See Fig. 2-3) a dynamic expression of luxury. And with plenty of space for passengers and cargo, it's an expression to be shared. The BMW 5 Series Gran Turismo 528i Vantage's aggressive stance is more than a good look. The low center of gravity makes for more precise handling, and more agility in corners. With up to a 4.4 L four-cylinder engine and 408 hp, its versatile 8-speed STEPTRONIC automatic transmission makes for a smooth ride at any speed.

Fig. 2-3　The BMW 5 Series GT 528i Vantage

Technical data

Take 528i Vantage for example (See Fig. 2-4 and Fig. 2-5 and Table 2-1 and Table 2-2):

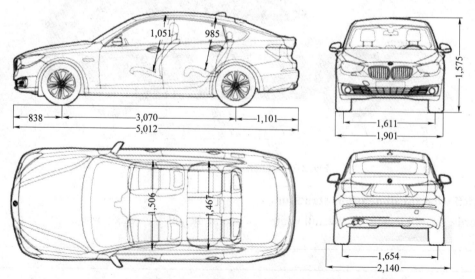

Fig. 2-4　Dimensions of the BMW 5 Series GT 528i Vantage

*Width measurements are indicated without outside mirrors (Overall width with mirrors unfolded).

Table 2-1 The Dimensions of the BMW 5 Series GT 528i Vantage

Terms	Data
Overall length	5,012
Overall width	2,140
Overall height	1,575
Wheelbase	3,070
Overhang front	838
Overhang rear	1,101
Track front	1,611
Track rear	1,654
Width (mirrors folded out)	1,901
Front seat room	1,506
Rear seat room	1,467

*The Dimension measurement of any automobile is expressed in millimeters.

Fig. 2-5 Side View of the BMW 5 Series GT 528i Vantage

Table 2-2 The Main Technical Parameters of the BMW 5 Series GT 528i Vantage

Fuel consumption	Data
Urban in L/100 km	9.6
Extra-urban in L/100 km	6.2
Combined in L/100 km	7.4
Tank capacity, approx. in L	70
Performance	
Top speed in km/h	240
Acceleration 0-100 km/h in s	7.0
Weight	
Unladen weight EU in kg	1,980

continued

Weight	Data
Max. permissible weight in kg	2,505
Permitted load in kg	525
Permitted axle load front/rear in kg	1,065/1,490
Engine	
Cylinders/valves	4/4
Capacity in mL	1,997
Stroke/bore in mm	90.1/84
Max. output in kW (hp) at 1/min	180/245/5,000–6,500
Max. torque in Nm at 1/min	350/1,250–4,800
Wheels	
Tyre dimensions front	245/50 R 18
Tyre dimensions rear	245/50 R 18
Wheel dimensions and material front	8 J×18
Wheel dimensions and material rear	8 J×18

English expressions of the related parts (See Fig. 2-6 and Fig. 2-7)

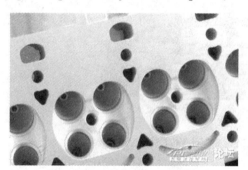

Fig. 2-6   A Cylinder

Fig. 2-7   Tyre Identification

(Four cylinders, four valves engine)

Continental: tyre brand

ContiSportContact 3: wheel tread

245: tire width

50: aspect ratio

R: radial ply tyre

18: rim diameter

100: load rating

Y: speed rating

SSR: self supporting runflat

Specification sheet

Compare the following four models of BMW 5 Series GT from safety, interior, exterior and other important sections.

■ Standard equipment   □ Optional equipment   — Not available

Safety (Table 2-3):

Table 2-3 Compare the Following Four Models of BMW 5 Series GT from safety

Models	528i* Vantage	528i* Luxury Line	535i* Vantage	535i* Luxury Line
Adaptive headlights	□	■	□	■
Adaptive drive	■	■	■	■
Airbags:	■	■	■	■
—Airbags for driver and front passenger	■	■	■	■
—Head airbags for driver and front passenger and rear passengers	■	■	■	■
—Side airbags for driver and front passenger	■	■	■	■
Alarm system with remote control	■	■	■	■
Anti-lock Braking System (ABS)	■	■	■	■
Child seat fastening, ISOFIX	■	■	■	■
Central locking	■	■	■	■
Dynamic Stability Control (DSC, incl. ABS and DBC, CBC, DTC)	■	■	■	■
Park Distance Control, front-to-rear (PDC)	■	■	■	■
Side impact protection (integrated, incl. roof crossbar)	■	■	■	■
Rain sensor and automatic headlights control	■	■	■	■
Xenon headlights for low and high beam	■	■	■	■
LED fog light	■	■	■	■
Headlight washer	■	■	■	■
Warning triangle and first-aid kit	■	■	■	■

English expressions of the related parts

The adaptive LED headlight includes the adaptive headlight with variable urban and motorway light distribution, cornering light and anti-dazzle high-beam assistant featuring automatic high-beam and low-beam headlight function.

Airbags are the passive safety device for the vehicle. They provide energy absorbing surfaces between the vehicle's occupants and any protruding parts in the car, so as to provide occupants protection and restraint during the crash event.

Fog lights are designed to increase the illumination at the low speed, esp. in conditions of poor visibility due to rain, fog, dust or snow (See Fig. 2-8 to Fig. 2-10).

Fig. 2-8　Adaptive LED Headlight

Fig. 2-9　Airbags

Fig. 2-10　Fog light

Interior (Table 2-4):

Table 2-4　Compare the Following Four Models of BMW 5 Series GT from Interior

Models	528i* Vantage	528i* Luxury Line	535i* Vantage	535i* Luxury Line
BMW navigation professional	■	■	■	■
Front, rear armrest	■	■	■	■
Automatic air conditioning	■	—	—	—
Automatic air conditioning, 4-zone	□	■	■	■
Cup holders, front and rear	■	■	■	■
Foot mats in velour	■	■	■	■
Interior and exterior mirror with automatic anti-glare function	■	■	■	■
Fine wood trim ash	■	—	■	—
Fine wood trim ash anthracite	—	■	—	■
Leather sports steering wheel	□	■	■	■
Leather steering wheel	■	■	■	■
Ambient lighting	□	■	■	■
Steering wheel heating function	□	□	□	□
Panorama roof	■	■	■	■
BMW professional radio	■	■	■	■
HiFi loudspeaker system	■	■	■	■

continued

Models	528i* Vantage	528i* Luxury Line	535i* Vantage	535i* Luxury Line
Rear-seat entertainment	□	□	□	■
Front comfort seat, electric, with memory on driver's seat	□	■	□	■
Seats, electric, seat adjustment with memory for driver's seat	■	—	■	—
Active seat ventilation at the front	□	■	□	■
Seat heating for driver and front passenger	■	■	■	■
Seat heating in the rear	□	□	□	□
Electric lumbar support	—	■	—	■
Smoker package	■	■	■	■
Dakota leather	■	—	■	—
Leather Nappa	—	■	—	■
Rear window lifts, electric with "open/close" toll-booth function	■	■	■	■
Roller sunblinds	□	□	■	■
Luxury line	—	■	—	■

English expressions of the related parts

With the aid of the multifunction steering wheel, drivers can operate various vehicle functions from the steering wheel. They needn't take their hands from the steering wheel and take their eyes away from the traffic situation, so as to increase safety for themselves.

If the sun is too intense, the double floating headliner of panorama glass roof can be closed electrically.

Rear-seat entertainment comprises two separate 9.2" color screens, which are electronics entertainment for your travelling (See Fig. 2-11 to Fig. 2-13).

Fig. 2-11　Multifunction Steering Wheel

Fig. 2-12　Panoramic Sunroof

Fig. 2-13　Rear-Seat Entertainment

Exterior (Table 2-5):

Table 2-5 Compare the Following Four Models of BMW 5 Series GT from Exterior

Models	528i* Vantage	528i* Luxury Line	535i* Vantage	535i* Luxury Line
Soft close	—	■	■	■
Two-part tailgate	■	■	■	■
Exterior components in body color (e.g. closing handle)	■	■	■	■
Metallic paintwork	■	■	■	■
Exterior mirrors, electrically adjustable, heated	■	■	■	■
Screen washer nozzles, heated				
Wheels	■	■	■	■
—BMW Light-alloy wheels in V-styling 425. 18 inch, 8Jx18, 245/50 R18	■	—	—	—
—BMW Light aluminum wheels in Multi-spoke 235.19 inch, 8.5Jx19, 245/45 R19, Rear 9.5Jx19, 275/40 R19	—	—	■	—
—BMW Light aluminum wheels in Multi-spoke 458.19 inch, 8.5Jx19, 245/45 R19, Rear 9.5Jx19, 275/40 R19	—	■	—	■
Run flat tyre	■	■	■	■
Wheel locking bolt	■	■	■	■

English expressions of the related parts

Electrically foldable side mirrors will help drivers to prevent rub from meeting on the narrow road. Moreover, it is necessary to save the park space.

Light-alloy wheels feature good heat dispersion for driving safety and lighter than steel wheel, so that they can reduce the fuel consumption.

Cars with run-flat tyres can drive on a flat for up to 150 miles, so as to avoid embarrassments if you have no spare tire (See Fig. 2-14 to Fig. 2-16).

Fig. 2-14   Side Mirror

Fig. 2-15   Light-Alloy Wheel

Fig. 2-16   Run-Flat Tyre

Engine/Transmission/Suspension (See Table 2-6):

Table 2-6 Compare the Following Four Models of BMW 5 Series GT from Engine/Transmission/Suspension

Models	528i* Vantage	528i* Luxury Line	535i* Vantage	535i* Luxury Line
Straight four-cylinder petrol engine	■	■	—	—
Straight six-cylinder petrol engine	—	—	■	■
Double-VANOS	■	■	■	■
Gearshift lever electrical transmission	■	■	■	■
8-speed automatic transmission	■	■	■	■
8-speed automatic transmission, including multifunction buttons	—	—	■	■
Lightweight double-joint spring strut front axle	■	■	■	■
Steering	■	■	■	■
—EPS	■	■	■	■
—Servotronic	■	■	■	■

English expressions of the related parts

The engine is the heart of an automobile. BMW TwinPower Turbo 6- and 4-cylinder petrol engines feature a TwinScroll turbocharger with Valvetronic, double-VANOS and high precision injection.

The chassis is the under body of an automobile. The sporty driving pleasure is transmitted from the road directly to your steering wheel, while guaranteeing safety and the highest possible comfort.

The 8-speed automatic transmission makes changing gears more convenient. There are four basic gears such as Drive, Neutral, Reverse and Park, but Park is activated by a button. Gears can also be changed manually using the selector lever (See Fig. 2-17 to Fig. 2-19).

Fig. 2-17 Engine

Fig. 2-18 Chassis

Fig. 2-19　8-speed Automatic Transmission

Exercises

I. Choose the correct answer according to the knowledge. (10')

1. Which equipment uses radar measurements to automatically maintain a preset speed and distance between your vehicle and the one ahead in both heavy traffic and highway driving?
   A. The navigation system.　　　　　　B. The DRL.
   C. The CCS.　　　　　　　　　　　　D. The TPMS.
2. Which device can monitor the pressure of all four tires and alert the driver?
   A. The ABS.　　B. The TPMS.　　C. The PDC.　　D. The brake assist.
3. Generally speaking, there are three types of headlights currently. Which of the following is not one of the three?
   A. The LED.　　　　　　　　　　　　B. The LCD.
   C. The halogen headlight.　　　　　　D. The xenon headlight.
4. Which light helps to increase visibility, especially in rainy or foggy weather conditions?
   A. The halogen headlight.　　　　　　B. The tail light.
   C. The turning light.　　　　　　　　D. The daytime running light.
5. Which equipment helps to prevent your wheels from locking up?
   A. The SRS.　　B. The EBD.　　C. The ABS.　　D. The ECU.
6. Which system will help the driver to choose the fastest route, the shortest route or the one that avoids traffic, and guide to the destination?
   A. The A/C.　　　　　　　　　　　　B. The ESP.
   C. The navigation system.　　　　　　D. The tire pressure monitor system.
7. Which parts are the main restraints that protect the occupants of a motor vehicle?
   A. The seat belt.　　　　　　　　　　B. The airbag.
   C. The sensor.　　　　　　　　　　　D. The adjustable seat.
8. If you see a statement like this "4-cyl.gasoline engine 1.4 L 16 V T FSI," what is the meaning of "16 V"?
   A. V type 16 cylinders.　　　　　　　B. 16 valves.
   C. 16 volts.　　　　　　　　　　　　D. W type 4 cylinders.
9. As for Audi Q7, which type of gearbox is equipped with?
   A. The automatic gearbox.　　　　　　B. The S-tronic gearbox.

C. The 8-speed Tip-tronic gearbox. D. The multi-tronic gearbox.

10. What does the number 1,424 mm stand for in the picture on the next page?

    A. The track front. B. The track rear.
    C. The wheelbase. D. The overhang rear.

1,424 mm

II. Match the following English phrases with the ir correct Chinese meanings. (10')

(   ) 1. interior length   A. 后备厢空间
(   ) 2. kerb weight   B. 离地间隙
(   ) 3. cargo space   C. 汽车总重量
(   ) 4. overall width   D. 室内长
(   ) 5. wheel base   E. 轴距
(   ) 6. gross vehicle weight   F. 空车重量
(   ) 7. ground clearance   G. 总宽
(   ) 8. overhang front   H. 乘坐人数
(   ) 9. seating capacity   I. 室内高
(   ) 10. interior height   J. 前悬

III. Interpret the following Equipment List of VW-EOS into Chinese. (50')

EOS Model China Equipment List		
	6 MT	DSG
Engine type	4-cylinder Ottomotor	4-cylinder Ottomotor
Displacement (CC)	1,984	1,984
Max. output, kW (bhp) at rpm	147(200)/5,000	147(200)/5,000
Max. torque, Nm at rpm	280/1,800	280/1,800
Transmission	6 MT	DSG
Dimension (mm)	4,407/1,791/1,443	4,407/1,791/1,443
Wheel base (mm)	2,578	2,578
Unladen weight, kg	1,557	1,557
Emission standard	EU4/E4	EU4/E4
Combined fuel consumption, L/100 km	8.2	8

EOS Model China Equipment List		continued
	6 MT	DSG
Acceleration from 0-100 kph (s)	7.8	7.9
Top speed, kph	232	229
Exterior equipments		
4 alloy wheels 7.5 J x 17"		S
Tires 235/45 R17"		S
Brake calipers front and rear		S
Body colored bumpers, outer mirrors and door handles		S
Electrically foldable exterior mirrors, dimming on driver's side		S
Chrome-plated radiator grille frame		S
Space and weight saving spare wheel		S
Interior		
Sport seats in the front		S
Front seats with electric adjustment		S
Heated front seats separately controlled		S
Electrically adjustable lumbar support, front		S
Leather multi-function steering wheel (3-spoke) w/control for gear shift, MFD, radio and telephone		S
Decorative aluminum inserts Brushed Black trim in center console		S
Pedal pads in brushed decorative aluminum		S
Leather hand brake lever handle		S
Front center armrest with storage box, 12-V-socket		S
Safety		
ABS incl. brake assistant ASR		S
Dual ton horn		S
Electromechanically powered steering, speed-related controlled		S
Safety-optimized front headrests		S
3-point seat belt for center rear seat, outer rear seats and for both front seats, with seat-belts tensioner and height adjustment		S
Driver's and front passenger airbag with front passenger airbag deactivation		S
Curtain airbag system for front passengers, incl. side airbags for front passengers		S

continued

EOS Model China Equipment List	6 MT	DSG
Anti-theft alarm system with back-up horn, electronic vehicle immobilization device		S
Tire pressure monitoring system		S
Warning tone and warning light for front seat belts not fastened		S
Park distance control		S
Rain sensor		S
Front/Rear fog light		S
Taillamps in LED technology		S
Warning triangle		S
Functionality		
Isofix preparation, mounting fixture for 2 child seats on outer rear seats		S
Interior mirror automatically dimming		S
CSC roof system in glass appearance with tilt/slide sunroof and net-fabric wind		S
Backrest release for front seats with "Easy Entry" function (electric)		S
Outer rear view mirrors: powered, separately heated and electrically foldable, automatically dimming		S
Power windows, front and rear		S
RNS 510 with MP3 function with 8 speakers		S
Automatic low beam mode with "Coming home" and "Leaving home" function		S
Climatronic		S
Multi-function display		S
Cruise control system (CCS)		S
Optional Packages		
Bi-Xenon headlight with automatic headlight-range adjustment dynamic/Headlight washer system		O

"S": Standard   "O": Option   "-": not available

IV. Fill in the blanks in English according to your auto knowledge. (30')

1. This is a basic information of Highlander LE. Give out the correct explanations.

LE
FWD 2.7 L   4-Cyl.   6-Speed
Automatic

(1) FWD:_____ (英文全称),_____ (中文).
(2) 4-Cyl.:_____ (英文全称),_____ (中文).
(3) 6-Speed Automatic:_____ (中文).

	Head room without moonroof
Interior dimensions, front/second-row/third-row seats (In.)	40.7/39.9/35.9

(4) 40.7:_____ (中文).
(5) 39.9:_____ (中文).
(6) 35.9:_____ (中文).
(7) Dose the auto have a standard sunroof? _____ (Yes/No).

GVWR (lb.)	5,665
EPA passenger volume (cu. ft.) without moonroof (front/second/third row)	61.7/52.8/30.4
Cargo volume (cu. ft.) behind front/second-row/third-row seats	83.7/42.3/13.8

(8) GVWR:_____ (英文全称),_____ (中文).
(9) 61.7:_____ (中文).
(10) 52.8:_____ (中文).
(11) 30.4:_____ (中文).
(12) 83.7:_____ (中文).
(13) 42.3:_____ (中文).
(14) 13.8:_____ (中文).
(15) As for passenger volume, the second row is larger than the front row. _____ (Yes/No).

2. This is a basic specification of Audi Q7,35 TFSI Quattro Vogue. Give out the correct explanations.

(1) 1,221:_____ (英文).
(2) 1,681:_____ (英文).

(3) 2,177: _____ (英文).

Approach angle in front [degree]	max 24.0
Approach angle in rear [degree]	max 25.4
Ramp angle [degree]	max 23.8
Climbing performance [%]	60
Ground clearance [mm]	204.8
Water fording [mm]	500

(4) Approach angle in front: _____ (数值).
(5) Approach angle in rear: _____ (数值).
(6) Ramp angle: _____ (数值).
(7) Climbing performance: _____ (数值).
(8) Ground clearance: _____ (数值).
(9) Water fording: _____ (数值).
(10) Dose "Water fording" have the same meaning as "wading depth"? _____ (Yes/No).
(11) The climbing performance for Q7,35 TFSI Quattro Vogue is better than BMW X5. _____ (Please give your opinion).
(12) The difference between approach angle in front and rear should be larger _____ (Yes/No).

Unit 3

Automobile Product Introduction

Learning Objectives

After learning this unit, you should be able to:
- know how to use FAB principle to introduce a car.
- get a good knowledge of Audi A3 sportback, BMW 3 series and Toyota RAV4 and related information.

Warm Up

Situation: The combination of Audi's daytime running lights and its classic headlights is appealing. Are DRLs attractive to customers just because of their nice appearance? What other functions can they serve? What benefits can customers reap? (See Fig. 3-1)

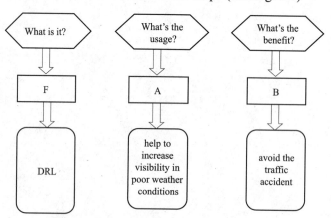

Fig. 3-1　FAB Principle for DRL

This is a selling principle or way: FAB way.

> FAB Principle in auto introduction
> F: Feature (What is it?)
> A: Advantage (What's the usage of it?)
> B: Benefit (What benefits can customers get?)

 FAB Statements

FAB stands for features, advantages and benefits. An FAB statement is explaining the feature, what it does (the advantage), and how that benefits the prospective client.

Features are one of the easier things to identify. These are facts or characteristics about your products and services. For example, the "daytime running lights" in the automobile is the feature.

Advantages are what the features do. These tend to be factual, and aren't connected to the prospect need. For example, "help to increase visibility in poor weather conditions."

Benefits answer why someone should value the advantage. It connects the facts about your product to a solution for your client. For example, "when the car is running on the road, daytime running lights will increase visibility and avoid the traffic accident."

 New Lesson

I. The Audi A3 Sportback.

The Audi A3 is a small family/compact car produced by the German automaker Audi since 1996. The All New Audi A3 sportback (See Fig. 3-2) is one of the A3 family members, which uses the Volkswagen Group MQB platform. It brings together coupe roof lines and sporty, tough body waistlines. Its rising wedge-shaped tornado lines and hatchback design highlight a progressive, sporty design style. Its remarkably angular classic family front grille and unique flying wing-like lights make its front face very sporty and charming. The New Audi A3 sportback, equipped with the new generation 1.4 TFSI® engine, only needs 8.4 seconds to easily realize the speed acceleration from static to 100 km/h. In addition, S tronic® dual-clutch transmission is used, which features a greater power but a lower energy consumption.

Fig. 3-2   An Audi A3 Sportback

New Technology

(1)The All New Audi A3 sportback is equipped with an engine start-stop system (See Fig. 3-3) which can turn off the engine at any time. When the car encounters red lights or other circumstances during the driving process, the engine will automatically turn off. Once you loosen the brake pedal, the engine will immediately restart. The entire engine start-stop process is carried out smoothly without your perception to ensure a comfortable driving while lowering fuel consumption and carbon dioxide emissions.

F: A start-stop system.

A: Encountering any red lights and traffic jams, the car need stop and stall the engine automatically.

B: It is easy to operate through the brake pedal, so the driver could concentrate on the road condition. In terms of fuel consumption, it can discourage petrol use more directly and efficiently. So it is an eco technology.

(2) The Danish Bang & Olufsen advanced sound system (See Fig. 3-4) specifically tailored for the All New Audi A3 sportback is equipped with a 5.1 surround sound system and 14 speakers, which can create realistic and stunning surround sound for you, making you feel like sitting in a professional concert hall to listen to the world's most beautiful sound.

Fig. 3-3　A Start-Stop System

Fig. 3-4　A Bang & Olufsen Sound System

F: The Bang & Olufsen sound system.

A: Audi was the first automaker to partner with Danish advanced sound expert Bang & Olufsen®, whose focus on both design and performance is a perfect match for the Bavarian luxury carmaker. High resolution and high quality voice frequency give value meaning in which the Audi brand innovates.

B: When you enjoy your journal inside the cabin, the Bang & Olufsen sound system shakes your heart and soul with its world stereo effect (See Fig. 3-5). You will feel like sitting in a professional concert hall to listen to the world's most beautiful sound.

(3) The A3 Sportback e-tron® (See Fig. 3-6) can operate on pure electric power, gas power or a combination of the two. The electric motor delivers 243 lb-ft of torque for nearly instantaneous response and an incredibly quiet and smooth drive. Combined with the gas engine, e-tron® delivers an impressive 204 hp for responsive acceleration.

Fig. 3-5 A Speaker

F: The A3 Sportback e-tron®.

A: Output large torque continuously and get an incredibly quiet and smooth drive.

B: Accelerate gradually fast and improve the driving comfort.

(4) The elegantly designed complimentary charger (See Fig. 3-7) can top off your battery at home in as little as 2 hours and 15 minutes when you use a 240-volt power source. A standard 110 V outlet takes about 8 hours, ideal for overnight charging.

Fig. 3-6 An A3 Sportback e-tron®

F: The A3 charger.

A: Charging the A3 Sportback e-tron® takes less time than 2 hours and 30 minutes. Meanwhile, it can be finished at home (See Fig. 3-8).

B: More convenient and efficient.

Fig. 3-7 A Charger

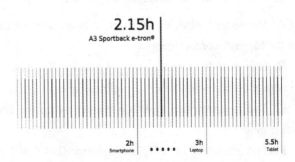

Fig. 3-8 A Charging Display Image

II. The BMW 3 Series.

The BMW 3 Series is a compact executive car manufactured by the German automaker BMW. In 1975, BMW sparked a revolution with the 3 Series. And 40 years later, it's still the benchmark of the segment it invented. Forever evolving, its style and handling make it the most popular Series in the lineup. Each of its three models—Sedan, Sports Wagon and Gran Turismo—guarantees the ultimate thrills. BMW's design language comes to life in each 3 Series model. From the telltale curve of the Hofmeister kink to the sight of the signature kidney grille rising up in a rearview mirror, every element contributes to the distinct look of the world's first, and most popular, sport sedan (See Fig. 3-9).

Fig. 3-9　A BMW 3 Series

New Technology

(1) When someone wants to open the luggage compartment after a shopping spree, they are nagged by searching for the key in their cluttered bags with their arms full. This is no longer necessary, thanks to the innovative comfort access system which allows the contactless opening of the tailgate (See Fig. 3-10): A quick, targeted wave of the foot under the rear bumper is all it takes for the tailgate to open via sensor.

Fig. 3-10　Contactless Opening of the Tailgate

F: The contactless opening of the tailgate.

A: The sensors installed at different heights in the rear bumper detect the wave of the foot and open the luggage compartment.

B: This is no longer necessary to awkwardly search for the key in your bags to open and lock the luggage compartment after a shopping spree.

(2) Fuel consumption and CO_2 emissions for the BMW 3 Series Sedan models with petrol or diesel engine:

Fuel consumption in l/100 km (combined): 3.8 to 7.9 (See Fig. 3-11).

CO_2 emissions in g/km (combined): 185 to 99.

F: The fuel consumption and CO_2 emissions.

A: Fuel consumption is low, and release less CO_2.

B: Reduce fuel consumption and save money for the customer, and protect the environment (See Fig. 3-12).

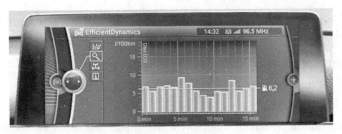

Fig. 3-11　Fuel Consumption Display

Fig. 3-12　ECO Button

(3) The full-color BMW Head-Up Display (See Fig. 3-13) projects all information relevant to the journey directly into the driver's field of vision, allowing them to fully concentrate on driving. The display includes data such as the current speed and — depending on the equipment — navigation tips, Speed Limit Info incl. no-overtaking indicator, telephone and entertainment lists, along with information and warnings from the various driver assistance systems.

Fig. 3-13　A Full-color BMW Head-Up Display

F: The full-color BMW Head-Up Display.

A: The icons and driving information projected onto the windscreen are displayed in a particularly high resolution and in full color, meanwhile they are displayed in the driver's field of vision.

B: Get the information directly and conveniently with minimal distraction.

(4) At speeds of 20 km/h or more, the radar-based Lane Change Warning (See Fig. 3-14) detects the approaching vehicles in the blind spot as well as the vehicles in the neighboring lane. The driver is

Fig. 3-14　A Lane Change Warning

alerted to the presence of vehicles in the critical zone by a triangular warning symbol on the exterior mirrors. If, in spite of this, the driver indicates the intention to change lanes by activating the indicator, they are alerted to the danger of the situation by a vibration in the steering wheel and a flashing triangular warning symbol on the exterior mirrors.

F: The Lane Change Warning.

A: It can detect the approaching vehicles in the blind spot as well as the vehicles in the neighboring lane and alert the driver to the accident.

B: The driver can be alerted by a vibration in the steering wheel and a flashing triangular warning symbol on the exterior mirrors, so as to avoid the car accident from the neighbor car.

III. The Toyota RAV4.

The Toyota RAV4 (See Fig. 3-15) is a sport utility vehicle (SUV) produced by Japanese automobile manufacturer Toyota. It was the first compact crossover SUV, making its debut in Japan and Europe in 1994 and in North America in 1995. The vehicle was designed for the consumers wanting a vehicle that had most of the benefits of SUVs, such as increased cargo room, higher visibility and the option of full-time four-wheel drive, along with the maneuverability and fuel economy of a compact car.

Fig. 3-15 A Toyota RAV4

New Technology

(1) We want you to enjoy your drive without worries. That's why RAV4 comes with eight airbags (See Fig. 3-16), including our driver and front passenger Advanced Airbag System, driver and front passenger seat-mounted side airbags, front- and second-row Roll-sensing Side Curtain Airbags (RSCA), and a driver knee airbag and a front passenger seat-cushion airbag.

F: Eight airbags.

A: They are the safety devices to provide the sole form of passive restraint in the car, and reduce the risk of dying in a direct frontal crash by about 30%.

B: They can save us in emergency and crash, and especially protect the children. Meanwhile, they reduce the risk of death.

(2) RAV4 Limited helps customers customize their comfort. Standard multi-stage heated SofTex®-trimmed front seats (See Fig. 3-17) help tame those chilly nights. And finding the perfect driving position is never an issue, thanks to an 8-way power-adjustable driver's seat with memory function and power lumbar support.

F: The power-heated front seats.

A: It has the heating function, an 8-way power-adjustable driver's seat with memory function and power lumbar support.

B: It will drive away coldness, and spread waist with power lumbar support to relieve fatigue.

Fig. 3-16   Eight Airbags

Fig. 3-17   A Power-heated Front Seat

(3) RAV4 Limited offers up to 42.6 inches of front leg room and 37.2 inches of rear leg room (See Fig. 3-18), so it can accommodate four of your favorite six-foot passengers with room to spare. The friends and family riding in the rear seat will feel like first-class passengers too. With the pull of a handle, they can recline the rear seatbacks and enjoy the ride.

F: The interior room.

A: As for RAV4 Limited, the head room with moonroof is 38.9 inches, rear shoulder room is 55.4 inches, rear hip room is 48.9 inches and rear leg room is 37.2 inches, let alone the spacious room for front passengers. Also, the rear seats can be reclined for individual demand.

B: It can accommodate four of your favorite six-foot passengers with room to spare. The rear seat passenger has the same comfort as first-class ones for 44 mm more leg room than the last generation. What's more, fold-down rear seat backs provide large-scale room for storage when shopping and travelling.

(4) No free hands? No problem. RAV4 is available with a power rear liftgate featuring jam protection, plus a handy height-adjustment feature (See Fig. 3-19). Simply raise the liftgate to your ideal height, then press and hold the cargo door button for two seconds until a confirmation beep sounds. Now, whether you open the liftgate via release or key fob, it will open to the desired height every time.

F: The height-adjustable power liftgate.

A: It is a power trunk lid that is integrated with intelligent memory function. The system can memorize the ideal height as we open each time.

B: It is benefit for shorter owners to close the tailgate, because they needn't stand on tiptoe any more.

Fig. 3-18   Interior Room

Fig. 3-19   Height-Adjustable Power Liftgate

Exercises

I. Choose the correct answer according to the knowledge. (10')

1. Which platform does the All New Audi A3 sportback use?
   A. The MLB.　　　B. The MQB.　　　C. The PQ35.　　　D. The PQ25.
2. What does "FAB" in "FAB principle" represent for?
   A. Future, Advantage, and Benefit.　　B. Future, Advantage, and Bargain.
   C. Feature, Advantage, and Benefit.　　D. Feature, Advantage, and Bargain.
3. Which gearbox is the All New Audi A3 equipped with?
   A. The CVT.　　　　　　　　　　　B. The Tip-tronic.
   C. The R-tronic.　　　　　　　　　　D. The S-tronic.
4. How long does the Audi A3 Sportback e-tron top off the battery when we use a 240-volt power source?
   A. Less than 2 hours.　　　　　　　　B. Less than 8 hours.
   C. 2 hours 15 minutes.　　　　　　　　D. Overnight charging.
5. Which type does the Audi A3 Sportback e-tron belong to?
   A. Hybrid power automobiles.　　　　B. Battery electric vehicles.
   C. Internal combustion engines.　　　D. Natural gas automobiles.
6. Which type does the BMW3 belong to?
   A. SUVs.　　　　　　　　　　　　　B. Compact cars.
   C. Roadsters.　　　　　　　　　　　D. Medium cars.
7. Which technology helps to open the trunk lid without hands?
   A. Bluetooth wireless technology.　　　B. One-touch power sunroofs.
   C. USB adapters.　　　　　　　　　　D. Contactless opening of the tailgate.
8. What advantage could BMW 3 series sedan provide for car owners?
   A. Emission reduction.　　　　　　　B. Cost saving.
   C. Fuel efficiency is 8.3.　　　　　　　D. 0～100 km/h, 4.1 s.
9. Which was the first compact crossover SUV appearing in Europe in 1994?
   A. CRV.　　　　B. Q5.　　　　C. RAV4.　　　　D. Tiguan.
10. What does "standard multi-stage heated SofTex®-trimmed front seats" mean as for RAV4?
    A. It has an 8-way power-adjustable driver's seat with heating function and power lumbar support.
    B. It has a massager, a 6-way power-adjustable driver's seat with heating function and power lumbar support.
    C. It has the heating function, an 8-way power-adjustable driver's seat, but without a power lumbar support.
    D. It has a 6-way power-adjustable driver's seat with heating function and power lumbar support.

II. Match the following English phrases with their correct Chinese meanings. (10')

(   ) 1. dual-clutch transmission   A. 腰部支撑
(   ) 2. energy consumption   B. 后备厢
(   ) 3. full-time four-wheel drive   C. 正面碰撞
(   ) 4. roof line   D. 燃油消耗
(   ) 5. fuel consumption   E. 副驾驶员
(   ) 6. luggage compartment   F. 紧凑型跨界车
(   ) 7. compact crossover   G. 双离合器
(   ) 8. frontal crash   H. 能量消耗
(   ) 9. front passenger   I. 顶线
(   ) 10. lumbar support   J. 全时四驱

III. Decide whether the following statements are true (√) or false (×) according to the professional knowledge. (10')

(   ) 1. Airbags, safety belts, and door beams are the passive safety devices in the car.
(   ) 2. Nowadays, no airbags are equipped for the driver's knees.
(   ) 3. The ABS is used to control brakes when a braking wheel goes into a locked condition. This is "benefit" in the FAB way.
(   ) 4. RAV4 stands for "Recreational Activity Vehicle Four-wheel Drive," which means all the RAV4 are the four-wheel drive.
(   ) 5. The Audi A3 is a crossover vehicle produced by the Volkswagen Group since 1996.
(   ) 6. The Audi S-tronic means a continuously variable transmission.
(   ) 7. Contactless opening of the tailgate is controlled by the sensors installed at different heights in the rear bumper.
(   ) 8. Features like Head-Up Display of BMW3 help you keep your eyes on the road, while iDrive lets you intuitively control the functions you care most about.
(   ) 9. The BMW3 series sports wagon combines ample room with the sleek design and sporty, responsive handling you expect from a BMW.
(   ) 10. BMW3 contains four models—Sedan, Sports Wagon, convertible and Gran Turismo.

IV. Fill in the blanks according to the text. (10')

1. _____ can save us in emergency and crash, and especially protect the children.
2. _____ installed at different heights in the rear bumper detects the wave of the foot and open the luggage compartment.
3. BMW's design _____ comes to life in each 3 Series model.
4. The electric motor delivers 243 lb-ft of _____ for nearly instantaneous response and an incredibly quiet and smooth drive.
5. _____® dual-clutch transmission is used, which features a greater power but a lower energy consumption.

6. The Audi A3 brings together coupe roof lines and sporty, tough body _____.
7. The Audi A3 is a _____ produced by the German automaker Audi since 1996.
8. A _____ is explaining the feature, what it does (the advantage), and how that benefits the prospective client.
9. The _____ of BMW3 series contributes to the distinct look of the world's first, and most popular, sport sedan.
10. _____ answer why someone should value the advantage.

V. Translate the following sentences into Chinese. (15')

1. The vehicle was designed for the consumers wanting a vehicle that had most of the benefits of SUVs, such as increased cargo room, higher visibility and the option of full-time four-wheel drive, along with the maneuverability and fuel economy of a compact car. (5')
2. When someone wants to open the luggage compartment after a shopping spree, they are nagged by searching for the key in their cluttered bags with their arms full. (3')
3. It brings together coupe roof lines and sporty, tough body waistlines. Its rising wedge-shaped tornado lines and hatchback design highlight a progressive, sporty design style. Its remarkably angular classic family front grille and unique flying wing-like lights make its front face very sporty and charming. (5')
4. The A3 Sportback e-tron® can operate on pure electric power, gas power or a combination of the two. (2')

VI. Fill in the blanks in English according to your auto knowledge. (30')

1. Audi A5 家族成员分别为轿跑（英文）_____、掀背（英文）_____和敞篷（英文）_____。
2. 福特（英文）_____翼博是一款小型城市化 SUV（英文名称）_____。它偏向运动、年轻的设计风格，家族化的大嘴进气格栅（英文）_____，犀利的前大灯（英文）_____造型都凸显出强烈的时尚气息。
3. Audi Q5 的真皮包裹方向盘（英文）_____采用四幅式（英文）_____设计。电动后备厢门（英文）_____作为 Audi Q5 全系标配，不但方便、好用，而且很显档次。
4. 在两轮驱动形式中，可根据发动机在车辆中的位置以及驱动轮的位置将其细分为前置后驱（英文缩写）_____、前置前驱（英文缩写）_____、后置后驱（英文缩写）_____、中置后驱（英文缩写）_____等形式。
5. 2013 年上市的本田（英文）_____杰德（英文）_____，搭载的1.8 L i-VTEC 发动机通过吸排气系统的最佳调校实现了与 2.0 L 同等水平的强动力。其中 VTEC 的英文扩展名为_____，中文意思是_____。
6. 天窗（英文）_____是个不错的配置，只是新途安的天窗面积较小，不能很好地照顾到前、后排的乘客（英文）_____。
7. 在驾驶者不干预的前提下，奥迪预防式整体安全系统（英文）_____可以对危险情况进行预判。这段话属于"FAB"原则中的_____（英文）。

8. FAB 语言原则，说出来非常简单，就是我们在介绍产品时，使用的语言是按照这样一个结构组成：**特点**（英文）_____+**优点**（英文）_____+**利益点**（英文）_____。

9. 全新奥迪 A3 Sportback e-tron 将独有的 e-tron 元素发挥得淋漓尽致，突出了当下生活的超高质感。带有 e-tron 标识的**翼子板**（英文）_____、进气格栅**镀铬**（英文）_____、S line 保险杠（英文）_____等完美地彰显了车型的动感与优雅，将低碳（英文）_____、环保（英文）_____融入时尚生活。

VII. Fill in the blanks with the words or phrases in the boxes, according to the new technology. (15')

radio, information, ahead, windshield, music, eyes, navigation

BMW i8 innovations, available in the BMW 6 series
full-color head-up display.

　　Keep your eyes on the road _____. With all your essential driving _____ like current speed, _____, and collision warnings projected on the _____ in your direct line of sight, you can keep your _____ where they belong — on the road. It even displays current _____ stations and _____ tracks so you'll never miss your favorite song.

emissions, brake, shifts, engine, foot, fuel consumption, start/stop, shut

The start/stop system optimizes the allocation of resources.

　　The All New Audi A7 sportback is equipped with the _____ system. When the vehicle state _____ from the driving state into the stop state, the system can automatically shut down the _____, thus reducing _____ and carbon dioxide _____. For example, when the driver steps down on the _____ pedal to stop the car before a red light, the system will _____ down the engine; when his _____ leaves the brake pedal, the engine will start immediately.

Unit 4

Automobile Manual Reading

Learning Objectives

After learning this unit, you should be able to:
- understand the English expressions of some useful parts on the auto.
- read some related *quick start guides* of other brand models.
- get to know some new functions and technologies of *Audi R8* and *Range Rover Sport*.

Warm Up

Situation: English automobile manuals are one kind of scientific-technical writing of practical style. Several owners are perplexed by the complimentary original edition manuals, even if figures, which are not an easy way to solve their problems. We frequently lose control of power windscreen wipers as driving high-end cars, because they can't be activated in a more efficient way. Manuals give the example of how to control the windscreen wiper efficiently (See Fig. 4-1), but English is the stumbling block.

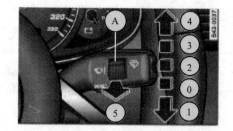

Fig. 4-1 An Audi R8 Windscreen Wiper Lever

Brief wipe
— Move the lever down to position ( ) to give the windscreen a brief wipe.

Intermittent wipe ※ (activating rain sensor)
— Move the lever up to the stop ( ).
— Move the control ( ) to set the wiper intervals or the sensitivity of the rain sensor.

Slow wiper speed
— Move the lever up to the stop ( ).

Fast wiper speed

— Move the lever up to the stop (   ).

Automatic wash and wipe

— Pull the lever to position (   ).

— Release the lever again. The washer will stop and the wiper will keep running for 4 seconds approximately.

Switching off the wipers

— Move the lever to the "off" position (   )

 New Lesson

Brief Introduction

Land Rover is a British car manufacturer which specializes in four-wheel-drive vehicles. It has been owned by the Indian company Tata Motors since 2008, forming part of their Jaguar Land Rover (JLR) group. It is the second oldest four-wheel-drive car brand in the world.

The Range Rover Sport (See Fig. 4-2) is a Land Rover mid-size luxury sport utility vehicle, which made its first appearance in late 2004, in concept car guise as the Range Stormer (See Fig. 4-3). This was a low-slung, short wheelbase 3-door coupe that depicted a significant aberration in design brief for a Land Rover.

Fig. 4-2 A Range Rover Sport   Fig. 4-3 A Range Stormer

A quick start guide of "Range Rover Sport" is as follows.

Part I Vehicle Access

1. Remote control (See Fig. 4-4)

1) Key blade

Press button (arrowed in illustration) to release the key blade.

2) Automatic relock

If the vehicle is unlocked with the remote control, it will automatically relock and arm the alarm if a door or the tailgate is not opened within one minute.

Fig. 4-4 A Remote Control

🔒 Press once to lock the vehicle and arm the alarm.

🔓 Press once to disarm the alarm and unlock the driver's door (single point entry).

A second press will unlock all other doors.

> **Single point entry:**
>
> This is a security feature that unlocks only the driver's door. It can be disabled on individual remote controls by simultaneously pressing and holding the lock and unlock buttons for three seconds. The vehicle will lock and then unlock in the currently selected mode to confirm the change.

2. Central locking (See Fig. 4-5)

1) Master lock and unlock switches

(1) Press button ① to unlock all doors and tailgate.

(2) Press button ② to lock all doors and tailgate.

Press and hold both buttons ① and ② for three seconds to release the tailgate.

2) Speed-related locking

If enabled, the doors and tailgate will automatically lock when the vehicle's speed exceeds 8 km/h. This feature can be disabled or enabled in the settings option accessed via the trip computer.

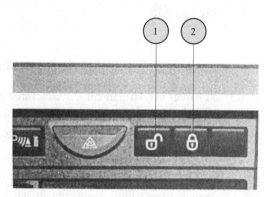

Fig. 4-5　Central Locking

3. Tailgate

1) Opening the tailgate

With all doors unlocked, press the release button ① on the tailgate to release (See Fig. 4-6).

2) Power closure

The tailgate latch has a power closure feature which fully closes the tailgate when lowered.

3) Opening the tailgate glass

With all the doors unlocked, press the touch pad ② on the exterior handle and pull to open (See Fig. 4-7).

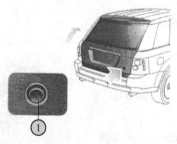 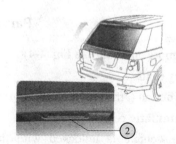

Fig. 4-6　The Tailgate　　　　　Fig. 4-7　Tailgate Glass

Part II Comfort and Safety

1. Driver's seat adjustment

(1) Seat fore/aft, cushion height and front tilt control switch.

(2) Seat recline adjustment switch.

(3) Lower backrest lumbar support switch (See Fig. 4-8).

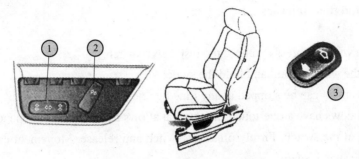

Fig. 4-8 Driver's Seat Adjustment

2. Driving position memory (See Fig. 4-9)

Once you have adjusted the driver's seat and exterior mirrors for your ideal driving position, the vehicle can memorise these settings for future use.

(1) Press the memory store button to activate the memory function for five seconds.

(2) Press one of the preset buttons within five seconds to memorize the current settings. MEMORY STORED will be displayed on the message centre accompanied by an audible chime to confirm the settings have been memorized.

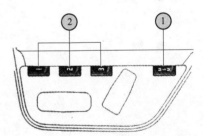

Fig. 4-9 Driving Position Memory

To recall a stored driving position, press the appropriate preset button ②.

Operating note:

A seat position will only be memorized during the five-second active period. Any existing setting will be over-written when we programme a memory position.

---

3. Steering column adjustment (See Fig. 4-10)

Turn the control on the left-hand side of the column clockwise and then move to adjust the height and reach.

Driver seat movement with starter switched off:

If the control is set to AUTO, the positions of the steering column and driver's seat will automatically adjust to provide greater clearance for exit and entry when the starter key is removed.

The positions of the steering column and seat will be returned to their previous positions next time when the key is inserted into the starter switch.

> **Automatic seat movement:**
> To prevent the automatic movement of the driver's seat when the starter switch is turned on or off, turn the control to its clockwise position.

4. Window and door mirrors
1) Windows
(1) To open a window, press and hold the respective switch.
(2) To close the window, pull and hold the switch.
Window movement can be stopped at any time by releasing the switch.

The front windows have a one-touch facility that allows them to be fully opened or closed with a single operation of the switch. Firmly press the switch and release. Movement can be stopped by briefly pressing the switch again.

Press the right-hand side of switch ① to inhibit the operation of the rear window switches (See Fig. 4-11).

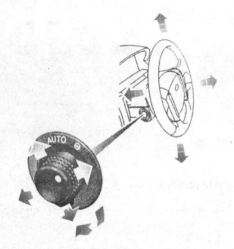

Fig. 4-10 Steering Column Adjustment

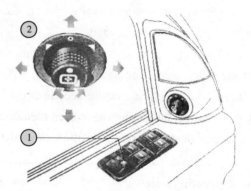

Fig. 4-11 Window and Door Mirrors

> **Resonance with lowered windows:**
> If a resonance/booming sound occurs when a rear window is open, lowering an adjacent front window about 25 mm will eliminate the condition.

2) Door mirror adjustment
To adjust the mirrors, rotate the mirror adjustment knob ② left or right to select the appropriate mirror (See Fig. 4-11). Move the knob in any direction to adjust the position of the

mirror glass.

3) Power fold mirrors

With the mirror adjustment switch knob in the central position, push the knob downwards to fold or unfold the mirrors.

5. Sunroof (See Fig. 4-12)

1) Open/close the sunroof

(1) Press and release the switch ① to open the sunroof fully.

(2) Press the switch ② to close.

2) Tilt the sunroof

(1) Press and release the switch ② to open the roof to the tilt position.

(2) Press and hold the switch ① to close.

If the sunroof is moving, it can be stopped by pressing the switch again.

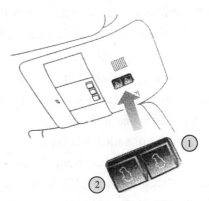

Fig. 4-12　A Sunroof

> **Operating note:**
> The sunroof can be operated with the starter switch in position I or II and position 0 has been selected for 40 seconds, providing that neither front door has been opened.
>
> With the starter switch in position I or 0, the switch will need to be pressed and held until the roof reaches the desired position.

6. Homelink transmitter (See Fig. 4-13)

The buttons(arrowed) can be programmed to transmit radio frequencies that can operate external devices, i.e. garage doors, entry gates, security systems, etc.

7. Seat belts and child restraints

A warning indicator (See Fig. 4-14) on the instrument pack will illuminate to alert you that the driver's and front passenger's seat belts are unbuckled. Dependent upon specification this may be accompanied by an intermittent chime.

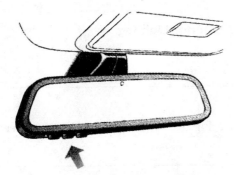

Fig. 4-13　A Homelink Transmitter

Fig. 4-14　A Seat Belt Indicator

Automatic Locking Reels (ALRs):

All passenger seat belts have ALRs fitted for use with child seats or securing large items.

(1) To engage: Extend the belt to maximum length to enable locking mechanism.

(2) Allow the seat belt to retract onto the child seat/item (A clicking sound will be heard as the belt retracts). Ensure there is no slack by pressing the seat/item firmly into the vehicle seat.

(3) To disengage: Unbuckle the belt and allow the belt to fully retract.

With ALRs enabled, as the seat belt retracts, it will automatically lock preventing re-extension. Ensure passengers do not fully extend the restraints and inadvertently engage this feature during normal use.

Recommended child seats:

The Land Rover strongly recommends the use of LATCH (Lower Anchors and Tethers for Children) child seats. LATCH child seats can only be fitted in the rear, outer seating positions.

---

8. Passenger airbags

The front passenger seat is fitted with an occupancy sensor system that determines the state of seat occupancy and sets the airbag status to suit (See Fig. 4-15 and Fig. 4-16):

(1) Seat unoccupied—airbag deactivated and indicator off.

(2) Seat occupied—airbag activated and indicator off.

(3) Seat occupied by a child seat or low weight object airbag deactivated and indicator on.

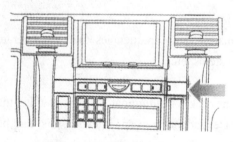

Fig. 4-15   Dashboard

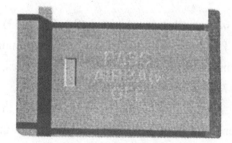

Fig. 4-16   An Airbag Button

Part III   Climate Control and Exterior Lighting

1. Climate control

Recommended mode:

Select AUTO as the normal operating mode (See Fig. 4-17). This will help to prevent window misting.

Fig. 4-17 Climate Control Inserts

AUTO (automatic) MODE:

Press AUTO (See Fig. 4-18) to select the automatic operation of the system. Both LEDs in the switch will illuminate.

The system will adjust the heat output, blower speed, air intake and airflow distribution to maintain the selected temperatures and reduce misting without further adjustments.

The air distribution and blower controls can be operated to override the automatic settings.

Fig. 4-18 An Auto Mode Switch

External water deposits:

The air conditioning system removes moisture from the air and deposits excess water beneath the vehicle. Puddles may form, but this is normal and no cause for concern.

---

1) Temperature selection

Rotate the controls to adjust the temperature for the respective side of the passenger compartment.

Operating note:

It is not possible to achieve a temperature differential of more than 4℃ between left and right.

---

2) Blower speed

Rotate the blower control 2 to adjust airflow through the vents.

3) Air distribution control

Press the following buttons to select the desired distribution settings:

(1) ▥ Windshield and side window vents.
(2) ▥ Face level vents.
(3) ▥ Foot level vents.

More than one setting can be selected to achieve the desired distribution.

4) [PROG] **Maximum defrost program**

Select to remove frost or heavy misting from the screens. The system will automatically adjust the blower output for maximum clearing and activate the screen heaters.

5) **Heated windshield**
6) **Heated rear window**

2. Exterior lighting

1) **Exterior lamps master switch (See Fig. 4-19)**

① Exterior lamps off.
② Side lamps.
③ Headlamps.
④ Auto lamps.

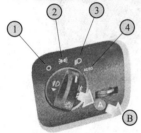

Fig. 4-19 An Exterior Lamps Master Switch

In AUTO mode and the starter switch in position II, a sensor monitors the exterior light levels and will automatically switch the side lamps and dipped headlamps ON and OFF as required.

Ⓐ Front fog lamps: Pull the switch to position A to switch on the front fog lamps.
Ⓑ Rear fog lamps: Pull the switch to position B to switch on the rear fog lamps.

Fog lamps cannot be operated if the lamps master switch is in AUTO.

2) **Direction/turn indicators**

Move the lever (See Fig. 4-20) up or down to activate the direction/turn indicators.

Moving the lever up or down against spring pressure and then releasing will flash the indicators three times. Useful for lane changing.

3) **Headlamp high beam**

Push the lever away from you to select headlamp high beam. A warning indicator will illuminate on the instrument pack. To flash the headlamps, pull the lever towards the steering wheel and then release.

Fig. 4-20 The Direction/Turn Lever

Part IV Facia Overview

Facia overview is shown in Fig. 4-21.

① Exterior lamps master switch.
② Direction/turn indicators/headlamps/trip computer switch.
③ Cruise control switch.
④ Instrument pack/ warning indicators and message centre.
⑤ Audio/telephone switch.
⑥ Wiper/washer switch.

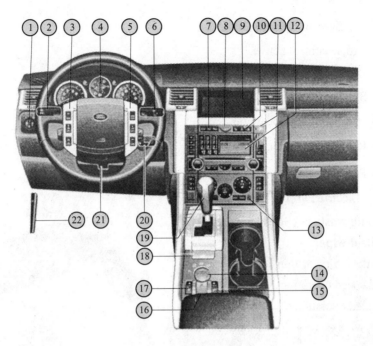

Fig. 4-21   Facia Overview

⑦ Dynamic Stability Control (DSC) switch.

⑧ Hazard warning switch.

⑨ Touch screen.

⑩ Master locking switch.

⑪ Passenger airbag status indicator.

⑫ Audio system.

⑬ Heater/air conditioning control.

⑭ Terrain response control switch.

⑮ Transfer gearbox switch.

⑯ Hill Descent Control (HDC) switch.

⑰ Air suspension control.

⑱ Electric Parking Brake (EPB).

⑲ Gear selector.

⑳ Starter switch.

㉑ Steering column adjustment.

㉒ Hood release.

1. Warning indicators (information)

The following will illuminate during normal driving to indicate that a particular system or feature is operating:

(1)   seat belt reminder.

(2)   low gear range selected.

(3) ![icon] Hill Descent Control (HDC) on.

(4) ![icon] Cruise control active.

(5) ![icon] Direction indicator.

(6) ![icon] Side lamps on.

(7) ![icon] Headlamp high beam on.

(8) ![icon] Rear fog lamps on.

(9) ![icon] Front fog lamps on.

(10) ![icon] Electric Parking Brake.

2. Wipers and washers (See Fig. 4-22)

1) Windshield wiper

① Intermittent wipe or rain sensor operation.

② Normal speed operation.

③ High speed operation.

④ Single wipe—press down and release to operate.

⑤ Rotate the collar to adjust the speed of intermittent wipe or the sensitivity of the rain sensor.

2) ![icon] Windshield washer

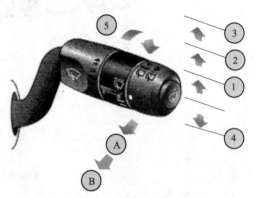

Fig. 4-22 Wipers and Washers' Control

Press and release the button on the end of the lever to operate the windshield washer. Press and hold the button to operate the windshield washer and wipers.

3) Rear wiper and washer

Pull the lever to position **A** for the intermittent operation of the rear wiper. Pull and hold the lever in position **B** to operate the rear washer and wiper.

Care point:

Before entering a car wash, turn the wipers off to deactivate the rain sensor. The automatic operation of wipers during the car wash program may damage the wipers.

Part V On-Road and Off-Road

1. Automatic transmissions

1) Gearshift interlock

The starter switch must be in Position II, the foot brake applied and the selector release button pressed before the gear selector can be moved from P (Park) to R (Reverse).

The gear selector must be in P position before the starter key can be removed.

2) Sport mode

In *Sport* mode, automatic gear changing is maintained but the gearshift changes are modified to improve performance.

To select *Sport* mode, move the gear selector from the D position towards the left-hand side of the vehicle.

The word SPORT will appear on the instrument pack display and the LED in the gear selector surround will illuminate.

> With the gear selector in Sport, the transmission will stay in lower gears for longer with downshifts occurring more readily.
>
> Fuel consumption will be adversely affected.

3) CommandShift™

CommandShift gear selection can be used as an alternative to automatic gear selection and is particularly effective when rapid acceleration or engine braking is required (See Fig. 4-23 and Fig. 4-24).

Fig. 4-23　Shift Button (1)　　　　　　Fig. 4-24　Shift Button (2)

(1) Select Sport mode. The transmission will automatically select the gear most appropriate to the vehicle's road speed and accelerator position.

(2) Moving the selector lever forward (+) or backward (-) and then releasing will manually select a higher or lower gear (when available). The message TRANSMISSION COMMANDSHIFT SELECTED will appear in the message centre.

(3) Subsequent gear selections will display the selected gear on the instrument pack display.

(4) To deselect CommandShift mode, move the selector lever back to D position.

2. Cruise control

Cruise control (See Fig. 4-25) enables the driver to maintain a constant road speed without using the accelerator pedal.

① **SET+**: to set a road speed or increase the speed in 2 km/h steps when cruise control is operating.

② **SET−**: to set a road speed or decrease the speed in

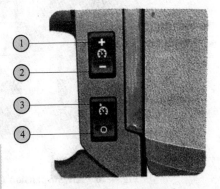

Fig. 4-25　Cruise Controls

2 km/h steps when cruise control is operating.

③ **RESUME**: to resume a SET speed retained in memory.

④ **CANCEL**: to cancel cruise control but retain the set speed in memory.

Cruise control will automatically disengage when the brake pedal is used or when the vehicle speed falls below 30km/h.

3. Air suspension

Vehicle height will be automatically adjusted according to road speed in order to maintain drivability and handling.

Some Terrain Response programs will automatically adjust the suspension height.

Vehicle height can be manually adjusted via the raise/lower Switch ①. Height changes may only be made when the engine is running and the driver and passenger doors are closed.

Indicators ② or ⑦ will illuminate to show the direction of movement. They extinguish when the height change movement is completed.

Off-road height ③ provides improved ground clearance and approach, departure and break over angles.

On-road height ④ is the normal height for the vehicle.

Access height ⑤ lowers the vehicle to provide easier entry, exit and the loading of the vehicle.

This position may be selected up to 40 seconds after the starter switch is turned off.

Crawl (locked at Access height) ⑥ allows the vehicle to be driven at low speeds at access height, to give increased roof clearance (See Fig. 4-26).

4. Hill descent control (HDC) (See Fig. 4-27)

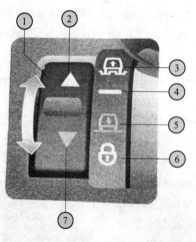

Fig. 4-26　Air Suspension Controls

Fig. 4-27　Hill Descent Control

The HDC operates in conjunction with the anti-lock braking system to provide greater control in off-road situations particularly when descending severe gradients.

Press the switch (arrowed in illustration) to select the HDC. The HDC can be selected at speeds below 80 km/h but will not be fully active until the vehicle speed reduces below 50 km/h, confirmed by a continuously illuminated HDC indicator on the instrument pack.

Press the switch again to deselect HDC.

Exercises

I. Choose the correct answer according to the knowledge. (10')

1. Which brand do these products belong to — Freelander, Evoque, Discovery, Range Rover, or Defender?
   A. Ford.   B. Land Rover.   C. Skoda.   D. Rolls-Royce.

2. Which country does Land Rover belong to nowadays?
   A. China.   B. USA.   C. Germany.   D. India.

3. What does 🔒 stand for?
   A. It means that "Press once to lock the vehicle and then lift the window."
   B. It means that "Press once to disarm the alarm."
   C. It means that "Press once to lock the vehicle and set the alarm."
   D. It means that "Press once to open the trunk lid."

4. How long should we press the memory store button in order to activate the memory function on the driver's seat for "Range Rover"?
   A. One minute.   B. Two seconds.   C. Five seconds.   D. Five minutes.

5. What does it mean "if the airbag of the front passenger is activated but the airbag indicator is off"?
   A. The seat is occupied by an adult.
   B. The seat is occupied by a child.
   C. The seat is unoccupied by an adult.
   D. The seat is occupied by a low weight object.

6. Which mode will help to prevent window misting?
   A. Select heating mode.   B. Select cooling mode.
   C. Select AUTO mode.   D. Select OFF mode.

7. What does [rear window icon] stand for?
   A. Heated front windshield.   B. Heated rear window.
   C. Clean windshield.   D. Maximum defrost program.

8. Why needn't we slam the tailgate on the Range Rover when we close it?
   A. Because it is a power closure.
   B. Because it is a mechanical device.
   C. Because it needs a key to close.

D. Because it has no tailgate at all.

9. How to eliminate the resonance when we open the rear window?

    A. Open the rear two windows about 45 mm.

    B. Open the adjacent front window about 25 mm.

    C. Open the rear two windows about 25 mm.

    D. Open the diagonal front window about 25 mm.

10. Which system does HDC cooperates with to provide greater control in off-road situations particularly when descending severe gradients?

    A. The Electric Spark Advance.

    B. The Supplemental Restraint System.

    C. The Anti-Slip Regulation.

    D. The Anti-Lock Brake System.

II. Match English phrases with the ir correct Chinese meanings. (10')

(　　) 1. remote control　　　　　　　　A. 出风速度

(　　) 2. driving position memory　　　　B. 空气悬架控制系统

(　　) 3. blower speed　　　　　　　　　C. 动态稳定控制系统

(　　) 4. audio system　　　　　　　　　D. 陡坡缓降控制系统

(　　) 5. front fog lamp　　　　　　　　　E. 前雾灯

(　　) 6. air suspension control　　　　　F. 遥控

(　　) 7. dynamic stability control　　　　G. 远光

(　　) 8. headlamp high beam　　　　　　H. 座椅位置记忆

(　　) 9. Hill Descent Control　　　　　　I. 风挡雨刮器

(　　) 10. windshield wiper　　　　　　　J. 音响系统

III. Decide whether the following statements are true (√) or false (×) according to the professional knowledge. (10')

(　　) 1. Pushing the headlamp lever away means to flash the headlamp.

(　　) 2. Fog lamps can't work if the lamps master switch is in AUTO mode.

(　　) 3. The front windows have a button to control the four windows open and close.

(　　) 4. Turn the control key on the left-hand side of the column anticlockwise and then move to adjust the height.

(　　) 5. The LATCH device will lock the seat belts automatically in order to avoid re-extension.

(　　) 6. The homelink transmitter system like a shortcut key can transmit radio frequencies to control the exterior equipment as required.

(　　) 7. A warning indicator on the dashboard will alarm when the driver's seat belt and the front passenger's seat belt are unfastened.

(　　) 8. ▨ means "low gear range selected."

(　　) 9. "Press to unlock all doors and tailgate and press to lock all doors and tailgate." indicates the function of central locking.

(　　) 10. 🀄 Pressing and releasing the button indicates the windshield washer is working.

IV. Fill in the blanks according to the text. (10')

1. Generally speaking, there are two _____ with integral keys supplied with your vehicle.
2. To close the window, pull and hold the _____. Window movement can be stopped at any time by releasing it.
3. There is an adjustment switch knob in the central position. When we push the knob _____, we can fold or unfold the mirrors.
4. The air conditioning system removes _____ from the air and deposits excess water beneath.
5. The front passenger seat is equipped with an occupancy _____ system that determines the state of the passenger.
6. As for the air conditioning, when we rotate the _____ to adjust the temperature for the passenger as required.
7. Before entering a car wash, turn the wipers off to deactivate the rain _____.
8. In _____ mode, automatic gear changing is maintained but the gearshift changes are modified to improve performance.
9. Vehicle height will be automatically adjusted according to road speed in order to maintain _____ and handling.
10. The _____ is automatically turned off when the vehicle's forward speed exceeds 16 km/h.

V. Translate the following sentences into Chinese. (15')

1. Land Rover is a British car manufacturer which specializes in four-wheel-drive vehicles. It has been owned by the Indian company Tata Motors since 2008, forming part of their Jaguar Land Rover (JLR) group. (3')
2. This is a security feature that unlocks only the driver's door. It can be disabled on individual remote controls by simultaneously pressing and holding the lock and unlock buttons for three seconds. (3')
3. This feature can be disabled or enabled in the settings option accessed via the trip computer. (1')
4. MEMORY STORED will be displayed on the message centre accompanied by an audible chime to confirm that the settings have been memorized. (2')
5. To prevent the automatic movement of the driver's seat when the starter switch is turned on or off, turn the control to its clockwise position. (2')
6. Ensure passengers do not fully extend the restraints and inadvertently engage this feature during normal use. (2')
7. The automatic operation of wipers during the car wash program may damage the wipers. (1')
8. Some Terrain Response programs will automatically adjust the suspension height. (1')

VI. Fill in the blanks in English according to your auto knowledge. (30')

1. 路虎（英文）_____独有的**全地形反馈适应系统**（英文）_____是目前同一级别车系所无法匹敌的高级配置，可以智能处理砂砾、车辙、雪地、草地等各种复杂路面。

2. 在高速路面行车时，**定速巡航系统**（英文）_____可有效帮助司机保证车速而不用踩**油门踏板**（英文）_____。

3. 在把**驾驶员座椅**（英文）_____、**转向柱**（英文）_____和车外**后视镜**（英文）_____调节到理想位置后，汽车的**驾驶位置记忆功能**（英文）_____可以记住这些调节位置，方便您将来使用。

4. 将插入驾驶员车门锁的**钥匙**（英文）_____朝车前方向转动，以解锁车门并解除**警报系统**（英文）_____。再次转动钥匙，可解锁其他**车门**（英文）_____。

5. 在汽车进入自动洗车房之前，请关闭**雨刮器**（英文）_____，以取消雨水传感器（英文）_____。否则，雨刮器会在洗车过程中误启动，并可能因而损坏。

6. 实现换挡互锁，要将换挡杆从**驻车挡**（英文）_____换到**倒车挡**（英文）_____，启动机开关必须位于位置II，同时踩下**制动踏板**（英文）_____且按下换挡杆，释放按钮1。

7. 如需要取消**安全气囊**（英文）_____，打开前乘客车门，并使用**启动机**（英文）_____钥匙将**乘客安全气囊**（英文）_____开关转动至**关闭**（英文）_____位置。

8. 打开**后车窗**（英文）_____时，如产生声音**共振**（英文）_____或声震情况，此时降低相邻前车窗高度25 mm，即可消除上述现象。

9. 车头的多层格栅以及独特的头灯外形保留了强大的**路虎揽胜**（英文）_____特征。但是，格栅的后向斜度、线条更加分明的边角，以及后斜顶**A柱**（英文）_____角度，使得全新一代揽胜的外形更加流畅。

10. 在车身尾部，全新一代揽胜的**尾灯**（英文）_____进行了层叠处理与醒目的设计，采用了**发光二极管**（英文）_____技术。主尾灯和**刹车灯**（英文）_____具有大胆的方形图案。**转向指示灯**（英文）_____进行了"三重直线"图形的全新解读。

11. 根据设备部件要求，**乙醇**（英文）_____含量超过10%的**燃油**（英文）_____将不适于本车。

VII. Fill in the blanks with the words or phrases in the boxes, according to the new technology of Audi R8. (15')

accident, engage, centre button, arrester hook, arms, safety, adjacent, spring, unlock switch, windscreen wipers, luggage lid, up, vehicle, close, damaged

The _____ must be switched off and the wiper _____ must be in contact with the windscreen when the _____ is opened. Otherwise the paint may get_____.

Opening luggage lid

— Press the _____ on the remote control key, or

— Press the _____ on the driver's door (Fig. 4-28).

— Pull the release lever (Fig. 4-29) in the direction indicated (arrow). This will release the _____.

— Pull the luggage lid_____.

Closing luggage lid

— To close the luggage lid, pull it down to overcome the _____ pressure.

— Close the luggage lid.

— Press down the luggage lid carefully with both hands until you hear it _____.

Fig. 4-28　Driver's Door: Unlocking the Luggage Lid　　Fig. 4-29　Luggage Lid Unlocked: Release Lever

⚠ **WARNING**

● For _____ reasons the luggage lid must always be completely closed when the vehicle is moving. After closing it always check that it is properly secured. The luggage lid must be flush with the _____ body panels.

● Should you notice that the luggage lid is not safely secured when the _____ is moving, stop the vehicle immediately and _____ the luggage lid properly, otherwise it could cause an_____.

Unit 5

Sales Procedure

 Learning Objectives

After learning this unit, you should be able to:
- grasp the English script about sales procedure.
- introduce one model by six-position demonstration skillfully.

 Warm Up

Please look at the following pictures about the sales consultants' appearances and behaviors carefully, and judge whether the appearances and behaviors are true or false (See Fig. 5-1 to Fig. 5-4).

(   )   (   )

Fig. 5-1

(   )   (   )

Fig. 5-2

( )　　　　　　　　( )

Fig. 5-3

( )　　　　　　　　( )

Fig. 5-4

New Lesson

First impressions are profound, long-lasting, and important in automobile sales for sales consultants. The first impressions of reception have a 30% impact on the closing of a deal. How to give customers perfect first impressions? Customers always would like to talk to those well dressed, properly smartened, polite yet knowledgeable sales consultants. Bland smile, decent appearance, and the right body language will be a plus for your professionalism to win trust from customers (See Fig. 5-5).

The first contact of a sales consultant with a customer is generally on the phone (See Fig. 5-6). If a potential customer calls, his sales consultant must collect the following information: ① the name of the customer; ② the contact number of the customer; ③ the model to which the customer pays most attention; ④ the appointment with the customer.

Fig. 5-5　Standard Smile　　　　**Fig. 5-6　Reception on the Phone**

Situation: Mr. Wang, a successful businessman, is very interested in BMW 5 series GT. His present car is Honda Accord that is mainly used to transport clients and friends and short trips. Mr. Wang enjoys the capacious space, excellent performance, high configuration of the car, and is willing to accept new things. He wants to leave his Accord to his families instead of replacing. At first, Mr. Wang calls for consulting and making an appointment, and then comes to the showroom directly to have a test drive.

For example:

Peng Zhang: Hello! This is Peng Zhang, sales consultant from Baoxinghang BMW Showroom. How can I help you?

Mr. Wang: Hello! I'd like to know when your new BMW 5 Series Li model is available.

Peng Zhang: Sir, the new BMW 5 Series will be available in August but you can pre-order it now. May I know your surname, please?

Mr. Wang: My surname is Wang. What is the pre-order price?

Peng Zhang: Sir, the advance sale price of our new BMW 5 Series Li model is between 489,600 and 791,600 RMB. BMW provided pre-sales brochures and a demo car to our showroom. You are welcome to order your car with us.

Mr. Wang: OK. What is the engine capacity of the new 5 Series?

Peng Zhang: The new BMW 5 Series consists of three levels of engine capacity 523, 528, and 535. Is this Saturday OK for you to have a look?

Mr. Wang: Let me see... No problem. Let's make it Saturday morning. I'm off this Saturday.

Peng Zhang: OK. Let me book Saturday morning for you. I'm your sales consultant "Peng Zhang." Please remember we are open from 8:00 a.m. to 5:00 p.m. To help you better, I need your contact number. I'll send you the address of our showroom by SMS.

Mr. Wang: No problem. My number is 13654311111.

Peng Zhang: Got it. Is it OK to give me your postal address? I can send you the latest BMW magazine.

Mr. Wang: No, thanks.

Peng Zhang: OK. Thank you for your call, Mr. Wang. Our appointment is on this Saturday. I'll wait for you in the showroom.

Mr. Wang: OK. Thank you. See you on Saturday.

Fig. 5-7 Show Room Reception

How to handle a customer in the showroom?

Greetings in the showroom are especially important. It will lay a good foundation for the closing of a deal and let customers feel that they can experience professional premium service here

(See Fig. 5-7 and Fig. 5-8).

(a) (b)

Fig. 5-8 Customer Reception

For example:

Tong Li: Good morning, sir! Welcome to Baoxinghang BMW Showroom.

Mr. Wang: Hello!

Tong Li: I'm your reception consultant. How can I help you?

Mr. Wang: I had an appointment with your sales consultant "Peng Zhang" to have a look at a car.

Tong Li: No problem. I'll tell him now. What's your name, sir?

Mr. Wang: My surname is Wang.

Tong Li: Mr. Wang, please take a seat here. We offer free drinks here. What would you like?

Mr. Wang: A coffee, please.

Tong Li: OK. Just a moment...Enjoy your coffee, sir.

Another example:

Tong Li: Peng Zhang, Mr. Wang is here for the appointment with you. Are you available for him now?

Peng Zhang: No problem. Let's go.

Tong Li: Hello, Mr. Wang. This is your sales consultant Peng Zhang.

Peng Zhang: Good day, Mr. Wang. I'm Peng Zhang. This is my business card.

Mr. Wang: Good day. You guys here are really friendly.

Peng Zhang: Sure. This is the standard of Baoxinghang.

In the early stage of sales, greetings will rapidly relax your customer.

For example:

It's hot today, isn't it? Would you like a cold drink?

Mr. Wang, where did you drive here from? Was there a traffic block?

Mr. Wang, your car is nice! Your cellphone number is also nice!

Mr. Wang, is the air condition too cold here? Shall we move somewhere else?

Mr. Wang, did I disturb you in the weekend?

Mr. Wang, you came on time even in such a rainy day. I promise to give you a detailed description of the car.

Mr. Wang, from your accent, I guess you're not local. How long have you been here?

Mr. Wang, you are really a young man with great achievements! You must have a successful business.

Mr. Wang, you really have a good taste. The vigor of BMW matches successful young men like you very well.

Sales today is customer centric and consultative in a highly competitive market. Therefore, we must understand the purchase motive of a customer, analyze his requirements, and recommend a car that fits him (See Fig. 5-9).

Fig. 5-9 Explanation to the Customer

There are so-called phenomotive and genomotive in the process theory of automobile sales. These two terms are also frequently referred to in requirement analysis of the iceberg theory. The requirements above the water are explicit ones that a customer knows and expresses. The requirements implicit under the water are those that a customer does not even know. A sales person must understand both explicit and implicit requirements of a customer to correctly analyze his requirements.

For example:

Peng Zhang: Mr. Wang, where did you drive here from?

Mr. Wang: The Pearl Complex.

Peng Zhang: It's not far from us. What car do you drive?

Mr. Wang: Honda Accord.

Peng Zhang: What is the mileage of it?

Mr. Wang: Over 60,000.

Peng Zhang: How old is the car? There is trade-in service available here.

Mr. Wang: No trade-in. It's three years old. I'll leave it to my family.

Peng Zhang: Around 60,000 km in three years, then you generally have short trips, right?

Mr. Wang: Yes. Generally, I don't drive out of the city.

Peng Zhang: Do you drive it to work generally? Do you need to pick up business partners?

Mr. Wang: Yes, sometimes I pick up friends at the airport. That's why I'd like to change it for a premium car. This is the way of business.

Peng Zhang: What were the advantages you like about the Accord three years ago?

Mr. Wang: I went with a few of my friends. It's a spacious car and fitted me well.

Peng Zhang: So you care about the space of a car?

Mr. Wang: Sure. A premium car must be spacious!

Another example:

Peng Zhang: Mr. Wang, do you purchase a new car for yourself?

Mr. Wang: Yes. I don't like a driver. It's not convenient at all.

Peng Zhang: How many passengers generally? (How many people do you generally pick up at the airport?)

Mr. Wang: Not too many. Mostly I drive myself. Sometimes I pick up a few friends, just two or three.

Peng Zhang: Did your friends around you recommend luxury cars of other brands to you?

Mr. Wang: Some recommended the new Mercedes Benz E Class Li. They said it's more spacious than A6 L. I'll go and have a look. My wife found on the Internet BMW also launched the All New 5 Series Li model. That's why I'm here. (The budget is around 500,000 RMB.)

Peng Zhang: Our new 5 Series is available for pre-order. When do you need the car?

Mr. Wang: As soon as possible. You know I want a new arrival. Of course, I'd like to be among the first batch of owners.

Peng Zhang: Thank you for your support to BMW! We don't have many business elite like you.

Mr. Wang: Well, when will the car be available for pick-up?

Peng Zhang: It depends on the ordering of the new 5 Series. It can be delivered in September at the soonest.

Mr. Wang: Anyway, it must be as soon as possible. You told me about brochures. Can I have a look?

Peng Zhang: No problem! I'll fetch it now. After reading the brochures, we can have a look at some similar models.

The six-position automobile introduction method is a classical automobile demonstration method. It is also a normalized automobile demonstration process. This method was first adopted by Mercedes Benz and then developed and improved by Lexus of Toyota. It has been a standard static demonstration method in automobile sales. A car is introduced at six-positions according to the six-position automobile introduction method. The entire process takes about 40 minutes. The actual duration depends on customers.

The mainline of six-position demonstration is customer requirements. The basic order is as follows (See Table 5-1).

Table 5-1 The Basic Order of the Six-Position Demonstration

Positions	Key Points
Position 1: 45 degrees from the front end	appearance, design, beltline, brand, and value
Position 2: the driver's seat	driving comfort and handling
Position 3: back seat	riding comfort and space
Position 4: the rear end	rear end design and trunk
Position 5: one side of the car	safety and side view
Position 6: engine room	features of the engine and dynamic performance

In the process of six-position introduction, let a customer truly experience good feelings that a car brings to him by demonstrating benefits of each item and position (See Fig. 5-10 to Fig. 5-15).

Fig. 5-10   45 Degrees from the Front End

Fig. 5-11   The Driver's Seat

Fig. 5-12   Back Seat

Fig. 5-13   The Rear End

Fig. 5-14   One Side of the Car

Fig. 5-15   Engine Room

Demonstration Procedure 1: 45 degrees from the front end (See Fig. 5-16)

Fig. 5-16　Introduction from 45 Degrees from the Front End

Peng Zhang: Good day, Mr. Wang. Let's have a look at this BMW 5 GT.

Mr. Wang: OK.

Peng Zhang: The market positioning of BMW 5 GT is a grand tourer.

Mr. Wang: What does a grand tourer mean?

Peng Zhang: Grand tourers are different from common tourers in positioning. They have flexible loading space, movement performance of sport cars, large inner space, high-end electronic equipment, and trafficability better than traditional cars. I'll explain them to you one by one later.

Mr. Wang: Please.

Peng Zhang: First of all, please have a look at the BMW logo on the bonnet hood. BMW is the initial of the Bavarian Motor Works. The blue and white pattern in the center means the blue sky and clouds are quartered by wheeling propellers. It symbolizes the aviation tradition of BMW.

Mr. Wang: Oh, the BMW brand is great! I only knew the two air inlets down there were the symbol of BMW.

Peng Zhang: Yes, sir. The dual-kidney grille has been a family feature of BMW since 1933.

Mr. Wang: It's a good design. Are the headlights around the grille adaptive?

Peng Zhang: Of course! They also have the light distribution function. At low speed in daily drive, the headlights give a wider lighting angle. At high speed, they give a longer lighting distance. Then we have proper lighting at both high and low speeds. How do you like the new feature?

Mr. Wang: It's really good. I haven't heard about it.

Peng Zhang: Lower there is the bumper of the BMW 5 GT. It is made of a special material. There is an external recovery layer on it. It can recover from a low speed collision and leave only a few surface scratches.

Mr. Wang: This is really great equipment.

Peng Zhang: Sure, sir! The grille throughout the lower part of the front gives the engine a powerful heat dissipation capability. In the design of the front end, fog lights on both sides highlight the stability and width of the car even better. The clear lines of the bonnet hood can effectively improve the ride stability of the car. Strong driving force is also highlighted in the design.

Mr. Wang: These designs are very good!

Peng Zhang: I believe you begin to like the car. Then please go to this side of the car with me along the beltline.

Demonstration Procedure 2: the driver's seat (See Fig. 5-17)

Fig. 5-17　Introduction from the Driver's Seat

Peng Zhang: Mr. Wang, our All New BMW 5 GT models all come with soft-close automatic doors. Doors can be automatically closed. This improves the safety. The entire 5 Series family comes standard with Keyless Go. It is more convenient to start your car.

Mr. Wang: Is this the so-called full-function key? I like this function.

Peng Zhang: Mr. Wang, please check the remote control function of the key. With the key of our BMW 5 GT, you can not only unlock or lock your car but also control vehicle tracking, trunk opening and trunk closing.

Mr. Wang: Really? I only heard about remote opening. Is there also remote closing?

Peng Zhang: Yes. Mr. Wang, please sit at the driver's seat. Let me adjust the seat for you. Our All New BMW 5 GT comes standard with a 24-way control seat system. It is the most comprehensive product in car seat adjustment.

Peng Zhang: Mr. Wang, the ALL function is also available on the air-con system of this car. That is, you can have zoning air conditioning. The driver also has control of it. This better fits big bosses like you driving yourselves.

Mr. Wang: Yes. Then it is much easier to operate.

Peng Zhang: You can easily operate the All New eight speed AMT with the electronic gear lever. This AMT is the same size as a six speed one but gives a more smooth shifting experience. It is also more fuel-efficient at high speeds.

Mr. Wang: OK. Great!

Peng Zhang: Besides, there are various driving modes available for customers on the BMW 5 GT: standard, sport, and enhanced sport. Then you have different types of driving experience. It's like you have three BMW's.

Mr. Wang: Nice. Let's try it later.

Demonstration Procedure 3: back seat (See Fig. 5-18)

Fig. 5-18　Introduction from the Back Seat

Peng Zhang: Mr. Wang, manual adjustment is available for the back seat of this car. Don't you feel the seats are especially comfortable?

Mr. Wang: Yes. I found the seats of my friends' BMW's hard. But this seat is really comfortable.

Peng Zhang: You're right! This is a grand tourer. It's terrible in a long distance trip if seats are uncomfortable enough. The BMW 5 GT comes with an anti-fatigue design. It is very comfortable.

Mr. Wang: BMW really has fine workmanship! These configurations fit me well. Zhang, why is the sunroof so big?

Peng Zhang: You noticed that, Mr. Wang? It is a panoramic sunroof. The passengers at the back can also feel the blue sky and white clouds!

Mr. Wang: A panoramic sunroof is nice. The car looks more spacious.

Demonstration Procedure 4: the rear end (See Fig. 5-19)

Fig. 5-19　Introduction from the Rear End

Peng Zhang: Mr. Wang, let's have a look at the rear end. This car has distinct features in trunk lid design. You have two choices to open it: full opening and partial opening. You can touch it. There are two sets of trunk lid switches.

Mr. Wang: Good. This design is really user friendly. It feels good.

Peng Zhang: You can open and close the trunk remotely. Besides, the BMW 5 GT also comes with a convenient button for full opening of the trunk. Your operation will be convenient with it.

Mr. Wang: It must be very convenient to open such a big trunk remotely.

Peng Zhang: The inner space of the trunk is well planned. There are also two independent storage places under the trunk cover. How do you like it? Mr. Wang, are you happy with the trunk of this grand tourer?

Mr. Wang: Very happy! I can't imagine this car has such a convenient trunk space.

Peng Zhang: Sure! Let's close the trunk and have a look at the overall effect of the tail lights. The tail lights come with LED beam tubes. Exhaust pipes on both sides under the tail lights highlight the car's sense of power. However, only the BMW models with turbocharged engines come with exhaust systems at this level. The tail bumper comes with an inlaid four-point reversing radar. The BMW 5 GT model also comes with a rear camera parking aid system. Your reversing will be very easy.

Mr. Wang: Nice. I like original rear camera parking aid. The one fitted later on my car was not good.

Peng Zhang: We can experience the PDC system of BMW later.

Demonstration Procedure 5: side view (See Fig. 5-20)

Fig. 5-20 Introduction from the Side View

Peng Zhang: Mr. Wang, can you find the difference of this car from your Honda Accord?

Mr. Wang: They are different some way. This car is taller and the tires are larger.

Peng Zhang: That's it. The BMW 5 GT model has a half-height body. The overall height is 1,559 mm. It provides a big inner space to passengers. The chassis height is also 40 mm higher than common sedans. This effectively improves the trafficability of the car.

Mr. Wang: That would be great! I worry about the low chassis height when I drive for an outing. The tires are also big.

Peng Zhang: Yes. This car comes with 245/55 tires with high performance 18 inch wheels. It has great comfort! Please also have a look at the wheelbase. Isn't it long?

Mr. Wang: I found that. It's much longer than my Accord.

Peng Zhang: The wheelbase of this car is 3,070 mm. The typical short front suspension of BMW makes such a long wheelbase car not bulky but agile. You also find it out in your test drive.

Mr. Wang: Sure. I must try it later.

Peng Zhang: Are the windows big? They give you a magnificent vision. These windows come with a frameless design. It can reduce wind noise at high speeds.

Mr. Wang: Sounds good. It looks like a sport car.

Demonstration Procedure 6: engine room (See Fig. 5-21)

Fig. 5-21   Introduction from the Engine Room

Peng Zhang: Mr. Wang, would you like to have a look at the engine room of the BMW 5 GT?

Mr. Wang: Sounds perfect. I'm just trying to have a look at the engine room.

Peng Zhang: Just a moment. Let me open the bonnet. Well, in front of you is the BMW 3.0 twin-power engine winning the best engine of the year in the 3.0 engine group in 2009. This engine gives you a 306 horse power. You can accelerate to 100 km per hour in only 6.3 seconds. The combined fuel consumption is only 8.9 liter.

Mr. Wang: It's powerful. One time faster than my Accord! It is also fuel-efficient.

Test drive is a dynamic display of a car. It is the most widely adopted method in automobile sales. A customer can have a most direct experience of the performance and driving feeling of a car through a test drive. For a sales consultant, it is also the best way to stimulate a customer to purchase a car. It can also develop an interest of those customers who are originally not interested.

Process of a Test Drive:

Step 1: Preparing a test drive (See Fig. 5-22)

Fig. 5-22　Preparation for the Test Drive

Peng Zhang: Mr. Wang, are you familiar with regular operations of the car? Are you happy with the functions?

Mr. Wang: Well enough. This car really has a lot of functions.

Peng Zhang: Now I'd like to invite you to test drive the car prepared for you, the BMW 535 GT deluxe model.

Mr. Wang: Sure. Let's go.

Peng Zhang: Just a moment. Please give me your driver's license for registration because the test drive is on common city urban roads.

Mr. Wang: No problem. Here you are.

Peng Zhang: Cool. Thank you for your support. Let me finish the test drive registration. Just a moment, please.

Mr. Wang: No problem. Go ahead.

Step 2: Introducing the test drive in advance

Peng Zhang: Mr. Wang, the registration is done. Please check and put away your license. This is the Test Drive Letter of Commitment. Please read the commitment in it carefully. Then please sign here at Customer Signature. Please also put your contact number.

Mr. Wang: OK. I got it. I must drive in your planned route and avoid accidents. All clear.

Peng Zhang: OK. Now the commitment is signed. Let's have a look at the test drive route. I'll explain the route and test drive items. Please follow me. The route map is at the gate.

Mr. Wang: OK.

Peng Zhang: This is the test drive billboard. Our test drive route is around 7 km long. First of all, we drive at medium and low speed in the first section to mainly feel sound insulation and ride performance. In the second section, we can test acceleration and braking performance. In Yangpu

Avenue, the third section, we can feel the capability of the chassis to block the noise of tires. In the fourth section, we can try the passing ability. In the bumpy fifth section, comfort of the 5 GT suspension will be reflected.

Mr. Wang: It's a good route. There are also many items.

Peng Zhang: Of course. The BMW brand cares about the driving experience of customers. So the test drive service here is very professional.

Mr. Wang: Then I must try it nicely.

Peng Zhang: No problem! This way, please. The car is in front of the showroom gate. Mr. Wang, please sit at the passenger seat. In the first lap, I will drive the car. It's your turn to experience riding. Let me adjust your seat...Is it comfortable for you?

Mr. Wang: Good. It's comfortable.

Peng Zhang: Now I'll go to the driver's seat. Please buckle up and close the door.

Mr. Wang: OK.

Peng Zhang: Mr. Wang, I'll press the brake, press the start button to switch on the engine, and then adjust the driver's seat and rear view mirrors. We must ensure we are driving in a safe posture and a good vision. BMW cars come with a three-spoke sport steering wheels. The best posture to drive a BMW is to hold three o'clock and nine o'clock positions on the steering wheel. This model comes with an electronic gear lever system. Is it like a plane joystick?

Mr. Wang: Interesting. How to use it?

Peng Zhang: Press the brake and then push the gear confirmation button. Push backward for Drive and forward for Reverse. Gear display is available on both the gear lever and the dashboard. This car also comes with an electronic braking system. You can release the hand brake by pressing this button. I'll show you later during the test drive.

Mr. Wang: OK. It sounds good.

Step 3: Driving experience of the sales consultant

Peng Zhang: Now we shift the gear lever to drive and then release the brake. The car begins moving. The starting is very smooth because the All New BMW 5 GT model comes with an eight-speed AMT. There will be a few heavy trucks in the first section. Now we drive at 30 km per hour and talk in a normal tone. If our talk is not interrupted, it means the sound-proofing and insulation of the car is very good. How do you feel?

Mr. Wang: Very good. This car is really quiet.

Peng Zhang: In the next section, we will test acceleration and deceleration. I'll shift the driving mode to sport. Let's feel the strong power of 5 GT! Are you ready?

Mr. Wang: Let's do it. Let me feel it!

Peng Zhang: How do you like it? Mr. Wang, don't you feel the car powerful?

Mr. Wang: Can't imagine! Such a big car is so powerful in acceleration! It's really fun! Deceleration is also very good!

Peng Zhang: Now you have an idea about our All New 5 GT?

Mr. Wang: Very good. It really is smooth and stable.

Peng Zhang: In the next turn, we can check the trafficability of the car.

Mr. Wang: On such a road...This car is really good!

Peng Zhang: This is the third section. We can experience the capability of the car to resist noise from the rough road.

Mr. Wang: Very good. This car is still quiet.

Peng Zhang: Then we can feel the passing ability of this car in urban roads. What music do you like? We have all types of music for you.

Mr. Wang: Any song is OK. Let me check the acoustics.

Mr. Wang: Good. The acoustics sounds good. This car has a good performance. Overtaking shouldn't be a problem.

Peng Zhang: Now we are on a narrow and bumpy urban road to experience suspension comfort.

Mr. Wang: Good. It's very comfortable.

Step 4: Driving experience of the customer

Peng Zhang: Mr. Wang, our company is ahead. Now we can swap. You will drive the car in the next lap.

Mr. Wang: Sure.

Peng Zhang: Please come to the driver's seat. Mr. Wang, please. Let me adjust the seat for you. Do you feel comfortable?

Mr. Wang: Very good. This position is good.

Peng Zhang: If you feel comfortable, we can save this position. The rearview mirror adjustment buttons are on the driver door.

Mr. Wang: I can manage it. It's the same as my car.

Peng Zhang: OK, Mr. Wang. I'll go to the passenger seat. Just a moment. Ok, Mr. Wang. You can switch on the engine. After adjusting the rearview mirror and buckling up, we are ready to go.

Mr. Wang: No problem. This position is perfect for me!

Peng Zhang: In the first section after car starting, we drive at a lower speed and turn the steering wheel gently to feel the steering capability.

Mr. Wang: Rest assured, Zhang. I've been driving for over a decade. But we don't drive as fast as you.

Peng Zhang: Actually, we don't drive that fast regularly. It was just to show you car performance. In this section, we can try acceleration and deceleration.

Mr. Wang: Very good. The braking and gas pedals are easy to press. I feel confident!

Peng Zhang: Please turn left in front. Then we can feel the quietness of the car.

Mr. Wang: This car is really quiet.

Peng Zhang: In this section, we can experience accelerated overtaking.

Mr. Wang: Good. Power is easy to come. I can also feel the solid chassis. You can not feel these if you haven't tried a BMW.

Peng Zhang: We are back to our company after this traffic light.

Step 5: Conclusion and Confirmation after the test drive

Peng Zhang: Mr. Wang, you can park at the parking bay given by the security to feel the BMW rear camera parking aid.

Mr. Wang: OK. The camera is very clear!

Peng Zhang: OK. We can pull the hand brake here. Are you clear about the operation of the car?

Mr. Wang: No problem. All clear.

Peng Zhang: Do you have any other questions for me?

Mr. Wang: Do you have stock now?

Peng Zhang: Yes. The colors are nice as well. Mr. Wang, let's talk about the details in the showroom.

Mr. Wang: OK.

Peng Zhang: Mr. Wang, what would you like to drink?

Mr. Wang: Tea, please.

Peng Zhang: Mr. Wang, this is your tea. Mr. Wang, here is a test drive feedback form. Please rate our test drive service and the performance of "Xiao ZHANG."

Mr. Wang: All good. You guys are really professional. I'm really happy with it. (It implies the sign to close a deal.)

Bargaining is a most common objection among clients. Buyers and sellers would all encounter the problems concerning quoting/negotiating prices in the whole process of automobile sales. When clients completely accept "the car model chosen by themselves" and think this car "fully satisfies their demands," and the sales consultant also explains all questions except prices, the discussion over price begins. At this stage, the sales consultant would try to avoid talking about its product value, as in the previous process of static and dynamic demonstration, the sales consultant has already made sure that the client understands the product value. It would be the wisest decision to reveal its added value. What constitutes the added value of a product? The added value includes: ① corporate services; ② scale and history; ③ personal service; ④ sufficient supply; ⑤ value-added services; ⑥ competitive products; ⑦ loans; ⑧ fast track to maintenance; ⑨ emergency hotline; ⑩ celebrity and famous cars; ⑪ replacement service; ⑫ group buying; ⑬ information of competitive products and so on.

For example:

Peng Zhang: Mr. Wang, are you satisfied with this BMW 5 Series GT?

Mr. Wang: Yes, I am quite satisfied and I love it. But, is there still room for discussion over price?

Peng Zhang: Mr. Wang, since you are so supportive for our BMW and you are so

straightforward, we certainly can discuss on price. But as BMW is famous for its high performance and excellent services, there is rarely big room for discussion over price.

Mr. Wang: Then how much discount can you offer?

Peng Zhang: Mr. Wang, the price we offer is the official price for presale (advance sale). When the car is delivered to our store, the price may be increased or reduced to a small extent. But if you reserve now, we will give you original factory automatic film and a navigation equipment as presents.

Mr. Wang: What about the price?

Peng Zhang: Mr. Wang, Xiao Zhang has tried my utmost to benefit you. Let's do it this way. If you make a reservation today, when you pick up the car in our store, I will ask for the manager whether he can give you more discounts. Is that OK with you?

Mr. Wang: All right, I will pay a deposit of 10,000 yuan today.

Peng Zhang: Thanks, Mr. Wang. This way, please. Let's pay the deposit and sign a contract.

❈ Exercises

I. Choose the correct answer according to the knowledge. (10')

1. Bland smile, (　　) appearance, and the right body language will be a plus for your professionalism to win trust from customers.
   A. dirty　　　　　B. excessive makeup　　C. decent　　　　D. sluttish
2. (　　) people are showing their preference in the lower-carbon vehicles.
   A. More and more　　B. Fewer and fewer　　C. Less and less　　D. Some
3. Before we get started, let's get more information about the classic car to (　　).
   A. exhibited　　　B. exhibiting　　　C. be exhibited　　D. exhibition
4. It is one of the most popular and (　　) cars in the world.
   A. succeed　　　B. success　　　C. unsuccessful　　D. successful
5. With a variety of mechanical and design improvements, race speeds had (　　) significantly.
   A. decreased　　B. decreasing　　C. increasing　　D. increased
6. As a sales consultant, what will you do when you receive a customer?
   A. Observe what he or she cares about.　　B. Judge him from his appearance.
   C. Greet him and his friends.　　D. Ignore him and his friends.
7. Why is it important for a sales consultant to collect information?
   A. For providing better service for customers.　　B. For decreasing the price.
   C. For comparing with another model.　　D. For giving an example to the customer.
8. As a sales consultant, how will you make an introduction about the model to your customers?
   A. In detail and professionally.　　B. Casually.
   C. Rudely.　　D. Abstractedly.
9. As a sales consultant, what will you do if a customer thinks the price is high?
   A. Let him go.　　B. Quarrel with him.

C. Tell him the advantages and benefits patiently.   D. Ignore him.

10. When a customer hesitates, the sales consultant should help him to make a decision by the following efforts except (   ).

    A. pointing out the importance of signing the contract now.

    B. discussing with him patiently.

    C. paying no attention to him.

    D. offering him a cup of tea and making him relax.

II. Match the following English phrases with their correct Chinese meanings. (10')

(   ) 1. 销售顾问   a. sunroof
(   ) 2. 六方位绕车   b. test drive
(   ) 3. 双肾式进气格栅   c. steering wheel
(   ) 4. 保险杠   d. sales consultant
(   ) 5. 天窗   e. chassis height
(   ) 6. 底盘高度   f. dual-kidney grille
(   ) 7. 试驾   g. brake system
(   ) 8. 悬架   h. six-position demonstration
(   ) 9. 转向盘   i. suspension
(   ) 10. 制动系统   j. bumper

III. Decide whether the following statements are true (√) or false (×) according to the professional knowledge. (10')

(   ) 1. First impressions are profound, long-lasting and important. The first impressions of reception have a 30% impact on the closing of a deal.

(   ) 2. Customers always would like to talk to those well dressed, properly smartened, impolite yet knowledgeable sales consultants.

(   ) 3. The first contact of a sales consultant with a customer is generally in the showroom.

(   ) 4. In the early stage of sales, greetings will not rapidly relax your customer.

(   ) 5. Sales today is customer centric and consultative in a highly competitive market.

(   ) 6. A sales person must understand both explicit and implicit requirements of a customer to correctly analyze his requirements.

(   ) 7. The mainline of six-position demonstration is sales consultants' requirements.

(   ) 8. Test drive is a dynamic display of a car. It is the most widely adopted method in automobile sales.

(   ) 9. Greetings in the showroom are especially important. It will lay a good foundation for the closing of a deal and let customers feel that they can experience professional premium service here.

(   ) 10. The basic order of six-position demonstration is: 60 degrees from the front end, the driver's seat, back seat, the rear end, the rear end, and the rear end.

IV. Fill in the blanks in English according to the knowledges you learned (See Table 5-2). (10')

Table 5-2 The Basic Order of the Six-Position Demonstration

Positions	Key Points
Position 1: 45 degrees from the _(1)_	appearance, design, beltline, _(2)_, and value
Position 2: the _(3)_	driving comfort and handling
Position 3: _(4)_ seat	riding comfort and _(5)_
Position 4: the _(6)_ end	rear end design and _(7)_
Position 5: one side of the car	_(8)_ and side view
Position 6: _(9)_ room	features of the engine and _(10)_ performance

V. Translate the following sentences into Chinese. (15')

1. Automobile sales consultants refer to those who provide customers with a consultative professional automobile consumption consultancy and sales guide.
2. Bland smile, decent appearance, and the right body language will be a plus for your professionalism to win trust from customers.
3. The six-position automobile introduction method is a classical automobile demonstration method. It is also a normalized automobile demonstration process.
4. You can easily operate the All New Eight Speed AMT with the electronic gear lever. This AMT is the same size as a six speed one but gives a more smooth shifting experience.
5. This engine gives you a 306 horse power. You can accelerate to 100 km per hour in only 6.3 seconds. The combined fuel consumption is only 8.9 liter.

VI. Fill in the blanks to complete the dialogues according to the words given in the boxes. (30')

Situation One: The customer is a fifty-four years old man, called Zhang Lixin. He is a professor in the Art Department of a university. He is straightforward and enjoys travelling. He wants to buy a car to do personal and business trip. Now the professor and his wife are coming.

Your task: You're a sales consultant called Sun Hao. Please receive the old couple, recommend the BENZ GLA (See Fig. 5-23) and make an overall introduction to them. Technical Data (See Table 5-3).

Fig. 5-23   A BENZ GLA

Table 5-3 The Technical Data of the BENZ GLA

Model	GLA 200 Dynamic	GLA 200 Style	GLA 220 4 MATIC Style
Rated Output(kW/hp/rpm)	115/156/5,300	115/156/5,300	135/184/5,500
Rated Torque (Nm/rpm)	250/1,250-4,000	250/1,250-4,000	300/1,200-4,000
Cyl./Displacement(cc)	L4/1,595	L4/1,595	L4/1,991
Fuel consumption,combined	6.4	6.4	7.2
Acceleration 0-100 km/h(s)	9.2	9.2	7.9
Top speed(km/h)	215	215	220
Tyres/wheels, front	235/50 R18	235/50 R18	235/50 R18
Tyres/wheels,rear	235/50 R18	235/50 R18	235/50 R18
Length/Width/Height(mm)	4,431/1,804/1,532	4,431/1,804/1,532	4,432/1,804/1,535

displacement	appointment	university	consultant	business
drinks	judgment	marketed	consumption	model
traveling	short-distance	economic	four-cylinder	acceleration

Sun Hao: Welcome to the Benz 4 S store. Can I help you?

Mr. Zhang: Hello. My wife and I want to shop around for a car here.

Sun Hao: Sir, have you made an __(1)__ by the phone or have you ever contacted your sales __(2)__ ?

Mr. Zhang: No. We have never been here before.

Sun Hao: Sir and Madame, do you mind me being your sales consultant?

Mr. Zhang: Of course not.

Sun Hao: Sir and Madam, here is my __(3)__ card. I'm Sun Hao. May I know your family name?

Mr. Zhang: My family name is Zhang.

Sun Hao: It is rather cold out there, so our showroom has prepared some warm __(4)__ for our customers. We have tea, coffee, and juice. What do you prefer, please?

Mr. Zhang: Two cups of tea, please.

Sun Hao: OK. Please wait a moment...

Sun Hao: Mr. Zhang, here are the teas for you. Hope you will enjoy them. Mr. Zhang, do you have any car models you like?

Mr. Zhang: I heard that Benz has __(5)__ a new model, GLA. I really want to have a look at this vehicle.

Sun Hao: I would say Mr. Zhang really follows up our Benz autos. Yes, GLA is a new __(6)__ just marketed in October. Sir, from your scholarly bearing I guess you must be a scholar.

Mr. Zhang: Haha, thank you for saying so. I'm a __(7)__ teacher. We two love __(8)__ very much, so we want to buy an SUV so that we may drive for __(9)__ tourism and I may

107

also drive it for my business trips to neighboring cities.

Sun Hao: Sir, you do have good __(10)__. The GLA is ideal for you not only in power, controllability, but also in room.

Mr. Zhang: Oh? Then, Mr. Sun, first tell us something about its power, please.

Sun Hao: Fine, this way please. This model in the exhibition hall is GLA220 4 Matic Style. It comes with an inline __(11)__ engine of 2.0 L __(12)__. The general fuel __(13)__ is 7.2 L/100 km. The vehicle __(14)__ from 0 to 100 km/h within 7.9 s and may run at 220 km/h at its top speed.

Mr. Zhang: Woo, according to your description, this model is quite __(15)__ on fuel and offers strong power.

Sun Hao: You are right, Mr. Zhang. Please take a rest. I will introduce more to you in a while.

Mr. Zhang: OK. That's great. I really love this vehicle more and more.

Situation Two: A pair of young lovers is coming to the showroom. They are both about 25 years old. The boy is a young boss, called Wu Di, and the girl is a postgraduate. They are preparing for their wedding, and they prefer the BMW 4 Series (See Fig. 5-24). They are willing to have a test drive today.

Your Task: You are the sales consultant Sun Hao. From the dialogue, you know the model is the wedding gift to the girl. Please introduce the model in detail during the test drive.

Fig. 5-24　A BMW 4 Series

Specification Sheet (See Table 5-4).

Table 5-4　The Specification Sheet of the BMW 4 Series

Safety		420i Life Style	420i Line Package	428i Line Package	428xDrive Line Package
Active Safety:					
	Active Protection (with Attention Assistant Monitors)	—	—	√	√
	Xenon Lights	√	√	√	√
	Headlight Washing System	√	√	√	√
	Safety Belt Unfastened Alert	√	√	√	√
	Electrical Seat Belt	√	√	√	√
	Dynamic Stability Control (DSC+)	√	√	√	√

continued

Safety		420i Life Style	420i Line Package	428i Line Package	428xDrive Line Package
	Runflat Tyres, Include Flat Tyre Indicator	✓	✓	✓	✓
	PDC, Rear	✓	✓	✓	✓
	PDC, Front and Rear	—	✓	✓	✓
	Door Automatic Lock when Driving Away	✓	✓	✓	✓
	Rain Sensor, Incl. Automatic Headlight Control	✓	✓	✓	✓
	Dynamic Braking Light (Decluding)	✓	✓	✓	✓
	Lights Package	✓	✓	✓	✓
	Fog Light	✓	✓	✓	✓
Passive Safety:					
	Driver and Front Passenger Airbags	✓	✓	✓	✓
	Side Airbags for Driver and Front Passenger	✓	✓	✓	✓
	Front-to-Rear Head Airbags	✓	✓	✓	✓
	Warning Triangle and First-Aid Kit	✓	✓	✓	✓
Vehicle Protection:					
	Alarm System with Remote Control	✓	✓	✓	✓
	Car/Key Memory	✓	✓	✓	✓
	Central Locking with Radio Remote Control	✓	✓	✓	✓

commitment	performance	run-flat	facilitate	test drive	airbags
license	DSC	registration	route	security	punctual
xenon	PDC	signature			

Sun Hao: Mr. Wu, welcome to our BMW 4 S store again. You are so __(1)__ that it's earlier as scheduled!

Mr. Wu: Hello, Sun. This is my fiancée I mentioned to you last time and this 428i is for her. So we come together today to feel its __(2)__.

Sun Hao: Nice to see you, madam. Mr. Wu has a good taste both for car and wife. It seems that your fiancée is a teacher. Am I right?

Mr. Wu: She is still in graduate school and hasn't graduated yet. This car is to __(3)__ her way to school and handling other affairs, including our wedding ceremony. I'm so busy that I don't have time to prepare the wedding ceremony. Everything is prepared by my fiancée.

Sun Hao: I see. Let's get ready for a __(4)__. Just a moment. Please give me your driver's __(5)__ for __(6)__ because the test drive is on common city urban roads.

Mr. Wu: No problem. This is the driving license of my fiancée. Here you are. She will drive later.

Sun Hao: Thanks Mr. Sun…Mr. Sun, the registration is done. Please check and put away your license. This is the Test Drive Letter of __(7)__. Please read the commitment in it carefully. Then please sign here at Customer __(8)__. Please also put your contact number.

Mr. Wu: OK. No problem.

Sun Hao: Now the commitment is signed. Let's have a look at the test drive route. I'll explain the route and test drive items. Please follow me. The route map is at the gate…

Mr. Wu: It's a good __(9)__. There are also many items.

Sun Hao: Of course. The BMW brand cares about the driving experience of customers. So the test drive service here is very professional.

Mr. Wu: Then I must try it nicely.

Sun Hao: No problem! This way, please. The car is in front of the showroom gate. Mr. Wu, you two please sit down. In the first lap, I will drive the car. It's your turn to experience riding. Now I'll go to the driver's seat. Please buckle up and close the door.

Mr. Wu: Sun, my fiancée is a green hand, so we put great emphasis on the safety performance of the car. Could you please show more __(10)__ configuration of this car to us?

Sun Hao: Of course, Mr. Wu. Security is the most important thing in driving. Firstly, this BMW 428i is of the same standard configuration with other models, such as __(11)__ Lights, Seat Belts Unfastened Alert, Electronic Seat Belts, etc. Besides, it's also equipped with __(12)__ (动态稳定控制系统), __(13)__ Tyre System, __(14)__ (停车距离控制系统) facilitating drivers to park, etc. All these active safety configurations provide all-around security assurance to drivers and passengers.

Mr. Wu: It sounds good.

Sun Hao: In terms of passive safety configuration, this car is equipped with front __(15)__, side airbags and head airbags for drivers and front passengers, so it's of high security. Mr. Wu, you two should have a certain understanding of the power and stability of this car after my driving. Now I will stop and let you have a try.

Mr. Wu: OK. My fiancée will have a test drive.

Unit 6

Derived Businesses

Learning Objectives

After learning this unit, you should be able to:
- understand the tips of buying a used car and auto insurance.
- purchase a used car or auto insurance in the oversea.

Warm Up

Situation: Charlie has been sent by his company to work in New York for a few years, and has to buy a car for temporary use. He cannot afford to buy a new car as the regular wage is approximately $ 8,000, moreover, the cost of car insurance is much higher. So a used car is his best choice. Now Charlie makes up his mind to buy a 2-year-old Chevrolet for sale at a price of $ 9,200. Which are the proper legal proceedings for purchase? What are the most significant considerations? Which types of auto insurance coverage should be chosen? (See Fig. 6-1)

Fig. 6-1 Used Car Trading

Write out our ideas:
(1) Used car purchase procedures: _____
(2) Matters needing attention in purchasing: _____
(3) Chosen auto insurance coverage: _____

New Lesson

Part I How to Buy a Used Car

A used car, a pre-owned vehicle, or a secondhand car, is a vehicle that has previously had one or more retail owners (See Fig. 6-2). Used cars are sold through a variety of outlets, including franchise and independent car dealers, rental car companies and leasing offices. Some car retailers offer "no-haggle prices," "certified" used cars, and extended service plans or warranties.

1. Why to buy used cars?

If carefully chosen, used cars can offer consumers a great deal on their transportation needs. Since new cars lose a great deal of their value as soon as you drive them, while used vehicles can offer a substantial value (See Fig. 6-3).

Fig. 6-2   Used Cars

Fig. 6-3   Used Cars' Value

2. Disadvantage of the used car

However, the consumer should take care not to buy somebody else's problem cars. Some used car sellers are dumping a car that has major issues or is about to have one! The majority, however, are just parting with older vehicles as they move on to a newer model. Keep in mind that problem cars can exist even if the car is brand new!

3. Before you start shopping

As with any vehicle purchase, keep in mind the following:

(1) How will you use the vehicle?

(2) How long will you plan to keep it?

(3) The size, style, features and appearance that you need or prefer.

(4) Your budget or financing options for the purchase.

(5) Your budget for maintenance.

(6) Don't expect perfection in a used car. Compromise on minor problems you can fix yourself, but don't overlook serious defects.

(7) Make safety a major priority. Older vehicles may not be equipped with airbags, child safety seat hook ups, seat belts, anti-lock brakes or security systems.

(8) Plan on a road test before you commit to buy. If you are not allowed to test drive the car,

consider very carefully before you take the risk of buying it.

(9) Have a trusted mechanic thoroughly inspect the car before you purchase it.

(10) Check with your car insurance company to make sure that you can afford to insure the vehicle.

4. Research

Take a little time to get to know more about your choice of car. The time you spend on research could save you big bucks and a lot of heart ache down the road.

(1) Ask friends and family for their experiences.

(2) Checkout any or all of the following (See Fig. 6-4):

① Edmund's Used Cars Price and Ratings (www.edmunds.com);

② Consumer Reports for reliability ratings;

③ National Highway Traffic Safety Administration (NHTSA) for safety defect reporting and recall information (www.nhtsa.dot.gov);

④ National Automotive Dealers Association (NADA) Official Used Car Guide (www.nadaguides.org);

⑤ Kelley Blue Book (www.kbb.com).

5. Where to look

When it comes to buying a used car, most people think just of the newspaper classifieds or word of mouth. Explore the rest of your options to make sure you get the best car you can get or the money!

Online:

(1) Used/new car dealerships;

(2) Car rental agencies;

(3) State and public auctions;

(4) Private owners;

(5) Bank and loan companies.

6. Looking at the car itself

Of all your other steps, this may be your most critical. Inspect the car in daylight and good weather (See Fig. 6-5). Bring someone you trust along to help you make a thorough appraisal.

Fig. 6-4　Used Car Research

Fig. 6-5　Used Car Inspection

1) Body (See Fig. 6-6)

(1) Rust, particularly at the bottoms of fenders, around lights and bumpers, on splash panels, under doors, in the wheel wells, and under trunk carpeting. Small blisters may indicate future rust sites.

(2) Check for paint that does not quite match, gritty surfaces, misaligned body panels and paint overspray on chrome — all possible signs of a new paint job, masking body problems.

(3) Look for cracks, heat-discolored areas, and loose bumpers — warning signs of a past accident.

(4) A welded seam may mean that the car is actually a body shop's "rebuilt" creation from salvaged parts. Look for welded seams in the trunk and on the floor; bumps under the paint around the windshield or rear window, or between doors, may indicate a rough welded seam beneath the paint.

(5) Look for hail damage. If the vehicle is dirty, have it washed for a better inspection.

2) Tires (See Fig. 6-7)

(1) Uneven wear on the front tires usually indicates either bad alignment or front suspension damage. Uneven wear on late model cars with radial tires may signal improper tire rotation.

(2) Do not forget to check the condition of the spare tire and make sure the correct jack is in the trunk and in working order.

Fig. 6-6 Used Car Body Inspection

Fig. 6-7 Used Car Tires Inspection

Fig. 6-8 Used Car Parts Inspection

3) Battery (See Fig. 6-8)

Look on the sticker for the guarantee date. A battery generally needs to be replaced after 25,000 miles.

4) Doors, Windows, Trunk Lid

Look for a close fit, ease of opening and closing, and secure latches. A door that fits unevenly may indicate that the car was involved in a collision.

5) Window Glass and Lights

Look for hairline cracks and tiny holes.

6) Tailpipe

Black, gummy soot in the tailpipe may mean worn rings, or bad valves and possibly expensive repairs.

7) Shock absorbers

Lean hard or "bounce" on a corner of the car and then release it. If the car keeps rocking up and down, the shocks may need replacing.

8) Fluids (See Fig. 6-9)

(1) The oil that is whitish or has white bubbles may mean that water has been introduced into the system and this can be a sign of major mechanical problems.

(2) Check the radiator fluid; it should not look rusty.

(3) With the engine idling, check the transmission fluid; it should not smell rancid or look dark brown.

(4) Check for leaks and stains under the car, on the underside of the engine, and around hoses and valve covers.

9) Mechanical parts (See Fig. 6-10)

(1) Be sure all headlights, taillights, brake lights, backup lights, and directional signals work properly.

(2) Test the radio, heater, air conditioner, and windshield wipers.

Fig. 6-9   Used Car Fluids Inspection

Fig. 6-10   Used Car Mechanical Parts Inspection

10) Interior

(1) Check the upholstery for major wear and tear; look under floor mats and seat covers.

(2) Check the adjustability of seats and make sure all seat belts work.

(3) Check the locations and working order of airbags. Ask whether they have ever been deployed.

(4) Check the steering wheel; unlocked, with the engine off, it should have no more than two inches of play.

(5) Lots of wear on the driver's seat and/or heavy wear on the brake and accelerator pedals of a car with low mileage may indicate tampering with the odometer (See Fig. 6-11).

Fig. 6-11   Poor Interior

Part II Auto Insurance

1. What is auto insurance?

Auto insurance protects you against financial loss if you have an accident. It is a contract between you and the insurance company. You agree to pay the premium and the insurance company agrees to pay your losses as defined in your policy (See Fig. 6-12 and Fig. 6-13).

Fig. 6-12　Auto Insurance (1)

2. Types of auto insurance coverage

Generally, auto policies include several different types of coverage, all of which may be priced differently. For instance, insurance may cover:

1) Bodily injury liability (See Fig. 6-14)

This type of coverage pays for medical bills, lost wages or income, pain and suffering, and even funeral expenses for those injured in an accident where you were legally responsible for their injuries. This coverage also pays for the legal and court costs to defend you in a covered lawsuit.

Fig. 6-13　Auto Insurance(2)

Fig. 6-14　Bodily Injury

2) Property damage liability (See Fig. 6-15)

If you are responsible for causing an accident, you are legally held responsible for repairs to another person's vehicle or property. Property damage coverage not only covers the cost to repair the other person's car, but it also covers repair costs of anything you hit with your vehicle, such as a street lamp, fence or building.

3) Collision (See Fig. 6-16)

This type of auto insurance coverage pays for damage to your car as the result of a collision with another vehicle. Even if you are at fault for causing an accident, this type of coverage will reimburse you for the cost of fixing your car once you have paid the out-of-pocket deductible amount. If you are not at fault, your insurance company can seek reimbursement from another driver to cover the cost of repairs to your vehicle. Collision coverage is optional in all states. However, if your automobile is financed, your bank or lending institution will require you to have this coverage.

Fig. 6-15   Property Damage

Fig. 6-16   Collision

4) Comprehensive (See Fig. 6-17)

This coverage protects you for losses due to hazards not caused by a collision with another vehicle. This includes the damages that are the result of theft, vandalism, fires, falling objects, earthquakes and storms, or contact with animals, such as deer. Comprehensive coverage is optional in all states. Though, like collision coverage, if your vehicle is financed, your bank or lending institution will require you to have this coverage.

Fig. 6-17   Car Combustion

5) Uninsured and underinsured motorist coverage (See Fig. 6-18)

If you, or anyone else permitted to drive your vehicle is involved in an accident caused by an uninsured or hit-and-run driver and submit an auto insurance claim, this coverage will reimburse you for damage to your vehicle. It will also cover you if the other driver does not have sufficient insurance coverage to pay for a total loss of your vehicle. This coverage also protects you if you are hit by a vehicle as a pedestrian.

6) What is medical payment or personal injury protection (PIP)?

If you or any passengers in your vehicle are injured in an accident, the PIP will pay for treatment. In some cases, a PIP may extend to further medical costs like rehabilitation, and may also cover other expenses resulting from accident injuries such as lost wages, and even funeral costs (See Fig. 6-19).

Fig. 6-18　Hit Someone with a Car

Fig. 6-19　Personal Injury

Exercises

I. Choose the correct answer according to the knowledge. (10')

1. What is the disadvantage if you buy used cars?
   A. The seller offers you a "no-haggle prices."
   B. You may buy a car with somebody else's problem cars.
   C. You can buy a "certified" used car.
   D. The seller can provide some extended service.

2. What's the major priority when you plan to buy a used car?
   A. Safety.   B. Financing options.
   C. Style.   D. Appearance.

3. Where can you look when you want to buy a used car?
   A. Bank.
   B. National Highway Traffic Safety Administration.
   C. Online.
   D. Edmund's Used Cars Price and Ratings.

4. Which is a derived business of an automobile sales company?
   A. Auto maintenance.   B. Auto sales.
   C. Auto insurance.   D. Car decoration.

5. You should look at the _____ on the body carefully when you buy a used car.
   A. leak, windows and welded seam   B. rust, glass and tires
   C. leak, paint and windows   D. rust, paint and welded seam

6. Uneven wear on the _____ usually indicates either _____ or front suspension damage.
   A. rear tires, good alignment   B. rear tires, bad alignment
   C. front tires, bad alignment   D. front tires, good alignment

7. Which statement about "auto insurance" is right?

A. Auto insurance prevents your property from damage.

B. Auto insurance prevents you from car accident.

C. Auto insurance protects you for all your losses if you have a traffic accident.

D. Auto insurance protects you against financial loss if you have an accident.

8. Which type of auto insurance coverage pays for damage to your car as the result of a collision with another vehicle?

   A. Collision.

   B. Property Damage Liability.

   C. Comprehensive.

   D. Uninsured and Underinsured Motorist Coverage.

9. Which type of auto insurance can pay for the damages that are the result of theft, vandalism, fires, falling objects, earthquakes, etc.?

   A. Collision.   B. Comprehensive.

   C. Property Damage Liability.   D. Bodily Injury Liability.

10. If you or any passengers in your vehicle are injured in an accident, _____ will pay for treatment.

    A. Bodily Injury Liability

    B. Comprehensive

    C. Personal Injury Protection

    D. Uninsured and Underinsured Motorist Coverage

II. Match the following English phrases with the ir correct Chinese meanings. (10')

(   ) 1. secondhand car   A. 试乘试驾
(   ) 2. hit-and-run driver   B. 汽车租赁代理
(   ) 3. test drive   C. 汽车保险
(   ) 4. car rental agency   D. 单边磨损
(   ) 5. uneven wear   E. 二手车
(   ) 6. medical bills   F. 医药费
(   ) 7. auto insurance coverage   G. 肇事逃逸驾驶员
(   ) 8. property damage liability   H. 保质期
(   ) 9. guarantee date   I. 个人伤害保护险
(   ) 10. personal injury protection   J. 财产损失责任险

III. Decide whether the following statements are true (√) or false (×) according to the professional knowledge. (10')

(   ) 1. A used car can be called pre-owned vehicle or secondhand car.

(   ) 2. All the secondhand car retailers can't offer "no-haggle prices," "certified" used cars, and extended service plans or warranties.

(   ) 3. If carefully chosen, used cars can offer consumers a great deal on their transportation needs.

( ) 4. You'd better have a trusted mechanic thoroughly inspect the car before you purchase it.

( ) 5. It's not necessary to inspect the car in daylight or good weather.

( ) 6. Uneven wear on late model cars with radial tires may signal improper tire rotation.

( ) 7. The cracks, heat-discolored areas, and loose bumpers are the warning signs of a past accident.

( ) 8. Property Damage Liability pays for the legal and court costs to defend you in a covered lawsuit.

( ) 9. Collision isn't optional. It is required in most states.

( ) 10. The oil that is whitish or has white bubbles may mean that water has been introduced into the system and this can be a sign of major mechanical problems.

IV. Fill in the blanks according to the text. (10')

1. You should consider your _____ or financing options for the purchase before buying a used car.
2. A battery needs to be _____ after 25,000 miles.
3. A door that fits unevenly may indicate that the car was involved in a _____.
4. A welded seam may mean that the car is actually a body shop's "_____" creation from salvaged parts.
5. Lean hard or "bounce" on a corner of the car and then release it. If the car keeps rocking up and down, the _____ may need replacing.
6. Black, gummy soot in the _____ may mean worn rings, or bad valves and possibly expensive repairs.
7. Auto insurance is a _____ between you and the insurance company.
8. You agree to pay the premium and the insurance company agrees to pay your _____ as defined in your policy.
9. Bodily Injury Liability also pays for the _____ to defend you in a covered lawsuit.
10. _____ not only covers the cost to repair the other person's car, but it also covers repair costs of anything you hit with your vehicle.

V. Translate the following sentences into Chinese. (15')

1. This type of auto insurance coverage pays for damage to your car as the result of a collision with another vehicle. Even if you are at fault for causing an accident, this type of coverage will reimburse you for the cost of fixing your car once you have paid the out-of-pocket deductible amount. If you are not at fault, your insurance company can seek reimbursement from another driver to cover the cost of repairs to your vehicle. (5')

2. Take a little time to get to know more about your choice of car. The time you spend on research could save you big bucks and a lot of heart ache down the road. (3')

3. If you are responsible for causing an accident, you are legally held responsible for repairs to another person's vehicle or property. Property damage coverage not only covers the cost to repair the other person's car, but it also covers repair costs of anything you hit with your vehicle, such as a street lamp, fence or building. (5')
4. With the engine idling, check the transmission fluid; it should not smell rancid or look dark brown. (2')

VI. Fill in the blanks in English according to your auto knowledge. (30')

1. 购买二手车（英文）_____ 时要注意的事项包括：
   ——是哪年的车？真实里程数（英文）_____ 是多少？
   ——确定其手续完备情况、车辆状况，能否过户。
   ——查询违章和欠交费用情况。
   ——弄清有没有年审，养路费、保险（英文）_____ 过期了没有。
   ——车辆车架和发动机号（英文）_____ 有没有更改。
   ——有没有锈蚀（英文）_____ 腐蚀，车面是否是原漆的。
   ——电喷？化油器？排放是不是达标？
   ——有无大的事故修复痕迹。
   ——与新车做对比，看发动机运转状况是否平稳，发动机有无漏油（英文）_____，有无跑偏或异响，加速是否平顺等。

2. 买二手车切记不能凭第一印象觉得车型时尚，表面无划痕就产生购买的冲动，而一定要细心地观察汽车外观（英文）_____。可按照由外到内的顺序，仔细观察车漆。一般原厂喷漆质感均匀，颜色协调；而经过修理厂修补的车漆（英文）_____，漆色或厚薄会与周围的不吻合。也可以打开后行李厢（英文）_____，根据行李厢内的颜色也可以判断出是否重新喷过漆。因此，要注意补漆处的颜色偏差以及橡胶密封件边缘的油漆残渣，还应注意门下边缘、车身纵梁等区域的漆面情况，以及有无腐蚀（英文）_____。除此之外，还要看前盖（英文）_____、车门及后备厢周边框间隙的均匀程度。

3. 我们在挑选二手车时，需要注意一下车辆的大灯（英文）_____ 灯组的新旧程度是否一样。如果出现了一侧的大灯外观及内部都很新，而另一侧灯罩泛黄，里面也比较旧的情况，很可能这辆车的大灯因为某种原因被更换过，比如发生过碰撞（英文）_____。这时我们就需要小心了。同样，车辆尾灯（英文）_____ 也可以通过这种方式加以判断。

4. 在试乘试驾（英文）_____ 过程中可以注意观察一下仪表盘（英文）_____ 内是否有常亮的故障灯（英文）_____。很多二手车商家会告诉你这是小毛病，但现在很多车型的仪表盘都是模块化设计的，集成度很高，一旦出现故障，很难修理，甚至会让你更换整个模块，价格非常昂贵。

5. 第三者责任保险（英文）_____：被保险人（英文）_____ 或其允许的合格驾驶员在使用保险车辆过程中，发生意外事故（英文）_____，致使第三者遭受人身伤亡或财产的直接损毁，依法应当由被保险人支付的赔偿金额，保险公司依照《道路交通事故处理办法》和**保险合同**（英文）_____的约定给予赔偿。

6. 车身尺寸方面，新一代 7 系长轴距版（底盘代号 G12）**长**（英文）_____、**宽**（英文）_____ **高**（英文）_____ 分别为 5,238 mm/2,169 mm（后视镜展开宽度）/1,479 mm，**轴距**（英文）_____ 为 3,210 mm。与老款车型相比，其车身长度和宽度均有所增加，而在轴距方面则没有变化。

7. 进口揽胜极光，一手自用车，因换车闲置出让。2.0 T **涡轮增压**（英文）_____、6 挡手自一体、3 门四座、闷骚红黑真皮内饰和座椅、全时四驱、**电动转向助力**（英文）_____、发动机电子防盗、车内中控、无钥匙启动及进入系统、全地形 5 种行驶模式、全景天窗、**多功能方向盘**（英文）_____、方向盘换挡、**巡航定速**（英文缩写）_____、GPS 导航、彩色显示大屏、座椅加热、**自动空调**（英文）_____、大灯清洗装置、20 寸轮毂。

VII. Fill in the blanks with the words or phrases in the box. (15')

> product recall; track record; customers; public record; maintenance; limited service; additional information; research

Vehicle history reports

In the United States, an estimated 34% of consumers (in 2006) are buying a vehicle history report for used cars. Vehicle history reports are one way to check the _____ of any used vehicle. Vehicle history reports provide _____ with a record based on the vehicle's serial number (VIN). These reports will indicate items of _____, such as vehicle title branding, lemon-law-buybacks, odometer fraud, and _____. The report may indicate minor/moderate collision damage or improper vehicle _____. An attempt to identify the vehicles which have been previously owned by hire car rental agencies, police and emergency services or taxi fleets is also made. Consumers should _____ vehicles carefully, as these reporting services only report the information to which they have access.

In some places the government is a provider of vehicle history, but this is usually a _____ providing information on just one aspect of the history.

In the UK, the DVLA provides information (Car check) on the registration of vehicles to certain companies for consumer protection and anti-fraud purposes. Companies may add to the reports _____ gathered from police, finance and insurance companies. Car check service is available online for the public and motor trade.

> vehicle owners; vary; insurance; accident; driving record; gender; reduce

BREAKING DOWN "Auto Insurance"

Auto insurance premiums, or the amount policyholders pay to be insured, _____ depending on: age, _____, years of driving experience, _____ and moving violation history, and other factors. Most states mandate that all _____ purchase a minimum amount of auto insurance, but many people purchase additional _____ to further protect themselves.

A poor _____ or the desire for more complete coverage will lead to higher premiums. However, you can _____ your premiums by agreeing to take on more risk, which means increasing your deductible.

Notes

1. Porsche:

保时捷,是德国汽车品牌。公司的创始人是费迪南德·保时捷(又译为"费迪南德·波尔舍")。其生产的保时捷 911 是迄今为止世界上在赛车中最畅销的一款。保时捷一直努力将种种可能性与看似不太可能的东西相组合。如今对于跑车而言,"保时捷"无异于一个全球意义上的代名词。

2. Neoplan:

尼奥普兰巴士公司(Neoplan Bus GmbH)是德国著名的客车生产商,1935 年成立于斯图加特。初期该公司为客车及卡车组装车身,1953 年开始生产一体化的客车。除此之外,尼奥普兰还生产 Apron 机场摆渡车。2001 年,尼奥普兰被 MAN 集团收购,现隶属于 MAN 旗下的 Neoman 汽车公司。

3. Bentley:

宾利是一家发迹于英国的豪华房车和 GT 车的制造商,是由沃尔特·欧文·本特利(1888—1971 年)在 1919 年 7 月于英格兰创立的。从 1919 年成立到 1924 年勒亡赛道上的所向披靡,再到 20 世纪 30 年代初期由于濒临倒闭而并入劳斯莱斯,直到 1998 年被大众收购,宾利饱经磨砺,但是每一辆宾利车都有着传奇的经历。在第一次世界大战中因制造、供应皇家空军飞机引擎而闻名。

4. Acura:

讴歌(曾译为"阿库拉")是日本本田针对美国成立的汽车品牌,起始于 1986 年。从诞生之日起,讴歌不断提升其豪华车型的性能标准——从高性能的跑车、轿车到 MDX 运动性实用车款,再到充满异国情调的 X 型运动车型的问世。美国本田汽车公司的豪华性能部门——讴歌——以其破纪录的先进技术、卓越的工程学,以及霸气十足的造型而著称。

5. Infiniti:

英菲尼迪是日产汽车公司旗下的豪华车品牌,于 1989 年诞生于北美地区。凭借独特前卫的设计、出色的产品性能,以及贴心的客户服务,英菲尼迪迅速成为全球豪华汽车市场中最重要的品牌之一。自诞生之日起,英菲尼迪便以独特前卫的设计、出色的操控表现,以及顶级的客户服务著称。如今英菲尼迪已拥有双门跑车、轿车、越野车和 SUV 等全系列车型。

6. Lexus:

雷克萨斯,全球著名豪华汽车品牌,创立于 1983 年,仅仅用了十几年的时间,在北美便超过了奔驰、宝马的销量。1999 年起至今,其连续位居北美豪华汽车销量第一的宝座。

7. Rolls Royce:

劳斯莱斯(Rolls-Royce)是宝马公司旗下的品牌,于 1906 年在英国正式成立。劳斯莱斯以一个"贵族化"的汽车公司享誉全球,同时也是目前世界三大航空发动机生产商之一。劳斯莱斯是车坛中的贵族,四轮的皇者。从诞生之日起就拥有高人一等的血统。劳斯莱斯成为英国王室专用车已有多年历史。爱德华八世、女王伊丽莎白二世、玛格丽特公主、肯特公爵等众多英王室成员的座驾都是劳斯莱斯。2003年劳斯莱斯汽车公司归入宝马集团。

8. MINI：

在BMW的集团范围内，迷你是一个独特、独立的品牌，诞生于1959年的MINI，设计别具一格。40年来MINI售出超过500万辆，世界各地也有MINI车迷组织。BMW在买下MINI成为旗下的一个品牌之后，投注了上百万美元的研发经费。迷你车被英国人誉为"国车"。

9. 8-speed STEPTRONIC automatic transmission：

8速Steptronic手自一体变速箱在舒适性和动态性能上设立了全新基准。极为精确的挡位传动比确保在所有车速下都能提供最佳动力输出。这不仅显著降低了耗油量，而且使驾驶者能够享受到更佳的运动性和动态性能。特别是在高转速下，附加的挡位可降低发动机转速，进而降低耗油量和发动机噪声。

10. ISOFIX：

ISOFIX的全称为"International Standards Organization FIX"，是指儿童约束系统与车辆连接的一种系统。它包括车辆上的2个刚性连接点，儿童约束系统上的2个相适应的刚性连接装置，还有一种抗翻转的方法（如顶部约束抗翻转、支撑脚抗翻转）。它是一个关于在汽车中安置儿童座椅的新标准。这一标准正在为众多汽车制造商所接受。

11. DSC：

全称为"Dynamic Stability Control"。其中文意思是动态稳定性控制系统。它不仅能够优化起步或加速时的行驶稳定性，还可以改进牵引力的特性。此外，这个系统还能够识别不稳定的行驶条件，如转向不足或过度，有助于汽车保持安全的行驶方向。

12. Double-VANOS：

双凸轮轴可变气门正时系统，是由BMW开发的双凸轮轴可变气门正时系统。这是BMW技术发展领域中的又一项成就：Double-VANOS双凸轮轴可变气门正时系统根据油门踏板和发动机转速控制扭矩曲线，进气和排气气门正时则根据凸轮轴上可控制的角度按照发动机的运行条件进行无级的精准调节。

因此，不仅可以在较低的发动机转速下获得巨大的扭矩，而且能够在较高的转速下获得极佳的功率。未燃烧的残余气体的减少进一步提高了发动机怠速运转的质量。这项卓越的技术确保在动态驾驶条件下以及放松的巡航模式下均可获得最佳的气缸充气效果。

13. DRL：

全称为"Daytime Running Lights"，是使车辆在白天行驶时更容易被人认出来的灯具。它的功效不是为了使驾驶员能看清路面，而是为了让别人知道有一辆车开过来了。因此，这种灯具不是照明灯，而是一种信号灯。

14. Volkswagen Group MQB platform：

大众集团MQB平台，是大众集团在2007年推出的平台化战略的一部分，是一款发动机横置平台。还有，MLB平台是纵置平台。它们将大部分平台整合成这两个平台。新款的奥迪A4，A6，A8都是在MLB平台上开发的。MQB主要开发奥迪、TT、高尔夫、POLO等车型。

15. TFSI：

涡轮增压缸内直喷，就是带涡轮增压（T）的FSI（Fuel Stratified Injection燃料分层喷射技术）发动机，简称TFSI。一般奥迪系列车型会这么称呼，而大众系列直喷且带增压的发动

机被简称为 TSI。FSI 是 Fuel Stratifed Injection 的词头缩写，意指燃油分层喷射。燃油分层喷射技术是发动机稀薄燃烧技术的一种。什么叫稀薄燃烧？顾名思义，就是发动机混合气中的汽油含量低，汽油与空气之比可达 1:25 以上，可达到燃烧效率高，经济、环保等目的。

16. start-stop system：

就是停车/起步系统。汽车在怠速工况下尾气的污染最大，而且白白消耗了汽油，但如果总是频繁地关闭发动机，再重新启动，又会给驾驶带来不便。于是，停车/起步系统应运而生。这种新型的发动机控制系统，可以在汽车遇到红灯或堵车时自动关闭发动机，但当驾驶员松开刹车板或脚踩油门后，发动机便又会自行启动。

17. eco：

这一名称由 Ecology（生态）、Conservation（节能）和 Optimization（优化）合成而得，从一诞生开始，便是以技术、环保和经济性为设计研发的基本理念。这三大性能也成为 ECO 智能发动机家族系列产品始终追求的品质。

18. B&O：

Danish Bang & Olufsen Advanced Sound System（Bang & Olufsen 高级音响系统）。

奥迪 Q7 装备的 Bang & Olufsen 高级音响起动时，声音从两个音源透镜装置中自动从仪表盘开始蔓延，精确而逼真地传播到车内的每一个座位，给您一种非凡的音响体验。两个音响系统与多媒体交互系统（MMI®）和整体 DVD 播放器相连，使您能够播放 5.1 环绕声。

19. e-tron：

涵盖了所有采用电力驱动行驶，即电动化技术的奥迪汽车。奥迪采用各种方法研究电动化模式，包括纯电动、插电式混合动力等。

20. GT：

拉丁文 Gran Turismo，英文翻译为 Grand Tourer。Grand 的意思是豪华，而 Tourer 的意思是旅行者、巡游者的意思。把 Grand 和 Tourer 加在一起，就是豪华旅行车。20 世纪 60 年代的汽车普遍不能胜任长途旅行的工作，机械可靠程度很低。由此，出现了一批高性能、高可靠性的大马力跑车，称为 GT。

21. Hofmeister kink：

被译为霍夫曼拐角。20 世纪 60 年代，为普通人群设计的 BMW1500 为宝马确立了几个重要标杆：双肾造型的中网第一次与横向贯通的隔栅组合在一起，直到今天依然是人们识别宝马的重要标志；从这款产品开始，所有宝马汽车 C 柱靠近后窗的位置都有一个小小的折弯。这个延续了近半个世纪之久的宝马基因被根据当时宝马总设计师的名字命名为"Hofmeister 拐角"。

22. SUV：

全称是"Sport Utility Vehicle"。其中文意思是运动型多功能汽车。这是一种拥有旅行车般的空间机能，配以货卡车的越野能力的车型。按照 SUV 的功能性，通常被分为城市型 SUV 与越野车。现在的 SUV 一般指那些以轿车平台为基础，在一定程度上既具有轿车的舒适性，又具有一定越野性的车型。由于带有 MPV 的座椅多组合功能，适用范围广。SUV 的价位十分宽泛，路面上的常见度仅次于轿车。

23. EPB：

电子驻车 EPB（Electrical Parking Brake）是指由电子控制方式实现停车制动的技术。

24. HDC：

全称是"Hill Descent Control"，陡坡缓降系统,也被称为斜坡控制系统。HDC 使驾驶员能在不踩制动踏板的完全控制情况下，平稳地通过陡峭的下坡坡段。根据需要，制动装置自动控制各车轮，以略快于行走速度向前移动。此时驾驶员可完全专注于控制方向盘。

25. Keyless Go：

又称一键启动，由发射器、遥控中央锁控制模块、驾驶授权系统控制模块 3 个接收器及相关线束组成的控制系统组成。当车主进入车内时，车内检测系统会马上识别智能卡。这时只需轻轻按动启动按钮（或旋钮），就可以正常启动车辆。整个过程中，无须拿出车钥匙。

26. eight speed AMT：

8 速自动变速箱，凭借更多的挡位、更加合理的齿轮比、更快的换挡时间、更平顺的挡位切换感，以及更为先进且智能的电子管理系统，进一步提高了整车的舒适性与运动性能。

27. reversing radar：

驻车雷达是倒车时或泊车时的安全辅助装置，一般被分为前雷达和后雷达。

28. electronic braking system：

与传统的汽车制动系统不同，电子制动系统以电子元件替代了部分机械元件，是一个机电一体化的系统。同时，液压的产生与传递方式也不一样。

Translations

第一单元 汽车文化

第一部分 汽车的分类

1886年德国人卡尔·本茨发明了汽车,宣告人类从此告别了马车时代,迎来了汽车时代。汽车的发明是人类交通史上的重要里程碑。汽车不仅改变了人们的交通方式和时空观念,也深刻影响了人们的生活和工作方式,推动着人类社会的现代文明进程。

现在,汽车已经成为人们生活不可或缺的一部分。为了能够更深入地了解汽车,首先让我们来谈一谈汽车的不同分类。

I. 根据汽车的用途分类

(1) 轿车 (Passenger Cars):以运送人员及其行李和物品为主要目的设计制造的,按照其结构,轿车可分为普通轿车、豪华轿车和旅行轿车三类(见图1-11~图1-13)。

图 1-11 奔驰轿车

图 1-12 沃尔沃轿车

(2) 跑车 (Roadster):以娱乐运动为目的而设计的轻便型高速轿车(见图1-14)。

(3) 客货两用汽车 (Multipurpose Passenger Cars):具有箱式、敞开式(或可敞开式)车身,为便于输送货物而设计的轿车(见图1-15和图1-16)。

图 1-13 福特轿车

图 1-14 兰博基尼跑车

图 1-15 马自达客货两用汽车

图 1-16 福特客货两用车

（4）载货汽车（Motor Trucks）：以运送货物为主要目的设计制造的汽车（见图 1-17 和图 1-18）。

图 1-17 载货汽车（I）

图 1-18 载货汽车（II）

（5）客车（Buses）：以输送人员及其行李为主要目的设计制造的，包括驾驶员坐席在内设有 10 个以上座位的汽车（见图 1-19 和图 1-120）。

图 1-19 客车（I）

图 1-20 客车（II）

（6）专用汽车（Special Purpose Vehicles）：在普通的汽车底盘上安装有特殊用途的专用车身的汽车（见图1-21和图1-22）。

图1-21　专用汽车

图1-22　专用汽车

（7）特种汽车（Special Vehicles）：为了特定的目的而加装特种装备（或装置）的汽车，如清扫车、医疗车、消防车、混凝土搅拌车等，还包括特为农业生产设计的农业作业车以及专供运动和竞赛用的竞赛汽车等（见图1-23～图1-28）。

图1-23　警车

图1-24　消防车

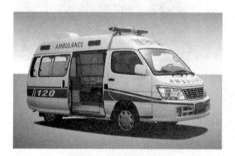

图1-25　急救车

图1-26　混凝土搅拌车

图1-27　清扫车

图1-28　拖拉机

II. 根据汽车的设计理念分类

（1）SUV（Sport Utility Vehicle，运动型多用途车）：SUV 离地间隙较大，在一定程度上既有轿车的舒适性，又有越野车的越野性（见图 1-29 和图 1-30）。

图 1-29　宝马 X6

图 1-30　保时捷卡宴

（2）CRV 是本田的一款车，国产的叫东风本田 CRV（City Recreation Vehicle，城市休闲车）（见图 1-31）。

（3）SRV（Small Recreation Vehicle，小型休闲车）一般指两厢轿车，如吉利豪情 SRV（见图 1-32）。

图 1-31　本田 CRV

图 1-32　吉利豪情 SRV

（4）RAV 源于丰田的一款小型运动车 RAV4。丰田公司的解释是 Recreation（休闲）、Activity（运动）、Vehicle（车），缩写就成了 RAV，又因为车是四轮驱动的，所以后面又加了一个 4（见图 1-33）。

（5）HRV 源于上海通用凯越 HRV 轿车，取 Healthy（健康）、Recreation（休闲）、Vigorous（活力）之意，是一个全新的汽车设计理念（见图 1-34）。

图 1-33　丰田 RAV4

图 1-34　别克凯越 HRV

（6）MPV（Multi-Purpose Vehicle 或 Mini Passenger Van，多用途汽车）集轿车、旅行轿车和厢式货车的功能于一体，车内的每一座椅都可以调整，并有多种组合方式。近年来，MPV趋向于小型化，并出现了所谓的 S-MPV，S 就是小（Small）的意思，车身紧凑，一般为5～7个座（见图1-35和图1-36）。

图1-35　东风本田艾力绅

图1-36　别克 GL8

（7）CUV（Car-Based Utility Vehicle）是以轿车为设计平台，融合轿车、MPV 和 SUV 特性为一体的多用途车，也被称为 Crossover（见图1-37和图1-38）。

图1-37　长城哈弗 CUV

图1-38　三菱欧蓝德

图1-39　奇瑞瑞虎5

（8）NCV（New Concept Vehicle，新概念轿车）以轿车底盘为平台，兼顾了轿车的舒适性和 SUV 的越野性（见图1-39）。

（9）RV（Recreation Vehicle，休闲车）是一种被用于娱乐、休闲、旅游的汽车。首先提出 RV 概念的国家是日本。从广义上讲，除了轿车和跑车外的轻型乘用车，如 MPV，SUV，CUV 等，都可归属于 RV。

从2002年3月份起，新的汽车分类国家标准实施。新国标在按用途划分的基础上，建立了乘用车和商用车概念，尤其是在轿车的划分上改革较大，解决了管理和分类的矛盾，是和国际接轨的标准。

A. 汽车
（a）乘用车（Passenger Car）
（b）商用车（Commercial Vehicle）
B. 拖车

第二部分　汽车外形的演变

从被发明到现在的 100 多年里，汽车无论是从车身造型，还是动力源或底盘、电气设备来讲，都有了翻天覆地的变化。其中最富特色、最具直观感的当数车身外形的演变（见图 1-40）。

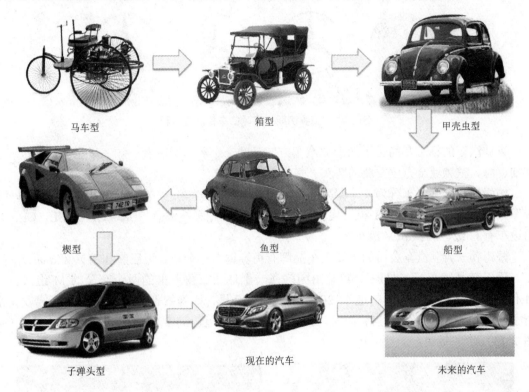

图 1-40　汽车外形演变

第三部分　汽车公司和品牌的介绍

I. 德国汽车公司和品牌

1. 梅赛德斯—奔驰汽车公司

梅赛德斯—奔驰汽车公司是世界十大汽车公司之一，也是世界上最著名的大客车和重型载重汽车的生产厂家。

梅赛德斯—奔驰汽车公司由奔驰、戴姆勒两家汽车公司于 1926 年合并而成，总部设在德国的斯图加特市。奔驰公司于 1883 年创建，创始人卡尔·本茨。戴姆勒公司由戈特利布·戴姆勒创建于 1890 年。

1926 年，奔驰公司和戴姆勒公司合并以后，两者的标志也结合在一起。图 1-41 所示是梅赛德斯—奔驰公司车标的演变过程。

图 1-41　梅赛德斯—奔驰的车标演变过程

奔驰汽车的标志是简化了的形似汽车方向盘的一个环形圈围着一颗三叉星。三叉星表示在陆、海、空领域全方位发展的势头。

戴姆勒—奔驰轿车分为4个级别："A级"代表微型轿车，"C级"代表紧凑型轿车，"E级"代表中等尺寸轿车，"S级"代表大型豪华轿车。跑车系列有SLK，CLK，SL，CL。多用途车有G级、M级和V级车等。

戴姆勒—奔驰汽车公司的主要汽车品牌有梅赛德斯—奔驰、迈巴赫和精灵（Smart）等。

迈巴赫品牌车标（见图1-42）由围绕在一个球面三角形里的两个交叉的M组成。双M代表的含义是"迈巴赫制造"。2014年11月19日，梅赛德斯—奔驰在广州正式发布全新子品牌梅赛德斯—迈巴赫；同时，该品牌首款车型迈巴赫S级也正式全球首发亮相（见图1-43）。

图 1-42　迈巴赫车标

图 1-43　迈巴赫 62 S

Smart是德国梅赛德斯—奔驰与手表巨头瑞士斯沃奇公司合作的产物。Smart中的S代表斯沃奇（Swatch），M代表戴姆勒集团（Mercedes-Benz），而ART在英文中则是"艺术"的意思（见图1-44），合起来可以理解为：这部车代表了斯沃奇和戴姆勒合作的艺术，而"smart"车名本身在英文中也有"聪明""伶俐"的意思，这也契合了Smart公司的设计理念。小巧的造型，配合智能化及人性化的操控设计，令Smart的车型如同一部聪明的大玩具（见图1-45）。

2. 奥迪汽车公司

奥迪是一个国际高品质汽车开发商、制造商，现为大众汽车公司的子公司。

图 1-44　Smart 车标　　　　　　　图 1-45　2015 Smart Fortwo 1.0 L

从 1932 年起，奥迪开始采用四环徽标。它象征着奥迪与小奇迹（DKW）、霍希（Horch）和漫游者（Wanderer）合并成的汽车联盟公司。其中每一个圆环都代表一个公司。4 个圆环同样大小，并列相扣，代表 4 家公司地位平等，团结紧密，整个联盟牢不可破。

目前，奥迪汽车公司生产的产品主要有 Q3，Q5，Q7（SUV），以及 R 系、敞篷车、跑车系列等。A 系列是奥迪最主要的车型。A3，A4，A6，A8 是目前最畅销的奥迪车型，分别是 A，B，C，D 级轿车。竞争对手分别是宝马 1，3，5，7 系和奔驰 B，C，E，S 级。奥迪轿车和 MPV 的型号均以公司英文（Audi）的第一个字母（A）打头。其后的数字越大表示价格越高（见图 1-46～图 1-49）。

图 1-46　奥迪 Q3　　　　　　　　图 1-47　奥迪 Q5

图 1-48　奥迪 Q7　　　　　　　　图 1-49　奥迪 R8

A1 系列是紧凑型掀背车（包括五门掀背、三门掀背和敞篷车）（见图 1-50）。

A2 系列是小型旅行车（见图 1-51）。

图 1-50　奥迪 A1

图 1-51　奥迪 A2

A3 系列也被称为小型旅行车（见图 1-52）。
A4 系列是运动轿车（见图 1-53）。

图 1-52　奥迪 A3

图 1-53　奥迪 A4

A5 系列是双门轿跑车（见图 1-54）。
A6（A6 L）系列是公务轿车（见图 1-55）。

图 1-54　奥迪 A5

图 1-55　奥迪 A6

A7 系列是大型豪华轿跑车（见图 1-56）。
A8 系列是大型公务轿车（见图 1-57）。

图 1-56　奥迪 A7

图 1-57　奥迪 A8

S 系列是基于 A 系列的较高性能车型（见图 1-58）。竞争车型为宝马的 135i, 335i, 550i, 以及其他低排放顶级车型。

RS 系列是基于 A 系列的顶级性能车型（见图 1-59）。

图 1-58　2015 奥迪 S8 Plus

图 1-59　2016 RS7 Sportback Gain

3. 宝马汽车公司

宝马汽车公司是由一个制造飞机发动机的公司于 1916 年 3 月注册的。宝马汽车公司的前身虽是宝马飞机公司，但后来被改为巴伐利亚发动机制造厂（Bayerische Motoren Werke），1918 年更名为宝马汽车公司。

BMW 是巴伐利亚发动机制造厂"Bayerische Motoren Werke"3 个单词首字母的缩写。宝马汽车公司以生产宝马跑车、宝马轿车、宝马摩托车为主，其产品享誉全球。

宝马采用了内外双圆圈的原型，并在双圆环标之间有 BMW 字样的商标（见图 1-60）。在内圆的圆形间隔图案中，采用蓝天、白云和运转不停的螺旋桨，寓示宝马汽车公司渊源悠久的历史，象征该公司过去在航空发动机技术方面的领先地位，又象征公司的一贯宗旨和日新月异的新面貌。

BMW 集团拥有 BMW，MINI 和 Rolls-Royce（劳斯莱斯）3 个品牌。这些品牌占据了从小型车到顶级豪华轿车各个细分市场的高端，使 BMW 集团成为世界上唯一一家专注于高档汽车和摩托车的制造商（见图 1-61～图 1-64）。

图 1-60　宝马车标

宝马的车系有 1，2，3，4，5，6，7，8（停产），i，M，X，Z 几个系列。其中 1 系是小型汽车，2 系是小型轿跑，3 系是中型汽车，4 系是中型轿跑（含敞篷），5 系是中大型汽车，

6 系是中大型轿跑（含敞篷），7 系是豪华 D 级车，i 系是宝马未量产的概念车系列，M 系是宝马的高性能跑车版本，X 系是宝马特定的 SUV（运动型多功能汽车）车系，而 Z 系则是宝马的入门级跑车（见图 1-65～图 1-76）。

图 1-61　MINI 车标

图 1-62　劳斯莱斯车标

图 1-63　Mini Countryman

图 1-64　劳斯莱斯幻影 6.7 Standard

图 1-65　宝马 1 系

图 1-66　宝马 2 系跑车

图 1-67　宝马 3 系

图 1-68　宝马 4 系

图 1-69　宝马 5 系

图 1-70　宝马 6 系

图 1-71　宝马 7 系

图 1-72　宝马 X6

图 1-73　宝马 i8

图 1-74　宝马 Z4

图 1-75　宝马 M6

图 76　宝马 1 系旅行车

4. 大众汽车公司

1937 年 3 月 28 日，费迪南德·保时捷（又译费迪南德·波尔舍，图 1-77）在奔驰公司的支持下创建了大众开发公司,并将其更名为大众汽车股份有限公司。大众汽车公司(Volks Wagenwerk, VW)是德国最大的,也是最年轻的汽车公司,是一家国际性集团公司,是全球领先的汽车制造商之一,同时也是欧洲最大的汽车生产商(见图1-78)。

图 1-77　费迪南德·保时捷

图 1-78　大众车标

大众汽车公司的德文 Volks Wagenwerk 意为大众使用的汽车。图形商标是德文 Volks Wagenwerk 单词的首字母"V"和"W"的叠合,表示大众公司及其产品"必胜—必胜—必胜"。

大众汽车公司生产的车型有甲壳虫(Beetle)、高尔夫(Golf)、捷达(Jetta)、帕萨特(Passat)、迈腾(Magotan)、CC、辉腾(Phaeton)、桑塔纳(Santana)、波罗(Polo)、文托(Vento)、卡拉维拉(Caravelle)等。大众汽车是大众集团(Volkswagen Group)的成员之一。其他集团公司包括奥迪、尼奥普兰、西亚特、斯柯达、宾利、布加迪、兰博基尼、保时捷、杜卡迪摩托、Man 卡车(见图1-79~图1-90)。

图 1-79　甲壳虫

图 1-80　帕萨特

图 1-81　迈腾

图 1-82　辉腾

图 1-83　西亚特车标

图 1-84　斯柯达车标

图 1-85　西亚特 IBE 电动概念车

图 1-86　斯柯达晶锐

图 1-87　宾利车标

图 1-88　布加迪车标

图 1-89　宾利添越

图 1-90　布加迪威航

II. 美国汽车公司和品牌

1. 福特汽车公司

福特汽车公司是世界最大的汽车企业之一，1903 年由亨利·福特（见图 1-91）创立。福特汽车的标志是采用福特的英文"Ford"字样,蓝底白字。由于创建人亨利·福特喜欢小动物,所以标志设计者把福特的英文画成一只小白兔样子的图案。1908年,福特汽车公司生产出世界上第一辆属于普通百姓的汽车——福特 T 型车(见图 1-92)。世界汽车工业革命就此开始。1913年,福特汽车公司开发出了世界上第一条流水线。福特先生因此被尊称为"为世界装上轮子"的人。

目前,福特汽车公司拥有福特(Ford)、林肯(Lincoln)、水星(Mercury)、阿斯顿·马丁(Aston Martin)、捷豹(Jaguar)、马自达(Mazda)、沃尔沃(Volvo)和路虎(Land Rover)。其中捷豹、路虎已被出售给了印度塔塔集团,马自达已被减持股份,沃尔沃出售给了吉利集团,阿斯顿马丁也已出售。水星系列停产(见图 1-93~图 1-98)。

你不能以你将来要做的事来建立信誉。

——亨利·福特

图 1-91　亨利·福特

图 1-92　亨利·福特和第一辆 T 型车

图 1-93　福特车标

图 1-94　林肯车标

图 1-95　福特翼虎

图 1-96　林肯 MKX

图 1-97　福特蒙迪欧

图 1-98　林肯 MKZ

2. 通用汽车公司

通用汽车公司的前身是 1907 年由戴维·别克（见图 1-99）创办的别克汽车公司。1908 年美国最大的马车制造商威廉姆·C·杜兰特（见图 1-100）买下了别克汽车公司并成为该公司的总经理，同时推出 C 型车（见图 1-101）。

图 1-99　戴维·别克

图 1-100　威廉姆·C·杜兰特

图 1-101　别克 C 型车

到 1908 年，别克汽车公司已经成为全美主要汽车生产商。杜兰特以别克汽车公司和奥兹汽车公司为基础成立了一家汽车控股公司——通用汽车公司（GM），并于 1909 年合并了另外两家汽车公司——奥克兰汽车公司和凯迪拉克汽车公司。

其标志 GM 是其英文名称（General Motors Corporation）前两个单词的第一个字母（见图 1-102）。

通用汽车在全球生产、销售包括雪佛兰、别克、GMC、凯迪拉克、宝骏、霍顿、五十铃、解放、欧宝、沃豪，以及五菱一系列品牌车型并提供相关服务（见图 1-103～图 1-110）。目前，通用汽车旗下多个品牌全系列车型畅销于全球 120 多个国家和地区，包括电动车、微车、重型全尺寸卡车、紧凑型车及敞篷车。

图 1-102　通用车标

图 1-103　雪佛兰车标

图 1-104　别克车标

图 1-105　雪佛兰科迈罗

图 1-106　别克昂科威

图 1-107　GMC 车标

图 1-108　凯迪拉克车标

图 1-109　GMC SAVANA

图 1-110　凯迪拉克凯雷德

3. 克莱斯勒汽车公司

克莱斯勒（Chrysler）汽车公司是美国第三大汽车工业公司，创立于1925年。创始人名叫沃尔特·克莱斯勒（见图1-111）。该公司在全世界许多国家设有子公司，是一个跨国汽车公司。公司总部设在美国底特律。

克莱斯勒公司的标志（见图1-112）是一枚五角星勋章，像一枚受勋的五角星奖章，体现了克莱斯勒人的远大抱负。它的商标为五边形，被五角星分割成5个部分，寓意亚、非、欧、美、澳五大洲，也意味着该公司的汽车遍布五大洲。

图1-111 沃尔特·克莱斯勒

图1-112 克莱斯勒公司标志

克莱斯勒汽车公司有道奇轿车部、顺风轿车部、克莱斯勒轿车部以及道奇载重车部、零部件部等（见图1-113～图1-116）。1998年，克莱斯勒和奔驰宣布合并，形成世界上又一大汽车集团。目前，它和奔驰共同拥有奔驰、克莱斯勒、JEEP、三菱、迈巴赫等品牌。

图1-113 克莱斯勒车标　　　　　　　　　图1-114 道奇车标

图1-115 克莱斯勒300C　　　　　　　　　图1-116 道奇酷威

III. 日本汽车公司和品牌

1. 丰田汽车公司

丰田（TOYOTA）汽车公司的前身是 1933 年在丰田自动织布机所设立的汽车部。创始人是丰田喜一郎（见图 1-117）。1937 年 8 月 28 日，正式改名为丰田汽车工业公司。1982 年 7 月 1 日，丰田汽车工业公司和丰田汽车销售公司合并为丰田汽车公司。总部设在日本爱知县丰田市。

20 世纪 80 年代后期，丰田汽车公司的商标图案（见图 1-118）被改成 3 个椭圆。3 个椭圆巧妙地组合在一起，象征着用户的心和汽车厂家的心是连在一起的，具有相互信赖感。标志中的大椭圆代表地球，中间由两个椭圆垂直组合成一个"T"字，是 TOYOTA 的第一个字母，代表丰田汽车公司。它象征丰田公司立足于未来，对未来充满信心，也象征着丰田重科技和革新。

图 1-117　丰田喜一郎

图 1-118　丰田车标

丰田品牌旗下的车型包括皇冠、卡罗拉、锐志、普锐斯、普拉多、RAV4、普瑞维亚、兰德酷路泽、威驰、柯斯达、酷路泽、汉兰达、雅力士等（见图 1-119～图 1-126）。

图 1-119　丰田皇冠

图 1-120　丰田卡罗拉

图 1-121　丰田锐志

图 1-122　丰田普锐斯

图 1-123　丰田普拉多

图 1-124　丰田 RAV 4

图 1-125　丰田汉兰达

图 1-126　丰田兰德酷路泽

雷克萨斯：原来被译为"凌志"，是 1989 年丰田汽车公司专门为向国外销售豪华轿车而成立的一个分部。"Lexus"发音与英文豪华"luxury"的读音相近，使人联想到豪华车的印象。

雷克萨斯的商标由图形商标和文字商标两部分组成。在一个椭圆中镶嵌着英文"Lexus"的第一个大写字母"L"。椭圆代表着地球，表示雷克萨斯轿车遍布全世界（见图 1-127 和图 1-128）。

图 1-127　雷克萨斯车标

图 1-128　雷克萨斯 LX570

2. 本田汽车公司

本田（HONDA）汽车公司的前身是本田技术研究所，1948年由本田宗一郎（见图1-129）创建。该公司是世界上最大的摩托车生产厂家，于1962年开始生产汽车。汽车产量和规模名列世界十大汽车厂家之列。公司总部在日本东京。本田公司先后在美国、亚洲各国、英国等建立了分公司。

本田标志中的H是"Honda"本田的第一个字母（见图1-130）。这个标志体现出本田公司年轻、技术先进、设计新颖的特点。

图1-129 本田宗一郎

图1-130 本田车标

本田公司旗下主要有本田（Honda）和讴歌（Acura）两大品牌（见图1-131～图1-136）。

图1-131 本田雅阁

图1-132 本田思域

图1-133 本田CR-V

图1-134 本田奥德赛

图 1-135　讴歌车标

图 1-136　讴歌 MDX

本田品牌主要车型有雅阁（Accord）、思域（Civic）、风范（City）、奥德赛（Odyssey）、飞度（Fit）、CR-V 等。

3. 日产汽车公司

日产汽车公司的前身是快进社和户烟铸造公司。1933 年，户烟铸造公司与日本产业公司合资建立汽车制造公司，于 1934 年更名为日产汽车公司。日产的 NISSAN 是日本产业的简称。

车标（见图 1-137）中圆表示太阳，而中间的字是"日产"两字的日语拼音形式。整个图案的意思是"以人和汽车的明天为目标"。

目前日产旗下车型主要有骐达、阳光、骊威、逍客、天籁、风度、公爵等（见图 1-138 和图 1-139）。

图 1-137　日产车标

图 1-138　日产天籁

图 1-139　日产逍客

英菲尼迪：车坛有"日产的科技，丰田的销售"的说法。英菲尼迪是日本汽车的高端品牌。英菲尼迪的标志是"一条无限延伸的道路"。椭圆曲线代表无限扩张之意，也象征着"全世界"；两条直线代表通往巅峰的道路，象征无尽的发展，象征着英菲尼迪人的一种永无止境的追求（见图 1-140 和图 1-141）。

图 1-140 英菲尼迪车标

图 1-141 英菲尼迪 QX70

IV. 韩国汽车公司和品牌

1. 起亚汽车公司

起亚汽车是韩国最老牌的汽车制造厂。成立于 1944 年 12 月的起亚汽车前身名为京城精密工业（Kyungsung Precision Industry）。1952 年 3 月制造出韩国第一辆自行车，公司更名为起亚汽车公司。

起亚的名字，源自汉语。"起"代表起来，而"亚"代表在亚洲。因此，起亚的意思，就是"起于东方"或"起于亚洲"。正反映了起亚的胸襟——崛起亚洲，走向世界。

起亚汽车现行的标志由白色的椭圆、红色的背景，以及黑体的"KIA"3 个字母构成，而更改后的标识变为亮红的椭圆、白色的背景，以及红色的"KIA"字样，给人以新鲜感。起亚汽车公司标志是英文"KIA"，形似一只飞鹰，象征公司如腾空飞翔的雄鹰（见图 1-142）。

这个改变并颠覆品牌的人叫彼得·希瑞尔（Peter Schreyer）（见图 1-143）。在入主韩国的起亚之前，他已经是欧洲三大汽车设计师之一。他曾设计了大众新甲壳虫、奥迪 TT、奥迪 A6，以及其他经典车型。希瑞尔为起亚带来的不仅是外观设计的变化，还包括整体设计思路的变革。起亚将迈向年轻活力的设计方向。

图 1-142 起亚车标

图 1-143 彼得·希瑞尔

主要车型：Quoris/K9（首款后驱车型，即将引入）、K4（即将推出）、K3、K2、

Picanto/Morning、锐欧、Venga、Cee'd、秀尔、速迈、福瑞迪、Oprius/K5、凯尊、索兰托、狮跑、智跑、霸锐、佳乐、威客、欧菲莱斯（停售）等（见图 1-144～图 1-147）。

图 1-144　起亚 K5

图 1-145　起亚 K9

图 1-146　起亚狮跑

图 1-147　起亚智跑

2. 现代汽车公司

现代汽车公司（HYUNDAI）是韩国最大的一家汽车公司，世界 20 家最大汽车公司之一，创立于 1967 年 12 月。创建人为郑周永（见图 1-148）。公司总部设在韩国首尔，汽车年产量达 100 多万辆。现代汽车公司已发展成为现代集团。其经营范围由汽车扩展到建筑、造船和机械等领域。

2002 年 10 月 18 日，现代汽车与北京汽车工业公司合资建立了北京现代汽车有限公司。现代汽车公司的标志（见图 1-149）由椭圆及椭圆内的斜字母 H 组成。H 是现代公司英文名 HYUNDAI 的首个字母。商标中的椭圆既代表汽车方向盘，又可以被看作地球。两者结合寓意了现代汽车将遍布全世界。

现代汽车的经营理念是：以创意的挑战精神为基础，创造丰富多彩的汽车生活，尽力协调股东、客户、职员以及汽车产业之间的利益关系。

现代主要有伊兰特、雅绅特、瑞纳、索纳塔、名图、ix35、圣达菲、途胜等车型（见图 1-150～图 1-153）。

图 1-148 郑周永

图 1-149 现代车标

图 1-150 现代伊兰特

图 1-151 现代名图

图 1-152 现代 ix35

图 1-153 现代途胜

V. 法国汽车公司和品牌

汽车诞生于德国,成长于法国。自德国人发明汽车后,法国汽车工业的先驱者们迅速开始制造汽车,完善汽车结构,创建汽车公司。1890 年,阿尔芒·标致(见图 1-154)制造出法国的第一辆汽车,开创了法国汽车工业的先河。

标致—雪铁龙汽车集团

1903 年,标致推出了摩托车并使用标致的品牌至今。1929 年,推出标致 201。这是标致第一次使用数字（中间为"0"的3个数字）对产品进行命名。这也成为以后标致汽车命名的方法。

1976年，标致汽车公司兼并了雪铁龙汽车公司，成立了标致—雪铁龙汽车公司。1980年，改为标致雪铁龙集团（PSA—Peugeot Societe Anonyme），包括标致汽车公司、雪铁龙汽车公司和塔伯特（TALBOT）汽车公司。PSA集团拥有标致和雪铁龙两大品牌，生产和销售汽车和摩托车。

标致汽车公司标志是一只站立的雄狮。雄狮是标志家族的徽章，后也是蒙贝利亚尔省的省徽。雄狮商标最初只用于锯条，1880年演变为标致公司的唯一商标。1850—2003年，标致的雄狮图案经过了9次演变（见图1-155）。目前采用的是前爪伸出做拳击状的立狮图案。雄狮商标既突出力量，又强调节奏，富有时代感，暗示着标志汽车像雄狮一样威武、敏捷，永远保持旺盛的生命力。

图1-154　阿尔芒·标致

图1-155　标志车标的演变

标致主要有206、207、307、308、308CC、3008、408、4008、508等（见图1-156～图1-159）。

图1-156　标致408

图1-157　标致508

图 1-158 标致 3008

图 1-159 标致 RCZ

雪铁龙汽车公司的商标（见图 1-160）是人字形齿轮的一对轮齿，象征着人们密切合作，同心协力，步步高升；同时，此商标图案也说明雪铁龙汽车公司的技术领先地位。

雪铁龙的主要车型有爱丽舍、C2、C3—XR、C4、C4 Aircross、C5、世嘉、DS5 等（见图 1-161～图 1-163）。

图 1-160 雪铁龙车标

图 1-161 雪铁龙 C4 L

图 1-162 雪铁龙爱丽舍

图 1-163 雪铁龙 C3-XR

VI. 意大利汽车公司和品牌

1. 菲亚特汽车公司

FIAT 是意大利都灵汽车制造厂（Fabbrica Italiana Automobili Torino）的缩写（见图 1-164）。经过一个多世纪的发展，菲亚特汽车集团已成为意大利规模最大的汽车公司。不仅汽车产量占意大利汽车总产量的 90%以上，而且控制着阿尔法·罗密欧、玛莎拉蒂、蓝旗亚、法拉利等汽车公司。为方便经营，1979 年菲亚特汽车成为菲亚特汽车集团中一个独立经营的公司。

菲亚特旗下的著名品牌包括菲亚特、蓝旗亚、阿尔法·罗密欧和玛莎拉蒂。其中法拉利也是菲亚特下的独立子公司。工程车辆公司有依维柯公司。

菲亚特品牌目前生产的主要车型有熊猫（Panda）、派力奥（Palio）、西耶那（Siena）、菲翔（Viaggio）、菲跃（Freemont）、乌诺（Uno）等（见图 1-165 和图 1-166）。这些都是意大利著名设计师乔治·亚罗（见图 1-167）设计的。

图 1-164　菲亚特车标

图 1-165　菲亚特菲翔

图 1-166　菲亚特菲跃

图 1-167　乔治·亚罗

2. 阿尔法·罗密欧汽车公司

阿尔法·罗密欧（ALFA ROMEO）汽车公司是意大利高级轿车、跑车和赛车的制造商，建于 1910 年，总部在意大利米兰市。

1911 年，阿尔法·罗密欧汽车公司采用了将"ALFA ROMEO"置于米兰市的圆形市徽外圈上半部的商标（见图 1-168）。采用该商标，是为了纪念米兰市的创始人维斯康泰公爵及其家族。红色的十字是米兰城盾形徽章的一部分，用来纪念古代东征的十字军骑士，而吃人的龙形蛇图案则来自当地一个古老贵族家族的家徽，象征着中世纪米兰领主维斯康泰公爵的祖先击退使城市人民遭受苦难的"龙蛇"的传说。

阿尔法·罗密欧公司的经典车型有阿尔法（Alfa）、蜘蛛（Spider）、阿尔菲塔（Alfetta）、吉利耶塔（Giulietta）、阿尔法苏（Alfasud）等（见图 1-169）。

图 1-168　阿尔法·罗密欧车标

图 1-169　阿尔法 C4

3. 法拉利汽车公司

法拉利（FERRARI）汽车公司是意大利超级跑车和赛车制造公司，创建于 1929 年（最早是赛车俱乐部，即法拉利车队的前身）。创始人是恩佐·法拉利（世界赛车冠军）（见图 1-170）。公司总部设在意大利的摩德纳。菲亚特集团拥有法拉利汽车公司 50%的股份。但法拉利现为菲亚特汽车公司旗下独立运营的子公司。

法拉利汽车公司及其汽车商标为一匹跃马（见图 1-171）。在第一次世界大战中意大利有一位表现出色的飞行员。他的飞机上就有一匹会给他带来好运的跃马。他曾多次击落敌人的战机。在法拉利最初的比赛获胜后，飞行员的父母亲（一对伯爵夫妇）建议：法拉利也应在车上印上这匹带来好运气的跃马。法拉利欣然同意。跃马成了法拉利赛车上的吉祥物。后来飞行员死了，马就变成了黑颜色，而标志底色为公司总部所在地摩德纳的金丝雀的颜色。红色是法拉利赛车的主色。因此，它也被称作红色的跃马或红魔。

图 1-170　恩佐·法拉利

图 1-171　法拉利车标

法拉利公司的经典车型有法拉利 F355 Spider、法拉利 F50 Ferrari、法拉利 F512 M，以及法拉利 458 等（见图 1-172～图 1-175）。

图 1-172　458

图 1-173　LaFerrari

图 1-174　法拉利 FF

图 1-175　F12 berlinetta

4. 玛莎拉蒂汽车公司

1914 年，玛莎拉蒂（MASERATI）家族的四兄弟（见图 1-176）创建了玛莎拉蒂汽车公司，总部位于意大利的博洛尼亚，主要生产轿车和跑车，在欧洲具有很高的知名度。目前它是菲亚特汽车公司的子公司。

意大利是跑车王国。亚平宁人特有的奔放性格使得他们所钟爱的跑车同样激情四溢。大多数中国人对于意大利跑车的认识都是从法拉利开始的，而对玛莎拉蒂跑车却不甚了解。其实，玛莎拉蒂的历史比法拉利还要早，更是比法拉利在赛场上先行取得过辉煌的成绩。

玛莎拉蒂汽车的商标是在树叶形的底座上放置的一件三叉戟（见图 1-177）。这也是公司所在地意大利博洛尼亚市的市徽。相传它是罗马神话中的海神纳普秋手中的武器（在希腊神话中则被称为海神波赛顿），显示出海神巨大无比的威力。该商标表示玛莎拉蒂汽车公司及汽车像浩瀚无垠的大海在咆哮，暗示了玛莎拉蒂汽车快速飞奔的潜力。

图 1-176　玛莎拉蒂四兄弟

图 1-177　玛莎拉蒂车标

玛莎拉蒂的车型主要有玛莎拉蒂 GT、Ghibli、MC 12、GTS 等（见图 1-178～图 1-181）。

图 1-178　玛莎拉蒂 Ghibli

图 1-179　玛莎拉蒂 GTS

图 1-180　玛莎拉蒂 GT

图 1-181　MC 12

5. 兰博基尼汽车公司

兰博基尼（LAMBORGHINI）汽车公司建于 1961 年。创始人是费鲁齐欧·兰博基尼（Ferruccio Lamborghini）（见图 1-182）。其总部设在意大利的圣亚加塔·波隆尼，主要生产跑车和赛车。

兰博基尼的骨子里有一种唯我独尊的霸气。这种霸气使其在汽车界树立起了显赫的地位。1998 年归入奥迪旗下，目前为大众集团（Volkswagen Group）旗下品牌之一。

兰博基尼的车标（见图 1-183）是一头浑身充满了力气、蓄势待发的犟牛，寓意该公司生产的赛车功率大、速度快、战无不胜。据说兰博基尼本人就是这种不甘示弱的牛脾气，也体现了兰博基尼公司产品的特点。

图 1-182　费鲁齐欧·兰博基尼

图 1-183　兰博基尼车标

兰博基尼的车型主要有埃文塔多、蝙蝠、盖拉多、穆拉、鬼怪、雷文顿等（见图 1-184～图 1-189）。

图 1-184　兰博基尼埃文塔多

图 1-185　兰博基尼鬼怪

图 1-186　兰博基尼穆拉

图 1-187　兰博基尼盖拉多

图 1-188　兰博基尼蝙蝠

图 1-189　兰博基尼雷文顿

第二单元　汽车配置单认知

宝马 5 系 GT 528i 领先型

多功能大尺寸全景天窗彰显了宝马 5 系 GT 528i 领先型（见图 2-3）奢华的动态理念。超大的车内空间可依据需求容纳多名乘客并载物。具备进攻姿态的宝马 5 系 GT 528i 领先型从外观上看十分抢眼。低重心底盘使它的操控更精准，特别是在转弯时操控更灵活。4.4 L 4 缸发动机，可达 408 马力①。搭载 8 速 STEPTRONIC 自动变速器，无论是高速行驶，还是低速行驶，车子都非常平稳。

图 2-3　宝马 5 系 GT 528i 领先型

---

① 1 马力≈0.735 499 千瓦。

技术参数

以宝马 5 系 528i 领先型为例（见图 2-4、图 2-5、表 2-1 和表 2-2）。

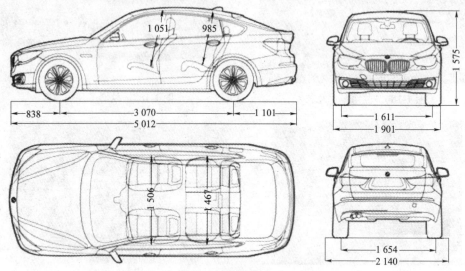

图 2-4　宝马 5 系 GT528i 领先型尺寸

*测量车宽不包括后视镜（总宽测量时展开后视镜）

表 2-1　宝马 5 系 GT 528i 领先型尺寸

名　　称	数　　据
总长	5 012
总宽	2 140
总高	1 575
轴距	3 070
前悬	838
后悬	1 101
前轮距	1 611
后轮距	1 654
宽度（后视镜折叠）	1 901
前排座椅宽度	1 506
后排座椅宽度	1 467

*汽车尺寸测量单位均为毫米。

图 2-5　宝马 5 系 GT 528i 领先型侧面

表 2-2　宝马 5 系 GT 528i 领先型的主要技术参数

燃 油 消 耗	数 据
市区内油耗 [L·(100 km)$^{-1}$]	9.6
高速路油耗 [L·(100 km)$^{-1}$]	6.2
综合油耗 [L·(100 km)$^{-1}$]	7.4
油箱容积/L	70
性能	
最高车速/(km·h^{-1})	240
由 0~100 km/h 加速/s	7.0
重量	
自重 欧盟标准/kg	1 980
最大载重量/kg	2 505
允许载量/kg	525
前/后轴允许承重/kg	1 065/1 490
发动机	
气缸数/气门数	4/4
排量/cm^3	1 997
冲程/气缸孔径/mm	90.1/84
额定最大功率 [kW (hp)]/额定转速/(r·min^{-1})	180/245/5 000~6 500
最大扭矩（Nm）/转速/(r·min^{-1})	350/1 250~4 800
车轮	
前轮胎尺寸	245/50 R 18
后轮胎尺寸	245/50 R 18
前轮圈尺寸	8 J×18
后轮圈尺寸	8 J×18

相关部件英文表达（见图 2-6～图 2-7）。

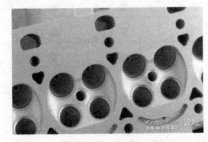

图 2-6　气缸

图 2-7　轮胎标识

（四缸四气门发动机）

马牌：轮胎品牌

ContiSport Contact 3：胎面

245：胎宽

50：扁平率

R：子午线轮胎

18：轮辋直径

100：载重率

Y：速率

SSR：自撑式防爆轮胎

配置单

从安全性、内部装备、外部装备和其他几个重要方面对宝马 5 系 GT 的 4 款车型进行比较。■ 标准装备　□ 选择装备　－无法供应

安全性（表 2-3）：

表 2-3　从安全性方面对宝马 5 系 GT 的 4 款车型进行比较

车　型	528i* 领先型	528i* 豪华型	535i* 领先型	535i* 豪华型
随动控制大灯	□	■	□	■
主动安全系统	■	■	■	■
安全气囊				
——双前座安全气囊	■	■	■	■
——驾驶者和前、后座乘客的头部安全气囊	■	■	■	■
——驾驶者和前座乘客的侧面安全气囊	■	■	■	■
报警系统，附遥控器	■	■	■	■
防抱死制动系统（ABS）	■	■	■	■
儿童座椅固定装置 ISOFIX	■	■	■	■
中央锁	■	■	■	■
动态稳定控制系统扩展型	■	■	■	■
前后部驻车距离报警器（PDC）	■	■	■	■
侧面撞击防护系统（一体式，包括车顶横梁）	■	■	■	■
雨量探测器和自动大灯控制	■	■	■	■
远、近光氙气前灯	■	■	■	■
LED 雾灯	■	■	■	■
大灯清洗系统	■	■	■	■
警告三角标志及急救包	■	■	■	■

相关部件英文表达

随动控制 LED 大灯包括带市区和高速公路可变光线分配功能的自适应大灯、转弯照明以及适用于自动远光和近光大灯功能的防眩远光辅助。因此,在所有情况下,系统均可提供最佳道路照明。

安全气囊是车上的被动安全装置。它有效地吸收车上人员与突出装置在撞车时产生的巨大冲击力,起到保护和防御的作用。

雨、雾、霾或雪天能见度低时,雾灯可在车子低速行驶过程中有效增加照明(见图 2-8～图 2-10)。

图 2-8 自适应 LED 前大灯

图 2-9 安全气囊

图 2-10 雾灯

内部装备(表 2-4):

表 2-4 从内部装备方面对宝马 5 系 GT 的 4 款车型进行比较

车型	528i* 领先型	528i* 豪华型	535i* 领先型	535i* 豪华型
BMW 专业导航系统	■	■	■	■
前后排中央扶手	■	■	■	■
高级自动空调	■	—	—	—
高级 4 区自动空调	□	■	■	■
前、后排杯座	■	■	■	■
丝绒脚垫	■	■	■	■
自动防眩功能的内、外后视镜	■	■	■	■
高光白蜡木纹理高级木饰(深色)	■	—	■	—
炫晶灰色细线纹高级木饰	—	■	—	■
多功能运动型真皮方向盘	□	■	■	■
多功能真皮方向盘	■	■	■	■

续表

车　型	528i* 领先型	528i* 豪华型	535i* 领先型	535i* 豪华型
环境灯	□	■	■	■
方向盘加热功能	□	□	□	□
全景式天窗	■	■	■	■
BMW 专业级收音机	■	■	■	■
高保真音响系统	■	■	■	■
专业级后排娱乐系统	□	□	□	■
前排舒适型座椅电动调节，驾驶者座椅具有记忆功能	□	■	□	■
座椅电动调节，驾驶者座椅具有记忆功能	■	—	■	—
前排主动通风座椅	□	■	□	■
前排座椅加热功能	■	■	■	■
后排座椅加热功能	□	□	□	□
电动腰撑	—	■	—	■
吸烟配套	■	■	■	■
Dakota 真皮	■	—	■	—
Nappa 真皮	—	■	—	■
后电动车窗，带触控、防夹和舒适开启/关闭功能	■	■	■	■
后侧窗电动遮阳帘	□	□	■	■
豪华设计套装	—	■	—	■

相关部件英文表达

有了多功能方向盘，驾驶者可以在方向盘上操作汽车上的相关功能，而无须将手脱离方向盘，眼睛可以专注观察路况，提高了驾驶安全系数。

如果阳光太过强烈，双浮动式车顶篷可电动关闭。

后座娱乐系统包括两个单独的 9.2 英寸彩色屏幕，为您的旅行增添色彩（见图 2-11～图 2-13）。

图 2-11　多功能方向盘

图 2-12　全景天窗

图 2-13　后座娱乐系统

外部装备（表 2-5）：

表 2-5　从外部装备方面对宝马 5 系 GT 的 4 款车型进行比较

车　　型	528i* 领先型	528i* 豪华型	535i* 领先型	535i* 豪华型
车门自动吸合功能	—	■	■	■
两段式行李厢盖	■	■	■	■
与车身同色的外饰部件（如：车门把手）	■	■	■	■
金属漆	■	■	■	■
电动调节外后视镜，可加热	■	■	■	■
风挡玻璃清洗喷嘴，可加热	■	■	■	■
车轮	■	■	■	■
——BMW 425 型铝合金 V 式轮圈,18 英寸,8Jx18, 245/50 R18	■	—	—	—
——BMW 235 型铝合金多轮辐，19 英寸，前轮 8.5Jx19，245/45 R19，后轮 9.5Jx19，275/40 R19	—	—	■	—
——BMW 铝合金 458 型多轮辐，19 英寸，前轮 8.5Jx19，245/45 R19，后轮 9.5Jx19，275/40 R19	—	■	—	■
防爆轮胎	■	■	■	■
车轮螺栓锁	■	■	■	■

相关部件英文表达

电动折叠后视镜在窄道会车时可防剐蹭，并且在停车时能节省空间。

铝合金轮毂具有良好的散热性，提高了行车安全，比钢轮毂轻，自然可以减少燃油消耗。

车轮瘪胎时，防爆轮胎可以继续前行 150 英里，避免无备胎时出现尴尬（见图 2-14～图 2-16）。

图 2-14　后视镜

图 2-15　铝合金轮毂

图 2-16　防爆轮胎

发动机/变速箱/悬架（表 2-6）：

表 2-6　从发动机/变速箱/悬架方面对宝马 5 系 GT 的 4 款车型进行比较

车　　型	528i* 领先型	528i* 豪华型	535i* 领先型	535i* 豪华型
直列 4 缸汽油发动机	■	■	—	—
直列 6 缸汽油发动机	—	—	■	■
双凸轮轴可变气门正时系统	■	■	■	■
e-Shift 电子换挡杆	■	■	■	■
8 速手自一体自动变速箱	■	■	■	■
8 速手自一体自动变速箱，带换挡拨片	—	—	■	■
双叉臂前悬挂	■	■	■	■
行驶机构	■	■	■	■
——电动助力转向系统	■	■	■	■
——伺服式助力转向系统	■	■	■	■

相关部件英文表达

发动机是汽车的心脏。BMW 双涡管单涡轮增压 6 缸和 4 缸汽油发动机带 Valvetronic 电子气门的双涡管涡轮增压器、double-VANOS 双凸轮轴可变气门正时系统，以及高精度直喷系统。

底盘在车的底部。运动般的驾驶乐趣可直接从路面传递至方向盘，同时具有安全性和最高水平的舒适性。

8 速手自一体自动变速器令换挡操作更为便捷。一共有 4 个基本挡：前进挡、空挡、倒车挡和驻车挡。其中，驻车挡通过按钮控制。换挡也可以使用换挡杆进行操作（见图 2-17～图 2-19）。

图 2-17　发动机

图 2-18　底盘

图 2-19　8 速手自一体自动变速器

第三单元 汽车产品介绍

FAB 原则，即配置、作用和益处。FAB 原则介绍所销售的产品、该产品的优势，以及给潜在客户带来什么样的利益。

配置是指人们最容易认知的物产，是你的产品及服务所具有的属性。比如，汽车上的日间行车灯就是配置。

作用就是这个产品的用途是什么，指向产品带来的实际需求，而非前景需求。例如，"日间行车灯在光线较差的情况下有效提升能见度"。

益处回答了客户为什么应该对你的产品买单，即你的产品给客户带来了哪些实惠、解决了他的哪些需求。例如，"车行驶时，日间行车灯有效地提升了能见度，规避了事故风险"。

I. 奥迪 A3 掀背跑车

奥迪 A3 是德国奥迪汽车制造商 1996 年以来生产的紧凑型家用小轿车。全新奥迪 A3 掀背跑车（见图 3-2）是 A3 家庭成员之一，使用了大众集团 MQB 平台。这款车汇聚了轿跑车般的车顶线条和动感硬朗的车身腰线，"旋风线"设计形成独特的光影效果，动感的掀背式造型设计突出了不断进取的运动设计风格。传承奥迪家族经典的一体式进气格栅，搭配独特的箭头造型前大灯，令它的前脸如此有动感而迷人。全新奥迪 A3 掀背跑车搭载了新一代 1.4 TFSI®发动机，只需 8.4 s 即可轻松实现从静止加速到 100 km/h。另外，它还配备了 S tronic®双离合变速箱，兼顾了更强动力与更低能耗。

图 3-2 奥迪 A3 掀背车

新技术

（1）全新奥迪 A3 掀背跑车配备了可随时关闭的发动机启停系统。当车辆在行驶过程中遇到红灯或其他情况时，发动机自动关闭；当你松开制动踏板时，发动机立即重新启动。整个开闭过程均在你毫无察觉的状态下流畅进行，确保舒适驾驭的同时，实现了更低油耗和更低的二氧化碳排放。

配置：发动机启停系统（见图 3-3）。

用途：路遇红灯或交通滞留的时候，停车时发动机可以自动熄火。

益处：利用踏板轻松操控该功能，驾驶员可专注开车，观察路面情况。从油耗的方面来看，能更直接、有效地降低燃油的使用，是一项环保技术。

（2）专门为全新奥迪 A3 掀背跑车量身定制的丹麦 Bang & Olufsen 高级音响系统（见图 3-4），配备了 5.1 环绕立体声系统和 14 个扬声器，可营造出逼真且震撼的环绕立体声，令你如同置身于专业的音乐演奏大厅，聆听世间最美妙的天籁之音。

图 3-3　发动机启停系统

图 3-4　Bang & Olufsen 音响系统

配置：Bang & Olufsen 音响系统

用途：奥迪是首家与丹麦专业音响品牌 Bang & Olufsen 合作的汽车厂商。后者对设计和性能的不懈追求与奥迪的品牌理念不谋而合。高分辨率和高质量音频赋予奥迪品牌革新理念。

益处：当您置身车中享受旅途的快感时，Bang & Olufsen 音响系统用世界级的立体声效果触及您的心灵，宛如置身专业音乐演奏大厅，聆听世间最美妙的天籁之音（见图 3-5）。

图 3-5　喇叭

图 3-6　A3 掀背 e-tron®

（3）奥迪 A3 掀背跑车的 e-tron®（见图 3-6）可以在纯电力、燃气动力，或两者的组合间操作。电动机几乎能提供 243 磅[①]·英尺[②]扭矩的瞬时响应，并且这一响应是令人难以置信的安静和平稳。联合燃气发动机，e-tron®提供了令人印象深刻的 204 马力的灵敏加速性能。

配置：奥迪 A3 掀背跑车的 e-tron®技术。

用途：持续输出大扭矩，并且是难以置信的安静和平稳。

益处：逐渐地加速，驾驶舒适感强。

（4）设计优雅的免费充电器（见图 3-7 和图 3-8）能让你在家里使用 240 V 的电源，在短短的 2 小时 15 分钟内完成充电。标准的 110 V 电源插座需约 8 小时，非常适合夜间充电。

配置：奥迪 A3 充电器。

用途：奥迪 A3 掀背跑车的 e-tron®技术令充电仅需不到两个半小时；同时，充电可以在

---

① 1 磅=453.592 37 克。
② 1 英尺=0.304 8 米。

家里完成。

益处：更方便，也更有效率。

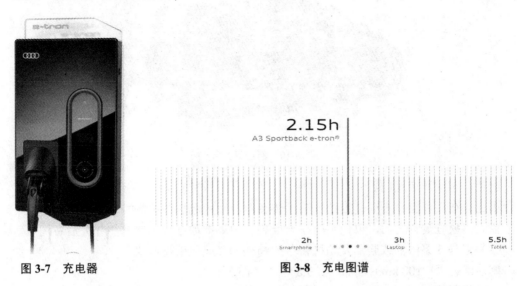

图 3-7 充电器　　　　　　　　图 3-8 充电图谱

II. 宝马 3 系

宝马 3 系是由德国宝马汽车制造商生产的紧凑型行政座驾。1975 年，BMW 引发了 3 系车的一次革命。40 年后的今天，这次变革仍然是这段历史的标杆。随着不断的发展，宝马 3 系的风格和操纵感使之成为宝马阵容中最流行的系列。3 款车型中的每一款——轿车、运动旅行车和 GT 赛车——都确保驾驶的刺激。宝马的设计语言在 3 系的每一款车型上都表现得栩栩如生。从霍夫迈斯特拐角的曲线到双肾格栅，再到后视镜，每一个元素都使 3 系有着世上最独特的外观，成为最流行的运动型轿车（见图 3-9）。

图 3-9 宝马 3 系

新技术

（1）疯狂购物之后，您双手提满购物袋，要寻找钥匙，希望将购物袋装入行李厢，会感到恼火吧。不过以后不需要这样做了。借助作为特殊装备提供的创新型便捷进入及启动系统，您可以感应开启尾门（见图 3-10）。您需要做的只是在适当的位置抬一下脚。

图 3-10　感应开启尾门

配置：感应开启尾门。
用途：在后保险杠不同高度处安装了传感器，感应到您的抬脚并打开后备厢。
益处：疯狂购物之后，再也不用在一堆袋子中笨拙地寻找钥匙就能开关后备厢了。
（2）宝马 3 系汽油或柴油发动机轿车的油耗和二氧化碳排放值：
燃油消耗（L/100 km）（综合）：3.8～7.9（图 3-11）。
二氧化碳排放 g/km（综合）：99～185。
配置：油耗和二氧化碳排放。
用途：油耗低，二氧化碳排放少。
益处：降低了油耗，既能给客户省钱，又能保护环境（图 3-12）。

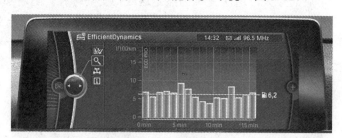

图 3-11　油耗显示器

图 3-12　ECO 按钮

（3）全彩色 BMW 平视显示系统（见图 3-13）会将所有相关的行驶信息直接投射在您的视野范围内，使您能够将注意力集中在路面上。全彩色 BMW 平视显示系统会显示当前车速（根据车辆功能的不同）、来自导航系统的指令，包括禁止超车指示的限速信息显示、电话和娱乐列表，以及来自驾驶者辅助系统的警告信息。

图 3-13　彩色 BMW 平视显示系统

配置：全彩色 BMW 平视显示系统。

用途：投射到挡风玻璃的图像以高分辨率和全彩进行显示，而且行驶信息直接投射在您的视野范围内。

益处：读取信息更方便、快捷，有助于驾驶员集中注意力。

（4）当速度达到或超出 20 km/h 时，基于雷达的车道变换警告系统（见图 3-14）会探测盲区的接近车辆以及邻近车道的车辆。系统通过在车外后视镜上显示三角警告符号来提醒您注意临界区的车辆；但如果您通过启动指示器表达变换车道的意图，系统将通过振动方向盘和在车外后视镜闪烁三角形警告符号来进行警示。

图 3-14　车道变换警告系统

配置：车道变换警告系统。

用途：该系统会探测盲区的接近车辆以及邻近车道的车辆，并警告司机防止交通意外。

益处：司机将通过方向盘振动和在车外后视镜闪烁的三角形警告符号得到警示，从而防止侧向车辆碰撞导致的交通意外。

III. 丰田 RAV4

丰田 RAV4（见图 3-15）是日本丰田汽车制造商生产的运动型多用途汽车。它是第一款紧凑型跨界车，1994 年在日本和欧洲首次亮相，1995 年在北美亮相。RAV4 车辆设计迎合顾客的需求，有 SUV 的大部分好处。例如它有增加了的货物空间、较高的视野和全时四轮驱动，还有紧凑型轿车的操控性和燃油经济性。

图 3-15　丰田 RAV4

新技术

（1）我们希望您无后顾之忧享受驾驶的感觉。这就是为什么RAV4配备有8个安全气囊（见图3-16），包括驾驶员和前排乘客座椅前的先进安全气囊系统、驾驶员和前排乘客座椅侧安全气囊、正面和第二排滚动感应侧帘安全气囊（RSCA），以及驾驶员膝部安全气囊和前排乘客座椅衬垫气囊。

配置：8个安全气囊。

用途：它们是车上唯一提供被动安全的安全设备，降低了约30%的正面碰撞的死亡率。

益处：它们可以在紧急情况和碰撞中保护我们，尤其是保护孩子；同时，它们减少死亡的危险。

（2）RAV4 Limited可以适度帮助客户定制舒适度。标准多级加热SofTex®前排座椅（见图3-17）帮助战胜那些寒冷的夜晚。由于有了带记忆功能及电动腰部支撑的8向电动可调驾驶员座椅，找到完美的驾驶位置也不是问题。

配置：电加热前排座椅。

用途：它具有加热功能、带记忆功能和电动腰部支撑的8向电动可调驾驶员座椅。

益处：这会赶走寒冷，靠电动支撑腰部，缓解疲劳。

图3-16　8个安全气囊

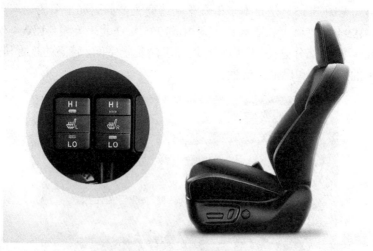

图3-17　电加热前排座椅

（3）RAV4 Limited 前排腿部空间达到 42.6 英寸，后排腿部空间达到 37.2 英寸，可容纳 4 位身高达 6 英尺的乘客入座且仍有余量（见图 3-18）。无论是您的家人，还是朋友，入座后排都如同入座头等舱一般。按动扳手，可大尺度倾斜后排座椅靠背，让您的旅途富有舒适感。

配置：内部空间。

用途：带天窗版的 RAV4 Limited 头部空间为 38.9 英寸，后排肩部空间为 55.4 英寸，后排容臀空间为 48.9 英寸，后排腿部空间为 37.2 英寸，更不用说宽大的前排空间了。同时，后排座椅可以根据个人需求倾斜到理想状态。

益处：宽大的内部空间能容纳 4 个身高达 6 英尺的乘客，并有余量。后排乘客仍然可以享受到头等舱一般的舒适空间，因为后排膝部空间相比上一代 RAV4 增加了 44 毫米。更值得一提的是，可折叠的后排座椅能为您的购物或出行提供大尺寸载物空间。

（4）东西多而腾不出手来？没问题。RAV4 研发了防夹电动后尾门，具有高度可调的性能（见图 3-19）。将尾门提升到理想高度，按压门边上的按钮，坚持 2 秒，你会听到蜂鸣声，高度被锁定。这样一来，无论您以后按门锁开门，还是用遥控钥匙开门，尾门都会开启至之前设定的理想高度。

配置：带记忆功能电动后尾门。

用途：该后备厢门具有智能化记忆功能，可以记忆预设的车门开启高度。

益处：它是个子矮小人士的福音，因为他们无须再费力踮起脚尖够尾门了。

图 3-18　内部空间

图 3-19　带记忆功能电动后尾门

第四单元　汽车使用手册阅读

简　介

路虎是英国专门从事生产四轮驱动车辆的汽车制造商。2008 年路虎被印度塔塔集团收购，成为捷豹路虎系列的品牌之一。它是世界上位居第二的资深四轮驱动车辆品牌。

路虎揽胜运动版（见图 4-2）是路虎旗下的一款中型豪华 SUV，于 2004 年年底以一款名为 Range Stormer 的概念车为雏形首次亮相（见图 4-3）。这是一款低底盘、短轴距的三开门双座版车型，是路虎在车型设计上具有重要意义的一次变革。

图 4-2　路虎揽胜

图 4-3　Range Stormer

路虎运动版快读指南如下。

第一部分　进入车辆

1. 遥控钥匙（见图 4-4）

1）钥匙芯

按下按钮（图中箭头所指），弹出钥匙芯。

2）自动上锁

如果遥控钥匙锁车失效，一分钟内若未开启车门或后备厢门，车辆将自动上锁且开启报警装置。

🔒 按一次锁车且开启报警装置。

🔓 按一次解除报警，并解锁驾驶员车门（单点进入）。

再次按下此按钮可以打开其他所有车门。

图 4-4　遥控钥匙

> **单点进入：**
> 单点进入可实现安保，因其只能开启驾驶员一侧车门。如若同时按住锁车键和解锁键 3 秒钟，则自动解除单点进入功能。车辆将会自动上锁并以现行选择的模式重新解锁。

2. 中央门锁（见图 4-5）

1）主锁及解锁开关

（1）按下①按钮，解锁所有车门及后备厢门。

（2）按下②按钮，所有车门及后备厢门上锁。

同时按住两个控制键 3 秒，后备厢门自动开启。

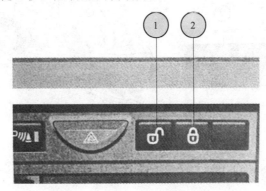

图 4-5　中央门锁

2）行驶中自动落锁

如果需要，行驶过程中车速超过 8 km/h 时，车门及后备厢门将自动上锁。这一功能可以在行车电脑设置选项中选择开启或关闭。

3. 后备厢

1）打开后备厢

在所有车门未被锁定时，按下后车厢上的按钮①，开启后备厢（见图 4-6）。

2）自动关闭

后备厢锁有电动关闭功能。若后备厢门处于较低位置时，它能完全自动关闭。

3）开启后备厢车窗

在所有车门未被锁定的条件下，按下外部把手上的触摸垫②，然后向上拉起窗户（见图 4-7）。

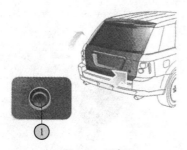

图 4-6　尾门

图 4-7　尾门玻璃窗

第二部分 舒适及安全装备

1. 驾驶员座位调整

（1）座椅前后调整，坐垫高度调整，以及座椅前倾控制开关。
（2）座椅倾斜度调整开关。
（3）降低靠背腰部支撑开关（见图 4-8）。

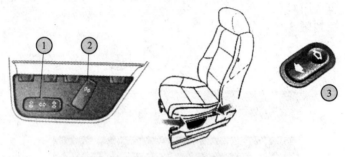

图 4-8 司机驾驶座椅按钮

2. 驾驶位置记忆控制（图 4-9）

若已将驾驶员座椅及外部后视镜调整到驾驶时的理想位置，汽车就可以记住这些调节位置，方便将来使用。

（1）按住记忆储存按钮 5 秒，以激活记忆功能。
（2）按住其中一个预置按钮 5 秒，以储存当前设置。"记忆储存"将会显示在信息中心并同时播放声音，以证明当前设置已经被储存。

按下图 4-9 中 2 部分的相应预置按钮，可以取消已储存的驾驶位置设置。

> **操作提示：**
> 座椅位置记忆只限于在 5 秒内调整完成。
> 重新记忆调节位置将覆盖现有设置。

3. 转向柱调整（图 4-10）

顺时针转动转向柱左边的控制按钮，然后调整方向盘的高度和远近。

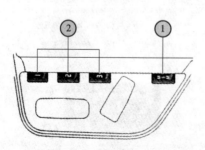

图 4-9 驾驶位置记忆控制　　　　图 4-10 转向柱调整

驾驶员座椅自动调整：
将转向柱左侧旋钮转至"自动挡"，拔出点火钥匙，汽车转向柱及驾驶员座椅能自动调整空间，方便驾驶员入门及下车。
方向盘及座椅将会在下一次钥匙插入钥匙孔时自动恢复到之前的位置。

电动座椅调整：
为避免发动机开启或关闭时驾驶员座椅自动调整，需顺时针旋转控制按钮。

4. 车窗及后视镜

1) 车窗

（1）分别按压并长按对应的开关，以打开车窗。
（2）分别提拉并长拉对应的开关，以关闭车窗。
松开开关，窗户将会立刻停止升降。
一键式触动可以完成前方两侧车窗完全打开或关闭动作。完全按下开关然后松开。再次短按相应开关时，车窗随时停止升降。
按下开关①右侧按钮，将后方车窗的升降功能完全锁死（见图4-11）。

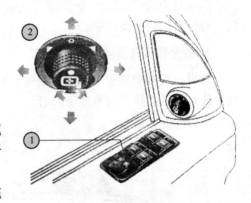

图4-11 车窗及后视镜

开车窗时产生共鸣声：
当打开某扇后车窗时，若产生共鸣声，则将邻近的前车窗降低25毫米，自然能消除该现象。

2) 后视镜调整

向左或向右旋转镜子的调整按钮②（图4-11），实现相应镜子的调整。可多方位旋转按钮调整某一后视镜，以达到理想位置。

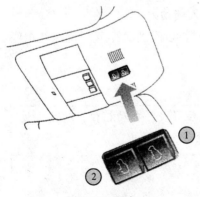

图4-12 天窗

3) 电动折叠后视镜

将后视镜调节按钮置于中心位置，推动该按钮，可将后视镜合拢或展开。

5. 天窗（图4-12）

1) 打开/关闭天窗
（1）按下并释放开关①，可完全打开天窗。
（2）按下开关②，可关闭天窗。
2) 天窗倾斜
（1）按下并释放开关②，将天窗开到倾斜位置。
（2）按下并长时间按住开关①，以关闭天窗。
天窗在移动时，可以再次按下开关，以使其停止移动。

> **操作注意：**
>
> 若想操控天窗，前车门都必须处于关闭状态，此时将点火开关拧至钥匙挡位置Ⅰ或者Ⅱ即可。再或者拧至钥匙挡位置0达40秒，也可以操控天窗。
>
> 将点火开关拧至钥匙挡位置Ⅰ或者0时，如若打开天窗，则需长时间按压开关，直到天窗到达想要的位置。

6. Homelink 发送器（图4-13）

图4-13所示箭头指向的按钮可以编程传送特定的无线电频率，以控制外部设备，如车库门、庭院门、安全系统等。

7. 安全带和儿童约束装置

如果司机和副驾驶乘客的安全带未被扣紧，则仪表组上的警告指示灯（见图4-14）将点亮。此时也可能伴有间歇性蜂鸣音。

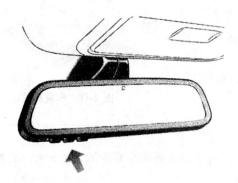

图4-13 Homelink 发送器

图4-14 安全带提示灯

自动锁定安全带卷收器：

所有乘客的安全带都有自动锁定安全带卷收器，可用于儿童安全座椅固定及对较大物品的束缚，以防脱落。

（1）插上安全带：将安全带伸拉至最大长度，将卡扣插入锁扣内。

（2）安全带能收回到符合儿童座椅的长度（安全带收缩时可以听到滴答声）。确保儿童座椅牢固安装，并无松动。

（3）释放安全带：解开安全带，让安全带完全缩回。

> 自动锁定安全带卷收器被激活后，安全带缩回到理想位置，并自动锁住，以防止过多拉伸。能有效防止顾客在正常使用安全带时不经意将安全带全部拉出。
>
> **建议使用的儿童座椅：**
>
> 路虎强烈建议使用扣栓式儿童安全座椅。
>
> 扣栓式儿童安全座椅仅适用于外侧后座椅的位置。

8. 乘客安全气囊

副驾驶座椅配有感应传感器，能够确定座椅被占用的状态并设定相应的气囊状态

（图4-15和图4-16）：

（1）座椅未被占用：气囊不起作用并显示不工作。

（2）座椅被占用：气囊起作用并显示不工作。

（3）座椅被小孩座椅或者低高度物体占用：气囊不起作用，显示灯亮。

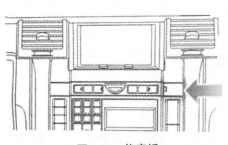 

图4-15　仪表板　　　　　　　　图4-16　安全气囊按钮

第三部分　车内气候控制和外部灯光

1. 气候控制

> 建议模式：
> 选择 AUTO 为正常运行模式（见图4-17）。这会防止车窗起雾。

自动模式：
按 AUTO（见图4-18）选择系统自动运行，开关上的 LED 灯会点亮。

图4-17　气候控制面板　　　　　图4-18　自动模式开关

系统会自动调节热量输出、风机速度、进气量及出风口气体流量，按照系统预设温度分配气流并保持温度，无须更多调节的情况下减小雾气产生。

气流分配和鼓风机控制可以在自动模式下手动操作。

> 外部排水：
> 空调系统除湿后将多余水分排出至车辆下部。该过程中可能会形成积水。此属正常现象，请勿担心。

1）温度选择

旋转控制按钮，可调节两侧乘客周围的温度。

> **操作注意：**
> 无法调节到左右两侧温差相差 4 ℃以上。

2）风扇转速

旋转风扇控制按钮②，可调整通过风口的气流。

3）气流分布控制

按如下按钮，可选择想要的气流分布设置：

（1） 挡风玻璃和两侧车窗通风。

（2） 水平通风。

（3） 向下通风。

可以选择不止一种方式，以实现理想的气流分布。

4） 最大限度除霜程序

可除去挡风玻璃上的霜或重雾。系统会自动将风机出风率调至最大，并激活挡风玻璃上的加热器。

5） 前挡风玻璃加热

6） 后挡风玻璃加热

2. 外部灯光

1）外部灯光总开关（见图 4-19）

① 外部灯光关闭。
② 侧灯。
③ 远光灯。
④ 自动车灯。
在自动模式下，将点火开关拧至钥匙挡位置 II 时，传感器会监测外部光线水平，并根据需要自动开启或关闭侧灯和近光前照灯。
⑤ 前雾灯：将开关拉至位置 A，打开前雾灯。
⑥ 后雾灯：将开关拉至位置 B，打开后雾灯。

当主灯开关在自动模式时，无法开启雾灯。

2） 方向/转向灯显示

向上或向下移动控制杆（见图 4-20），激活方向/转向指示灯。

用与弹簧力相反的方向朝上或朝下移动拨杆，然后释放，指示灯将闪烁 3 次。在变换车道时使用该功能。

3） 前照灯远光

向外推拨杆，可选择前照灯远光。此时仪表组上的警告指示灯将点亮。要使前照灯闪烁，朝方向盘方向拉动拨杆，然后松开即可。

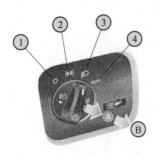

图 4-19　外部灯光总开关

图 4-20　转向灯拨杆

第四部分　仪表盘总览

仪表盘总览见图 4-21。

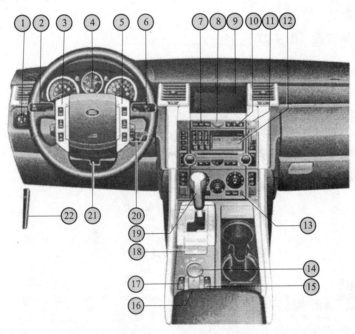

图 4-21　仪表盘总览

①—外部灯光主开关。②—方向/转向灯/远光灯/行车电脑开关。③—巡航控制开关。④—仪表盘/报警指示器和信息中心。⑤—收音机/电话开关。⑥—雨刷器和清洗器开关。⑦—动态稳定性控制开关。⑧—危险警报开关。⑨—触摸屏。⑩—主锁开关。⑪—乘客气囊状态指示器。⑫—音频系统。⑬—加热器/空调控制。⑭—地形响应控制开关。⑮—分动箱开关。⑯—陡坡缓降开关。⑰—空气悬挂控制。⑱—电子驻车。⑲—换挡杆。⑳—点火开关。㉑—转向柱调节器。㉒—引擎罩开启。

1. 报警灯（信息）

在正常行车时，以下指示灯会亮起，以显示某个特定功能在运行：

(1) 安全带提醒。

(2) 选择低速挡。

(3) 陡坡缓降控制开启。

(4) 巡航控制开启。

(5) 方向指示。

(6) 侧灯开启。

(7) 远光灯开启。

(8) 后雾灯开启。

(9) 前雾灯开启。

(10) 电子驻车制动开启。

2. 雨刷器和清洗器（图 4-22）

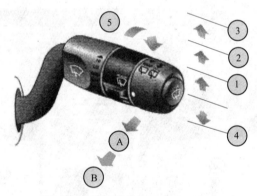

图 4-22 雨刷器及清洗器控制开关

1）挡风玻璃雨刷器

① 间歇刮水或者雨水感应器的操作。
② 正常速度刮水。
③ 高速刮水。
④ 单次刮水——按下并释放拨杆来操作。
⑤ 旋转开关可调整间歇刮水的速度或者雨水感应器的敏感度。

2) 挡风玻璃清洗器

按下并释放控制杆末端的按钮，可操作前挡风玻璃清洗器。按下并保持该按钮，可操作挡风玻璃清洗器和雨刷器。

3）后车窗雨刷和洗涤器

将控制杆拉到 A 位置，可实现后车窗雨刷的间歇性动作。将控制杆拉到 B 位置并保持住，可操作后车窗的洗涤器和雨刷器。

> **维护要点：**
> 在汽车进入自动洗车房之前，请关闭雨刷器，以取消雨水传感器功能。否则，雨刷器会在洗车过程中误启动，可能因此损坏。

第五部分　行车与越野

1. 自动变速装置

1）换挡互锁

必须将点火开关放置在钥匙挡位置 II，踩下脚刹车，释放换挡杆上的锁止按钮，方可将挡位从 P 挡（停车挡）移至 R 挡（倒车挡）间的各个挡位（图 4-23 和图 4-24）。

图 4-23　换挡旋钮（1）

图 4-24　换挡旋钮（2）

在将启动机钥匙拔出之前，换挡杆必须在 P 挡位置。

2）运动模式

这是自动挡位变换模式，但也将对挡位变换点进行修正，以充分利用发动机功率。

选择运动模式时，将换挡杆从 D 挡向左侧移动。

此时仪表板会显示 SPORT 字样，并且换挡杆周围的 LED 灯也会亮。

> 在运动模式下，变速器将长期保持在低挡位状态，以保证车辆更容易减速。
> 运动模式下会耗费更多燃料。

3）手动变速挡

可以选择手动变速挡与自动变速挡两种模式。在汽车需要快速加速或在发动机需要制动的情况下，使用手动变速挡尤为有效。

（1）选择运动模式。变速器会自动选择适用于当前车速和加速的挡位。

（2）通过向前（+）或向后（−）移动变速杆，然后释放变速杆，可以达到手动换低挡或高挡的目的。此时"变速器手动选择"字样将会显示在仪表的信息中心上。

（3）随后，仪表盘上将会显示当前选择的挡位。

（4）如需解除手动模式，请将换挡杆移回 D 挡位置。

2. 巡航控制系统

巡航控制系统（图4-25）可以使驾驶员在不使用踏板加油的情况下，按照某一特定速度在路面上行驶。

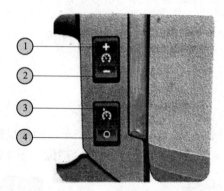

图4-25 巡航控制系统

①—SET+：在使用巡航控制系统时，此按键可用来设置所需的道路速度，或以 2 km/h 的步长增加速度。

②—SET-：在使用巡航控制系统时，此按键可用来设置所需的道路速度，或以 2 km/h 的步长降低速度。

③—RESUME：此按键可用来恢复保存在记忆中的一个设定速度。

④—CANCEL：取消巡航控制系统，但是设定的速度会保留在存储器中。

踏下制动踏板或车速低于30km/h时，巡航控制系统功能将会自动解除。

3. 空气悬挂

汽车将根据道路速度自动调整高度，以维持最佳的车辆行驶性和操控性。
有些地形响应程序将自动调整悬架高度。

通过提高/降低按钮①可以手动调节汽车高度。只有在发动机运行并且驾驶员和乘客车门关闭的时候才能实现此功能。

②或⑦指示灯亮起，指示运动方向。当移动结束时指示灯关闭。

③指示灯亮起，指示越野高度，提供更大的离地间隙，以及接近角、离去角和跨越角。

④指示灯亮起，指示路面的高度，即汽车正常行驶的高度。

⑤指示灯亮起，指示进入高度、降低汽车的高度，以便出入车辆和装载货物。

点火开关关闭后40秒时，可以选择此高度位置。

⑥指示灯亮起，指示缓行（锁定到进入高度），允许汽车在进入高度下低速行驶，提供更大的车顶间隙（图4-26）。

4. ![icon] 陡坡缓降控制（图 4-27）

陡坡缓降控制系统与防抱死制动系统结合，对在越野路面上行驶的车辆能提供更好的控制，尤其是当遇到极度陡坡时。

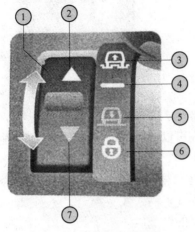

图 4-26 空气悬挂控制器

图 4-27 陡坡缓降控制

按图 4-27 中箭头所指按钮，选择 HDC。HDC 在车速低于 80 km/h 时，有效工作；但速度降到 50 km/h 以下时，此功能失效。可以通过仪表盘上持续点亮的 HDC 指示灯确认此功能是否运转。

再按一次此按钮，以取消 HDC 功能。

第五单元 销售流程

在汽车销售中，对于销售顾问而言，第一印象往往是深刻、长久而重要的。接待的第一印象影响成交的 30%。如何做到留给客户完美的第一印象呢？客户总是希望与那些衣着整齐、修饰有度、彬彬有礼而又具有专业知识的销售顾问进行交流。和蔼的笑容、得体的外表、恰到好处的肢体语言，都会为你的专业形象加分，从而取得客户的信赖（见图 5-5）。

作为销售顾问，与客户的初次接触可能是通过电话（见图 5-6）。如果来电话的是一位潜在客户，销售顾问就必须收集以下信息：① 客户姓名；② 客户联系方式；③ 客户关注车型；④ 客户预约情况。

情境：王先生，一位成功的生意人，对宝马 5 系 GT 非常感兴趣。他现在的座驾是本田雅阁，主要用来接送客户和朋友以及短途旅行。他喜欢空间宽敞、性能卓越、配置较高的车，容易接受新鲜事物。对于原来的本田雅阁车，不打算进行置换，想要把其留给家人用。王先生最初打来电话咨询和预约，而后就直接来到展厅看车并进行试乘试驾。

例如：

张鹏：您好！这里是宝兴行宝马展厅。我是销售顾问——张鹏。请问有什么可以帮到您？

图 5-5　标准的微笑　　　　　　　图 5-6　电话接待

王先生：你好，我想咨询一下你们新款的宝马 5 系列加长型什么时候上市。

张鹏：新款的宝马 5 系在 8 月份上市。现在可以接受车辆预订了。请问先生您贵姓呢？

王先生：我姓王。现在的预定价格是多少？

张鹏：我们的新款宝马 5 系列加长型的预售价格在 489 600～791 600。厂商为我们展厅提供了一些预售资料和展示样车。欢迎您到店预订车辆。

王先生：好的。那新款的 5 系都是多大排量的？

张鹏：我们新款的宝马 5 系列拥有 523、528、535 共 3 种排量级别。这个周六您方便来看一看吗？

王先生：我想一下……没有问题。那就周六上午吧。这周六我正好休息。

张鹏：好的。我帮您预约周六上午。我是您的销售顾问——张鹏。提醒您一下，我们展厅的营业时间是早 8 点至晚 17 点。为了我们更好地为您提供服务，我需要记录您的联系方式。稍后我将我们展厅的地址以短信的形式发送给您。

王先生：好的，我的号码是 13654311111。

张鹏：我记下了。王先生您方便留一下通信地址吗？我可以为您邮寄本期的宝马杂志。

王先生：谢谢你，不需要了。

张鹏：好的，王先生，感谢您的来电。我们的预约时间是本周六上午。我会在展厅等您。

王先生：好的，也谢谢你。我们周六见。

如何应对来店客户呢？

展厅接待的问候语尤为重要，将为未来成交打下良好的基础，因此要让客户感受到在这里可以体验到职业化的高级服务（见图 5-7 和图 5-8）。

图 5-7　展厅接待

(a) (b)

图 5-8　客户接待

例如：
李彤：先生，上午好！欢迎光临宝兴行宝马展厅。
王先生：你好！
李彤：我是前台咨询员。请问有什么可以帮到您？
王先生：我预约了一位销售顾问"张鹏"，今天过来看车。
李彤：好的。我马上通知他。请问先生怎么称呼您？
王先生：我姓王。
李彤：王先生，请这边稍坐。我们展厅为您免费提供饮料。您想喝点什么？
王先生：来一杯咖啡吧。
李彤：好的。请您稍等。热咖啡到了，请您慢用。
又如：
李彤：张鹏，你预约的王先生到展厅看车了。你现在有时间接待吗？
张鹏：好的。我马上跟你过去。
李彤：王先生，您好！这位就是您预约的销售顾问张鹏。
张鹏：王先生，您好！我是张鹏。这是我的名片。
王先生：你好。你们展厅的服务很热情呀。
张鹏：当然了。这是我们宝兴行的标准。
在销售过程的初期，寒暄可以迅速让客户放下紧张的心情。
例如：
王先生，今天很热吧？给您来些冷饮吧？
王先生，刚才从哪里开车过来的呀？路上塞车了吧？
王先生，您开的车子不错呀！电话号码也不错呀！
王先生，这边空调是不是有点冷？我们用不用换个地方说话？
王先生，周末打扰您休息了吧？
王先生，下雨天您都如约过来，我一定为您详细讲解一下车辆。
王先生，听口音，您不像本地人呀，来这里多久了？
王先生，年轻有为呀，您的事业一定很成功！
王先生，真是有眼光。宝马品牌的活力很适合您这样的年轻人。

今天的销售是以客户为中心的顾问式销售,是在市场竞争非常激烈的情况下进行的。因此,我们要了解客户的购买动机,分析他的需求,为客户提供一款适合他的车型(图5-9)。

图 5-9　为客户讲解

在汽车销售流程理论里存在显性动机和隐性动机的说法。需求分析的冰山理论也经常提到这两种动机。水面以上的部分是显性的,就是客户自己知道的,能表达出来的那一部分;水面以下的是隐性部分,就是有的客户连他自己的需求是什么都不清楚。销售人员既要了解客户的显性需求,也要了解他的隐性需求。只有这样,才能正确分析客户的需要。

例如:

张鹏:王先生刚才从哪里开车过来的呀?

王先生:明珠小区。

张鹏:那里距离我们公司很近呀!王先生开什么车过来的呢?

王先生:本田雅阁。

张鹏:这台雅阁跑多少公里①了?

王先生:跑了有6万公里多了。

张鹏:那部车用几年了?我们这里可以为您提供置换服务。

王先生:用了3年了,不置换了,留给家里人开。

张鹏:3年开了6万公里,就是短途驾驶比较多,是吗?

王先生:是的,基本不怎么出城。

张鹏:平时就是上下班开那台车吗?需要接一些生意上的朋友吗?

王先生:有时候去机场接一下朋友。就是因为这个,想换一台高档车。生意场没办法。

张鹏:那3年前您购置了那辆雅阁,当时感觉那辆车哪方面不错呢?

王先生:几个朋友一起去看的车,感觉空间挺宽敞,挺适合我。

张鹏:您很注重车辆的空间,是吧?

王先生:当然了。空间大才像高档车!

又如:

张鹏:王先生,您现在购置的新车还是由您自己驾驶吧?

王先生:是的。我不喜欢用司机开车,不方便。

张鹏:平时车辆的乘客多吗?(去机场接朋友的时候,大部分是几个人呀?)

---

① 1公里≈1 000米。

王先生：不多，大部分就是我自己，偶尔接一下朋友，就两三个人吧。

张鹏：您身边的朋友向您推荐过一些其他品牌的豪华车吗？

王先生：有朋友向我推荐新款奔驰 E 级加长型。他们说比现在的 A6 L 还要宽敞。我准备去看看。我妻子上网看到宝马也刚出了全新的 5 系列的加长型。所以，今天就先来看看你们的车（基本预算 50 万元左右）。

张鹏：我们新款 5 系正在接受预定中。您什么时间要用车呀？

王先生：越快越好。你也知道我要的都是新款。当然我想当第一批车主呀！

张鹏：感谢您对宝马汽车的支持！我们的车主中也很缺少您这样的商业精英。

王先生：呵呵，那你们这里几月份能提车呀？

张鹏：那要看现在新款 5 系列的预订状况。最快 9 月份就可以交付您使用。

王先生：无论如何，越快越好。你说过有不少资料。我能看看吗？

张鹏：好的！我这就去取过来。看过资料后我们可以看看一些类似的车。

六方位绕车介绍法是一种汽车展示的经典方法，也是一个比较规范的汽车产品展示流程。这一方法最早被奔驰汽车公司采用，后来被日本丰田汽车公司的"雷克萨斯"品牌予以发展和完善，如今已经成为汽车销售的标准静态展示方法。六方位介绍法主要把汽车分为 6 个方位，逐一进行介绍，通常全程需要 40 分钟左右完成。具体的时长需要视客户的情况而定。

六方位展示的主线是客户的需求。基本顺序见表 5-1。

表 5-1 六方位展示的基本顺序

方　　位	重点介绍内容
1 号位：车头 45°	车辆的外观造型、设计、腰线伸展、品牌、价值所在
2 号位：前排驾驶座	驾驶的舒适性和操控性
3 号位：后排座	乘坐的空间及舒适性
4 号位：车尾部	车尾设计特色、后备厢
5 号位：车侧身	汽车的安全性及侧视效果
6 号位：发动机室	发动机特点、动力性能

在六方位介绍过程中，通过各项目、部位的利益展示，让客户真正体验汽车带给他的良好感受（见图 5-10～图 5-15）。

图 5-10　车头 45°

图 5-11　前排驾驶座

图 5-12 后排座

图 5-13 车尾部

图 5-14 车侧身

图 5-15 发动机室

展示流程一：车头 45°（见图 5-16）

图 5-16 为客户介绍车头 45°

张鹏：王先生，您好！我们看一下这台宝马 5 系 GT 车型吧。
王先生：好啊！
张鹏：宝马 5 系 GT 的市场定位是超级旅行车。
王先生：超级旅行车是什么意思呀？

张鹏：超级旅行车和普通旅行车的定位有所不同。它具备灵活的装载空间、跑车化的运动性能、宽敞的内部空间、高端的电子装备，以及优于传统轿车的通过能力。等一下我将一一为您解答。

王先生：好的，你说说吧！

张鹏：首先请看镶嵌在发动机盖上的宝马徽标。BMW 代表巴伐利亚州发动机工厂的缩写。蓝白相间的中心图案象征蓝天与白云被旋转的螺旋桨划分成 4 等份。这也象征宝马曾经飞行的血统。

王先生：原来宝马品牌这么厉害啊！我就知道这下面的两个进气口是宝马标志。

张鹏：是的，先生。双肾型进气格栅是宝马从 1933 年至今一直沿用的家族特征。

王先生：这个设计真的不错。旁边的大灯有随动功能吗？

张鹏：有的！同时大灯还有光源分配能力。在日常低速行驶时它的照亮角度更宽，而高速行驶时照亮的范围更远。这样，无论是高速或低速，我们都有适合的灯光。您感觉这样的新产品怎么样？

王先生：那可真是不错。还真没听说过这个。

张鹏：再向下就看到了我们宝马 5 系 GT 的保险杠。它是由一种特殊材料制成的，外部复原层可以在低速撞击后慢慢修复，最多只留下一些表面划痕。

王先生：那确实是挺好的装备。

张鹏：是的，先生！贯通整个下部的进气格栅，为发动机提供了强大的散热能力。两侧的雾灯在整个前部设计中更能突出车辆的稳定性与车身宽度。发动机盖上清晰的设计线条，可以有效提高车辆行驶稳定性。在设计上也突出了强劲的动力！

王先生：这些设计都不错！

张鹏：我相信您已经开始喜欢这辆车了！下面请您与我一同沿着车辆的腰线来到车身侧面。

展示流程二：前排驾驶座（见图 5-17）

图 5-17　为客户介绍前排驾驶座

张鹏：王先生，我们全新的宝马 5 GT 车型都配备了电动拉紧车门的电吸门。门可以自动关闭。这样，就增加了用车的安全性。全系都配备了无钥匙启动系统，它使我们启动车辆更加方便了。

王先生：这就是全功能钥匙？我喜欢这个功能。

张鹏：王先生，请看看我们钥匙的遥控功能。我们宝马 5 GT 的钥匙除了可以进行传统的开启和关闭车锁外，还可以控制车辆的寻车功能，开启和关闭后备厢。

王先生：是吗？只听说有遥控开后备厢，还有遥控关闭呀？

张鹏：好的，王先生。请您坐在驾驶席。我为您调节一下座椅。我们全新的 5 GT 车型，标配 24 向调节的座椅系统，是现今汽车座椅调节最全面的一款产品。

张鹏：王先生，这辆车的空调系统提供了 ALL 这个功能，也就是说，可以分区调节，还可以由驾驶员控制。这更适合您这种喜欢自己驾车的老板。

王先生：是啊，这样操作就简单多了。

张鹏：电子挡杆可以轻松操作全新的 8 速手自动一体变速箱，体积和 6 速变速箱一样，但是换挡的效果会更加平顺，高速形式也更加省油。

王先生：哦！很好！

张鹏：此外，5 GT 的车型还为顾客提供了不同的驾驶模式选择，有正常、运动、运动加强。这样，您在驾驶时就可以体验不同的驾驶感觉，相当于拥有了 3 辆宝马车啊！

王先生：不错，等会儿体验一下。

展示流程三：后排座（见图 5-18）

图 5-18　为客户介绍后排座

张鹏：王先生，这款车的后排座椅提供手动调节功能。您没感觉到这辆车的座椅特别舒适吗？

王先生：是的，以前坐朋友的车总感觉宝马的座椅硬。这座椅坐上去很舒服呀。

张鹏：对了！这款车的市场定位是超级旅行车。长途旅行时座椅不舒服是最可怕的。宝马 5 GT 的座椅采用了抗疲劳设计，非常舒适。

王先生：宝马的做工真不错！这些配置很适合我。小张，这款车的天窗这么大呀？

张鹏：王先生，您注意到了吗？这款车采用的是全景天窗，在后排的乘客也可以感受到蓝天和白云了！

王先生：全景天窗好呀，看起来就宽敞很多。

展示流程四：车尾部（见图5-19）

图5-19 为客户介绍车尾部

张鹏：王先生，请和我一同看一下车辆的尾部。这辆车的后备厢盖的设计非常有特点。打开它有两种选择模式：整体开启和部分开启模式。请摸一下，打开后备厢的开关有两组！

王先生：不错。这样的设计实在太人性化了！感觉不错。

张鹏：后备厢具备遥控开启和遥控关闭功能，同时，宝马5 GT还提供了后备厢最大开启的快捷按钮。这样，操作起来就更方便了。

王先生：遥控开启这么大的后备厢很方便呀。

张鹏：后备厢内部空间的设计非常规整，而且在后备厢隔板下还提供了两个独立的储物空间。怎么样？王先生，您对这款超级旅行车的后备厢还满意吗？

王先生：太满意了！没想到这车还有这么方便的后备厢空间。

张鹏：好的。我们关闭后备厢，看一下尾灯的整体效果。尾灯内部集成了LED的灯光束管。下方的双侧排气管凸显了这辆车的力量感，只有配备涡轮增压发动机的宝马车型才配备这个等级的排气系统。后保险杠上面镶嵌了四点式的倒车雷达，并且宝马5 GT车型也配备了倒车影像系统，您倒车时将会非常容易操作。

王先生：不错！我就是喜欢原厂的倒车影像。我总感觉后加装的设备不太好用。

张鹏：等下我们可以体验一下宝马的这套停车辅助系统。

展示流程五：车侧身（见图5-20）

张鹏：王先生，请看这款车和您现在开的本田雅阁有什么不同？

王先生：是有一些不同。这车感觉有点高，然后轮胎很大。

张鹏：是的，宝马5 GT车型采用的是半高式车身。其整车高有1 559毫米。这就为乘客提供了宽敞的内部空间。其底盘高度比一般轿车要高出40毫米，有效地增加了车辆的通过能力。

王先生：那就太好了。出去郊游的时候就怕车子的底盘太低。这车的轮胎也很大呀！

张鹏：是的，这款车使用的是245/55的轮胎，还采用了高性能的18英寸轮毂。舒适性没的说！您再看一下车辆的轴距是不是很长呀？

图 5-20　为客户介绍车侧身

王先生：发现了。比我的雅阁长了很多呀！

张鹏：这款车的轴距是 3 070 毫米。宝马典型的短前悬设计会使这样长轴距的车非但不笨重，反而更加灵活。等会试驾的时候您就会发现。

王先生：好的，等一下一定要试一试！

张鹏：车窗面积是不是很宽敞？它们可以为您带来极佳的视野。车窗采用无框式设计，能降低高速风燥。

王先生：嗯，看起来不错。看起来像跑车呀！

展示流程六：发动机室（见图 5-21）

图 5-21　为客户介绍发动机舱

张鹏：王先生，您有兴趣看一下宝马 5 GT 的发动机舱吗？

王先生：很好呀，我正想看看发动机舱呢。

张鹏：稍等一下。我先把发动机盖打开。好，现在呈现在您面前的就是获得 2009 年度全球 3.0 升组最佳发动机的宝马 3.0 双涡管增压发动机。这款发动机可以为您带来 306 马力的功率，可以在 6.3 秒的时间加速至 100 公里/小时。综合油耗仅有 8.9 升。

王先生：动力不错。比我原来的雅阁要快一倍呀！还省油。

试乘试驾是汽车的动态展示方法，也是在汽车销售中运用最广泛的一种方法。客户通过试乘试驾可以对汽车的性能、驾乘感受有最直接的体验；而对于销售顾问来说，试乘试驾是刺激客户购买欲望的最佳途径，更可以让那些本来没有兴趣的客户产生兴趣。

试乘试驾的流程：

第一步：试乘试驾准备（见图 5-22）

图 5-22　试乘试驾准备

张鹏：王先生，您对车辆的日常操作都了解了吗？您对车辆的功能还都满意吗？

王先生：还不错。这车的功能真的很多。

张鹏：接下来我邀请您试驾一下为您准备的车辆。试驾车就是您喜欢的宝马 535 GT 豪华型。

王先生：可以呀。我们去试驾吧。

张鹏：请您稍等。因为试驾是在普通的城市公路，所以请您先出示驾照。我们做一下试驾登记。

王先生：没问题。给你驾照。

张鹏：好的。感谢您对我们工作的支持。我这就去做一下试驾登记。请您稍等片刻。

王先生：好的。你去吧。

第二步：试乘试驾前的介绍

张鹏：王先生，已经为您登记完毕驾驶执照。请您检查一下并收好您的驾照。这里是试乘试驾承诺书。请您认真看一下这份文件的承诺部分，然后请在以下客户签名处签名，还有联系电话。

王先生：好的。看明白了，就是按你们的路线开，别出事故。都明白。

张鹏：好的。已经签好试驾承诺书。接下来请看一下我们的试驾路线图。我为您讲解一下试驾路线和试驾项目。请跟我来。路线图就在展厅门口。

王先生：好的。

张鹏：这就是我们的试乘试驾看板。我们的试驾路线大约 7 000 米。首先，第一段路，我们以中低速驾驶,主要感受一下车辆的隔音性能和车辆行驶的平顺性。第二路段,我们可以测试一下车辆的加速性能和车辆的刹车性能。第三路段为杨浦大街,我们可以感受一下车辆的底盘隔绝胎噪的能力。第四路段,我们可以试驾车辆的超车能力。比较颠簸的第五路段,这里主要体现 5 GT 的悬挂舒适性。

王先生:这条试驾路线还不错的,项目也很丰富。

张鹏:当然了。宝马品牌是很关注客户驾驶感受的,所以提供的试驾服务的专业性很强。

王先生:那我一定要好好试驾一下!

张鹏:没问题!这边请。车辆已经停在展厅门口。王先生,请您先坐在副驾驶席。第一圈是由我驾驶车辆,您试乘。我为您调整一下座椅……对这个位置您感觉舒适吗?

王先生:还不错,挺舒服的。

张鹏:现在我要去驾驶席。请您系好安全带,关好车门。

王先生:好的。

张鹏:王先生,我首先踩下刹车踏板,按启动按钮,启动车辆,调节驾驶员座椅和后视镜角度。我们必须确定我们以安全的姿态驾驶车辆,而且有良好的视野。宝马车采用了三幅式运动型方向盘,所以驾驶宝马最好采用方向盘的 3 点和 9 点位置进行驾驶。这款车采用的是电子挡杆系统。它的造型很像飞机操纵杆吧?

王先生:有意思。怎么使用呀?

张鹏:踩下制动踏板,按下挡位确认按键。向后就是行驶挡,而向前就是倒车挡。挡位在挡杆和仪表盘都有显示。这款车也采用了电子刹车系统。按下这个按钮,车辆就解除手刹车了。下面的试驾过程中我会一一为您展示。

王先生:好的。听起来不错。

第三步:销售顾问的驾车体验

张鹏:现在我们将挡杆置入行驶挡,放开制动器,车辆就开始行驶了。因为全新的宝马 5 系 GT 车型采用的是 8 速手自一体变速箱,所以启动非常平顺。试驾的第一段路会有一些载重车辆。我们现在用 30 km/h 行驶,正常语调聊天。如果我们的交谈没有被打扰,就证明车辆的静音和封闭效果非常优秀。您现在感觉如何?

王先生:不错。这车真的很静音。

张鹏:在下一路段我们要进行车辆的加速和减速测试。我将车辆调节成运动模式,让我们感受 5GT 的强大动力!准备好了吗?

王先生:开始吧,让我感受一下!

张鹏:怎么样?王先生,您感觉动力性是不是很强?

王先生:没想到呀,这么大的车加速这么有劲!太过瘾了!减速也不错!

张鹏:对我们全新 5 系 GT 了解了吧?

王先生:不错。这车真的很平顺很稳。

张鹏:下一个转弯处就可以看一下车辆的通过能力了!

王先生:就是这种路况……这车真的不错。

张鹏:这里是第三段路。我们可以体验一下车辆在粗糙路面上抵制路面噪声的能力。

王先生:不错。这车还是这么静呀。

张鹏:接下来我们可以感受一下车辆在城市道路行驶的超车能力。您喜欢什么风格的音乐？我们为您准备了各式风格的音乐。

王先生：随便来一首歌曲。我顺便听听音响好不好。

王先生：不错。音响的感觉不错。这车性能这么好，超车肯定没问题了。

张鹏：现在我们行驶到了狭窄、颠簸的城区道路，体验车辆的悬挂舒适性。

王先生：不错。还是很舒服的。

第四步：客户的驾车体验

张鹏：王先生，前方就是我公司。我们可以换一下位置了。接下来的一圈由您驾驶车辆。

王先生：好的。

张鹏：请您到驾驶位。王先生，您请。我帮您调节一下座椅吧！您感觉舒服吗？

王先生：不错！这个位置就可以。

张鹏：如果您感觉舒服，我们就可以保存这个位置。后视镜的调节按钮在驾驶员车门上。

王先生：这个，我会。和我的车一样！

张鹏：好的，王先生。我现在去副驾驶席。您稍等。好了，王先生。您可以启动发动机了。调节好后视镜，系好安全带之后，我们就准备开车了。

王先生：没问题。这个位置很适合我！

张鹏：启动车辆后，第一段路，我们速度不要太快，小幅度打方向盘。我们感受一下车辆的转向性能。

王先生：放心，小张，我开车十多年了！但是我们开车没有你们那么快。

张鹏：其实，平时开车我也不会那么快，刚才只是为您展示车辆性能。现在这个路段，我们可以试一下加速、减速性能。

王先生：不错。踩刹车、油门都这么轻松呀。感觉心里有底呀！

张鹏：行驶到前方我们要向左。然后感觉一下车辆的安静程度。

王先生：这车真的很静呀。

张鹏：在这一路段我们可以体验一下加速超车。

王先生：不错。车的动力来得很快，底盘也很扎实。没开过宝马的，真感觉不到这些东西。

张鹏：通过这个红绿灯后我们就可以回到公司了。

第五步：试乘试驾后的总结与确认

张鹏：王先生，您可以停在保安指定的停车位，正好可以感受一下我们宝马的驻车辅助摄像。

王先生：好的。摄像头很清晰呀！

张鹏：好的。我们在这里可以拉好手刹车。您对车辆的操作都清楚了吗？

王先生：没有什么问题了。各方面都很清楚了。

张鹏：您还有没有什么问题需要我为您解答？

王先生：这款车有现车吗？

张鹏：有现车，而且颜色也不错！王先生，我们回展厅详细聊吧！

王先生：好的！

张鹏：王先生，想喝点什么饮料？

王先生：来点茶水吧！

张鹏：王先生，这是您的茶水。王先生，我们展厅这里有一份试乘试驾反馈表。请您对我们为您提供的试乘试驾服务和"小张"的表现进行打分。

王先生：都不错。你们的服务很专业呀！我真的很满意（这里体现出成交迹象）。

议价是一种最常见的客户异议。汽车买卖双方在整个销售过程中都会遇到报价与议价的问题。当客户完全接受了"自己挑选的车型"，并认为这辆车是"完全符合需求"的，销售顾问也完全解释除价格以外的所有疑问时，关于价格的讨论就可以开始了。在此阶段，销售顾问尽量少谈及产品本身的产品价值，因为在之前的静态及动态展示过程中，已经确认客户知道了产品本身的价值。揭示其附加价值是最明智的选择。什么是产品的附加价值呢？附加价值包括：① 公司服务；② 规模与历史；③ 个人服务；④ 货源充足；⑤ 增值服务；⑥ 有竞争力的产品；⑦ 贷款；⑧ 快修通道；⑨ 救援热线；⑩ 名人名车；⑪ 置换服务；⑫ 团购；⑬ 竞品信息等。

例如：

张鹏：王先生，您对这款宝马 5 系 GT 还满意吗？

王先生：很满意，我非常喜欢。只是价格上，还有商量的余地吗？

张鹏：王先生，既然您对我们宝马这么支持，您又这么爽快，价格上肯定会有商量。但是宝马车是以高性能和优质的服务著称，所以价格商量的余地肯定不会很大。

王先生：那能优惠多少呢？

张鹏：王先生，我们给出的价格是预售官方指导价格。等实车到店以后，价格会有小幅度的增加或者减少。但是如果您现在就预订的话，我们会赠送给您原厂车膜和导航。

王先生：那价格上呢？

张鹏：王先生，小张已经竭尽全力了。这样吧，如果您今天能预订的话，等您到店里提车的时候，小张再跟经理申请，看看还能否给您优惠了。您看这样行吗？

王先生：那好吧，那我今天先交一万元定金吧。

张鹏：谢谢，王先生。您这边请。我们去交款、签合同。

第六单元　衍 生 业 务

第一部分　怎样购买二手车

二手车，顾名思义，一部车子曾经被转手买卖过一次或多次。它们的买卖可以经由多种途径：汽车经销商、个体车贩、租赁公司。有些汽车经销商也提供"一口价"二手车服务，代办全套手续服务和售后保修服务（见图 6-2）。

1. 为什么购买二手车？

如果仔细挑选，二手车给客户带来的运输需求方面的实惠很多。因为一旦新车买到手，它的价值就会折损不少，而二手车却能带来更多的实惠（见图 6-3）。

图 6-2　二手车　　　　　　　图 6-3　二手车价值

2. 二手车的劣势

购车者应注意不要买到问题车。一些二手车卖家很可能隐瞒车上因碰撞而导致的安全隐患。更严重的是，将车内的重大隐患隐瞒下来，当优质二手车买卖。值得警惕的是，即使车外观已焕然一新，但故障并没有被排除。

3. 购买前的规划

买车前应注意如下内容：

（1）买车的用途是什么？

（2）计划用车多久？

（3）所需或偏好的尺寸、型号、配置及外观。

（4）预算及支付方式的选择。

（5）维修预算。

（6）对二手车的期望值不能过高。在一些小瑕疵上不要过于计较，但不能忽视严重问题。

（7）安全问题是优先处理事项。有些二手车可能没有配备安全气囊、儿童座椅卡扣、安全带、ABS 等安全装备。

（8）买之前一定要在路面上试乘试驾。如果卖方拒绝试乘试驾，则请慎重考虑。

（9）购买前一定要进行全车检验。

（10）和您的汽车保险公司联系并核实一下您是否可以为该车上保险。

4. 调查研究

花些时间去了解你选的车，可以为您节省一大笔开销，免于日后后悔。

（1）问问有经验的朋友及亲人。

（2）查找如下资料中的一些或全部（见图 6-4）：

① 《埃德蒙二手车价格与评级》（www.edmunds.com）。

② 《消费者可靠性评级报告》。

③ 《国家公路交通安全管理局安全报告及召回信息》（www.nhtsa.dot.gov）。

④ 《美国汽车经销商联合会官方二手车指南》（www.nadaguides.org）。

⑤ 《凯利蓝皮书》（汽车价值评估网

图 6-4　二手车调查

（www.kbb.com）。

5. 去哪儿看

一说起买二手车，大多数人都会想到看看报纸上的分类广告及口碑。拓展你的选择范围，这样不仅可以选到最符合自己的车，还可以为你有效地省钱。

上网在线查看：

（1）二手车或新车经销商。

（2）汽车租赁代理。

（3）拍卖公司。

（4）个人出售。

（5）银行及贷款公司。

6. 关注二手车本身

与其他事项相比，这是非常重要的。一定要在光线好的情况下检查车况（见图6-5）。带着你身边比较懂车且值得你信任的人帮你做全面评估。

1）车身检查注意事项（见图6-6）

（1）注意是否有生锈痕迹，尤其是在翼子板下方、车灯及保险杠周围、翼子板上、车门下方、轮罩内侧，以及后备厢毛垫底下。即使是小的砂眼，也很可能引起未来大面积生锈。

图6-5　二手车查看

图6-6　二手车车身查看

（2）检查一下车漆是否匹配，漆面上是否有砂砾出现。车身嵌板是否偏移，车漆是否喷到了镀铬格栅上——以上这些都是重新喷过漆的标志，表明对车身漆面上的某些问题做过处理。

（3）查看一下车身是否有裂缝，是否有遇热后出现的褪色区域以及保险杠松动等现象——这些预示着曾经遭遇过交通碰撞事故。

（4）车身上有焊接缝意味着汽车的车身经过焊接重新处理过。查寻后备厢和地板上有没有焊接痕迹，再查查挡风玻璃周边或后窗以及车门间是否有撞痕。如果有，就说明漆面下方一定有粗糙的焊接缝存在。

（5）查看车子是否遭受过冰雹灾害。如果车子外观不整洁，将车清洗干净，以便更好地检查。

2）轮胎检查注意事项（见图6-7）

（1）前轮胎出现单边磨损通常预示车轮定位不准确或前悬挂有破损现象。新车型子午线轮胎出现了单边磨损预示汽车轮胎安装错位。

（2）别忘记检查一下备胎的情况及后备厢内千斤顶是否完好。

3）蓄电池检查注意事项（见图6-8）

检查一下蓄电池标签上的保质期。一般情况下，在汽车行驶25 000英里[①]后需要更换蓄电池。

4）车门、车窗及后备厢检查注意事项

检查车门的密封度，开和关是否自如，门锁是否好用。如果车门关闭不严实，预示着车子曾经遭遇过交通碰撞事故。

图6-7　二手车轮胎查看

图6-8　二手车部件查看

5）车窗玻璃与车灯检查注意事项

检查车窗玻璃及车灯上是否出现了毛细裂纹及微孔。

6）汽车排气管检查注意事项

如果排气管出现黑色黏胶状烟灰物质，则意味着气缸内活塞环磨损或气门损坏，很可能需要对车子进行大修。

7）汽车减震器检查注意事项

用力（靠）按压或在车上一角起跳，再松开。如果车子仍不停地上下晃动，说明该减震器需要更换了。

8）油液检查注意事项（见图6-9）

（1）若机油发白或有白色泡沫出现，说明液体已渗入系统内部，很可能导致重大机械故障。

（2）检查冷却液，不应是铁锈色液体。

（3）让发动机处于怠速状态，检查一下变速器油。变速器油不应有腐臭的气味，也不应该看上去色泽呈现出深褐色。

图6-9　二手车油液查看

（4）检查车下方及发动机下方有无漏点及污点，同时检查软管周围及发动机盖周围有无漏点。

9）机械部件检查注意事项（见图6-10）

（1）检查大灯、尾灯、制动灯、倒车灯和转向灯工作是否正常。

（2）检测收音机、暖风、空调及雨刮器工作是否正常。

---

① 1英里≈1.609 3千米。

10）内饰检查注意事项

（1）检查座套是否有大面积的磨损和撕扯现象；同时，看看地垫下方和座椅垫是否有磨损。

（2）检查座椅的调节情况是否正常，并试试每条安全带工作是否正常。

（3）检查安全气囊的位置及是否能正常工作。问问卖主是否曾经在车子发生交通意外的情况下弹出过。

（4）检查方向盘。插入点火钥匙，挂入附件挡，发动机处于非工作状态，方向盘不应旋转超过 2 英寸。

（5）司机座椅有多处磨损或制动踏板及油门踏板也存在严重的磨痕，但仪表板上的里程数却显示很少的里程，说明该里程表被调过（图 6-11）。

图 6-10　二手车机械部件查看

图 6-11　糟糕的内饰

第二部分　汽 车 保 险

1. 什么是汽车保险？

如果发生交通意外，汽车保险可以帮助您减少经济损失。它以保险合同的形式呈现，是您与保险公司间的一份契约。您交保险费，而保险公司会按合同中的条款向您进行赔付（见图 6-12 和图 6-13）。

2. 汽车保险类型

一般来说，汽车保险有多种类型，价格也截然不同。例如，保险包括：

图 6-12　汽车保险（1）

图 6-13　汽车保险（2）

1）身体伤害险（见图 6-14）

这类保险一般承担因车祸导致对方伤残而产生的医药费、误工费、精神损失费，同时包含因车祸致死而产生的殡葬费。如果产生官司，则这类保险可以为您承担法律诉讼费。

2）财产损失责任险（见图 6-15）

假如您是肇事方，从法律的角度，您需要对对方的车或财产等进行赔偿，如修车。财产损失责任险可以帮您承担对方修车的费用，也可以承担您的车子因碰撞而导致公物受损的费用，例如路灯、栏杆或房屋等。

图 6-14　撞伤他人

图 6-15　财产损失

3）碰撞险（见图 6-16）

这类汽车保险支付您的车与另一辆车发生交通碰撞后造成损坏的保险费用。即使您是导致事故的过错方，并且您已经支付了维修车款，这种类型的保险也会如数赔偿您已垫付的维修款项。如果您不是过错方，您的保险公司会要求过错方司机支付您的车辆修理费用。碰撞险是自选险种。但是，如果您的汽车是借贷买的，您的银行或贷款公司也会要求您参保碰撞险。

4）综合险（见图 6-17）

此险种负责除车辆碰撞之外所产生的危险型损失。这些损失是由盗窃、破坏、火灾、高空坠物、地震、风暴，或与动物，如鹿，产生碰撞造成的。综合险是自选险种。然而，就像碰撞保险，如果您的汽车是借贷买的，您的银行或贷款公司也会要求您参保综合险。

图 6-16　碰撞

图 6-17　汽车自燃

5）未保险和保险不足驾驶人险（见图 6-18）

您或任何经您允许驾驶您的车辆的人员发生了事故，而肇事方驾驶员未保险或者肇事逃逸，若要索赔车险，此险种会赔偿您的车辆损失。如果对方司机没有足够的保险金来支付您的车辆的全部损失,该险种也会赔付给您。此外,如果您作为行人被车辆撞伤,此险种也会对您进行赔付。

6)什么是医疗费用或个人伤害保护险(PIP)

如果您或您车上的乘客在交通意外中受伤,个人伤害保护险将替您支付治疗费。在某些情况下,个人伤害保护险可以为您垫付如医疗康复等辅助医疗项目的费用,也可以赔付一些如意外伤害所造成的误工费,甚至丧葬费(见图6-19)。

图6-18 开车伤人

图6-19 人身伤害

Answers

Unit 1 Automobile Culture

I.
1. C 2. A 3. D 4. B 5. D 6. A 7. B 8. C 9. A 10. C

II.
1. i 2. b 3. f 4. c 5. a 6. j 7. d 8. e 9. h 10. g

III.
1. √ 2. × 3. × 4. √ 5. × 6. √ 7. × 8. × 9. √ 10. ×

IV.
1. Passenger Cars
2. Sports Cars
3. Special Vehicles
4. Mercedes Benz
5. compact hatchback
6. Rolls-Royce
7. Volks Wagenwerk
8. Ford Motor Company
9. Smart
10. Ferrari S. p. A.

V. 见译文。

VI.
1. A Passenger Car
2. A Roadster
3. A Multipurpose Passenger Car
4. A Motor Truck
5. A Bus
6. A Special Purpose Vehicle
7. A Special Vehicle
8. A Special Vehicle
9. An SUV
10. An MPV
11. An NCV
12. A Special Vehicle
13. A CUV
14. An SRV
15. A Special Vehicle

VII.
(1) Volks Wagenwerk
(2) Ferdinand Porsche
(3) people's car
(4) win-win-win
(5) City
(6) Recreation
(7) Vehicle
(8) 城市休闲车
(9) Honda Motor Company
(10) youth
(11) developed technology
(12) Acura
(13) Sport
(14) Utility
(15) Vehicle
(16) 运动型多功能车
(17) 巴伐利亚发动机制造厂
(18) motorcycles
(19) MINI
(20) Toyota Motor Corporation
(21) "Recreation"
(22) "Activity"
(23) "Vehicle"
(24) four-wheel drive
(25) compact
(26) MPV-styled
(27) supermini
(28) Horch
(29) Wanderer
(30) subsidiary

Unit 2 Automobile Specifications Reading

Warm up

I.

前保险杠　front bumper
与车身同色系车门　body-colored door
前大灯　headlight
后轮　rear wheel
后翼子板　back fender
尾灯　tail light
前风挡　front fender

发动机舱盖　engine hood
门把手　handle
进气格栅　grille
三角窗　quarter window
车顶　roof
后视镜　outside mirror
门柱　roof post

II.

Overall length is 4,629.
Overall width is 1,880.
Overall height is 1,653.
Wheel base is 2,807.
Track front is 1,617.
Track rear is 1,613.
Width (mirrors folded out) is 2,089.
Overhang front is 895.
Overhang rear is 927.
Front seat room is 1,043.
Rear seat room is 990.
Ground clearance is 603.

Exercise:

I.
1-5　CBBDC　　6-10　CABCB

II.
1-5　DFAGE　　6-10　CBJHI

III.

EOS China Equipment List EOS 装备表	6速手动版	DSG 自动版
Engine type 发动机	4-cylinder Ottomotor 4缸汽油机	4-cylinder Ottomotor 4缸汽油机
Displacement (CC) 排量（CC）	1 984	1 984
Max. output, KW (bhp) at rpm 最大输出功率，（hp）/转速	147(200)/5 000	147(200)/5 000

continued

EOS China Equipment List EOS 装备表	6速手动版	DSG自动版
Max. torque, Nm at rpm 最大扭矩，Nm/转速（r/min）	280/1 800	280/1 800
Transmission 变速箱	6MT 6速手动挡	DSG 双离合器变速箱
Dimension (mm) 外形尺寸（mm）	4 407/1 791/1 443	4 407/1 791/1 443
Wheelbase (mm) 轴距（mm）	2 578	2 578
Unladen weight, kg 整备质量，kg	1 557	1 557
Emission standard 排放标准	EU4/E4	EU4/E4
Combined fuel consumption, L/ 100 km 平均综合油耗，L/100 km	8.2	8
Acceleration from 0-100 kph, (s) 0-100 km/h 加速时间（s）	7.8	7.9
Top speed, kph 最高时速（km/h）	232	229
Exterior equipments 外部装备		
4 alloy wheels 7.5 J×17" 17 英寸铝合金轮毂 7.5 J×17"		S
Tires 235/45 R17" 轮胎规格 235/45 R17		S
Brake calipers front and rear 前、后碟式刹车盘		S
Body colored bumpers, outer mirrors and door handles 与车身同色保险杠、外后视镜以及门把手		S
Electrically foldable exterior mirrors, dimming on driver's side 电动外后视镜，电动折叠，自动防炫目		S
Chrome-plated radiator grille frame 镀铬散热器隔栅		S
Space and weight saving spare wheel 压缩备胎		S
Interior 内部装备		
Sport seats in the front 前排运动座椅		S
Front seats with electric adjustment 前排电动调节座椅		S
Heated front seats separately controlled 前排座椅独立控制加热功能		S
Electrically adjustable lumbar support, front 前排座椅电动腰部支撑		S
Leather multi-function steering wheel (3-spoke) w/ control for gear shift, MFD, radio and telephone 带换挡、收音机调节和电话功能的三辐多功能方向盘		S
Decorative aluminum inserts Brushed Black trim in center console 中央操控台全铝装饰		S
Pedal pads in brushed decorative aluminum 铝饰的刹车踏板		S
Leather hand brake lever handle 真皮手刹		S
Front center armrest with storage box, 12-V-socket 前排中央扶手储物箱带 12 V 插座		S
Safety 安全装备		
ABS incl. brake assistant ASR ABS 和 ASR 电子刹车稳定系统		S

continued

EOS China Equipment List EOS 装备表		
	6速手动版	DSG自动版
Dual ton horn 双音鸣嘀		S
Electromechanically powered steering, speed-related controlled 电子随速助力转向		S
Safety-optimized front headrests 前排主动性头枕		S
3-point seat belt for center rear seat, outer rear seats and for both front seats, with seat-belts tensioner and height adjustment 所有座椅带三点式张紧式安全带，高度可调节		S
Driver's and front passenger airbag with front passenger airbag deactivation 前排双气囊，带乘客气囊控制开关		S
Curtain airbag system for front passengers, incl. side airbags for front passengers 前排侧气囊和前排头部帘式气囊		S
Anti-theft alarm system with back-up horn, electronic vehicle immobilization device 防盗警报系统带倒车鸣音，电子防拖车系统		S
Tire pressure monitoring system 轮胎压力流失警告系统		S
Warning tone and warning light for front seat belts not fastened 前排座椅未系安全带提醒装备		S
Park distance control 驻车雷达控制系统		S
Rain sensor 雨水感应雨刮		S
Front/Rear fog light 前后雾灯		S
Tail lamps in LED technology LED的后尾灯		S
Warning triangle 三角警示牌		S
Functionality 操控装备		
Isofix preparation, mounting fixture for 2 child seats on outer rear seats ISO-FIX儿童座椅安装系统，固定后排外侧2个儿童座椅		S
Interior mirror automatically dimming 自动防炫目内后视镜		S
CSC roof system in glass appearance with tilt/slide sunroof and net-fabric wind CSC敞篷系统带上翘可移动功能的天窗		S
Backrest release for front seats with "Easy Entry" function (electric) "轻松进入"上车帮助（电动调节）		S
Outer rear view mirrors: powered, separately heated and electrically foldable, automatically dimming 电动外后视镜，可独立加热，电动折叠，自动防炫目		S
Power windows, front and rear 前、后电动升降车窗		S
RNS 510 with MP3 function with 8 speakers RNS 510带MP3播放功能的中文收音机导航系统，带8个扬声器		S
Automatic low beam mode with "Coming home" and "Leaving home" function 大灯近光自动开启和"回家，离家"照明模式		S
Climatronic 双区自动空调		S
Multi-function display 多功能显示屏		S

EOS China Equipment List EOS 装备表	6速手动版	DSG 自动版
Cruise control system (CCS) 定速巡航		S
Optional Packages 选装包		
Bi-Xenon headlight with automatic headlight-range adjustment dynamic/ Headlight washer system 双氙气大灯带照明距离的自动调节，带前大灯清洗功能		O

仅供参考，具体请以实车为准

"S": Standard 标准装备   "O": Option 选装装备   "-": not available 不提供

IV.

1.

(1) Front Wheel Drive 前轮驱动

(2) Four-Cylinder 四缸

(3) 六速自动变速器

(4) 前排座椅空间

(5) 第二排座椅空间

(6) 第三排座椅空间

(7) No

(8) gross vehicle weight rating；总体车重标准值

(9) 前排座椅空间

(10) 第二排座椅空间

(11) 第三排座椅空间

(12) 前排座椅后方载物空间

(13) 第二排座椅后方载物空间

(14) 第三排座椅后方载物空间

(15) No

2.

(1) Width of the trunk

(2) Track rear

(3) Overall width

(4) 最大 24.0

(5) 最大 25.4

(6) 最大 23.8

(7) 60

(8) 204.8

(9) 500

(10) Yes

(11) Q7 is equipped with quattro.

(12) No

Unit 3 Automobile Product Introduction

Exercises

I.
1-5 BCDCA   6-10 BDACA

II.
1-5 GDJID   6-10 BFCEA

III.
1-5 √××××   6-10 ×√√√×

IV.

1. Airbags

2. Sensors

3. language

4. torque

5. S-tronic

6. waistlines

7. small compact car

8. FAB principle

9. Hofmeister kink

10. Benefits

V. 见译文。

VI.

1. coupe; sportback; cabriolet

2. Ford; Sports Utility Vehicle; grille; headlights

3. leather-wrapped steering wheel; four-spoke; power trunk lid

4. FR; FF; RR; MR

5. Honda; Jade; Variable Valve Timing and Valve Lift Electronic Control System；可变气门正时和升程电子控制系统

6. sunroof; passengers

7. Pre-sense; Advantage

8. Feature; Advantage; Benefit

9. fender; chrome; bumper; low carbon; eco/ environmental protection

VII.

ahead, information, navigation, windshield, eyes, radio, music, start/stop system, shifts, engine, fuel consumption, emissions, brake, shut, foot.

Unit 4　Automobile Manual Reading

Warm up

1, 2, A, 3, 4, 5, 0.

Exercises

I.

1-5　BDCCA　　6-10　CAABD

II.

1-5　FHAJE　　6-10　BCGDI

III.

1-5　×√√××　　6-10　√√×√√

IV.

1. remote controls

2. switch

3. downwards

4. moisture

5. sensor

6. controls

7. sensor

8. Sport

9. drivability

10. parking aid

V. 见译文。

VI.

1. Land Rover; Terrain Response System

2. cruise control system; gas pedal

3. driver's seat; steering column; side mirror; driving position memory

4. remote key; alarm; doors

5. wipers; rain sensor

6. park; reverse; brake pedal

7. airbag; starter; passenger's airbag; off

8. rear window; resonance

9. range rover; A-pillar

10. tail light; light emitting diode; brake light; turning indicator

11. ethyl alcohol; fuel.

VII.

windscreen wipers; arms; luggage lid; damaged; centre button; unlock switch; arrester hook; up;

spring; engage; safety; adjacent; vehicle; close; accident.

Unit 5 Sales Procedure

I.
1. C 2. A 3. C 4. D 5. C 6. C 7. A 8. A 9. C 10. C

II.
1. d 2. h 3. f 4. j 5. a 6. e 7. b 8. i 9. c 10. g

III.
1. √ 2. × 3. × 4. × 5. √ 6. √ 7. × 8. √ 9. √ 10. ×

IV.

(1) front end	(2) brand	(3) the driver's seat	(4) back	(5) space
(6) rear	(7) trunk	(8) safety	(9) engine	(10) dynamic

V. 见译文。

VI.

Situation One:

(1) appointment	(2) consultant	(3) business	(4) drinks
(5) marketed	(6) model	(7) university	(8) traveling
(9) short-distance	(10) judgment	(11) four-cylinder	(12) displacement
(13) consumption	(14) acceleration	(15) economic	

Situation Two:

(1) punctual	(2) performance	(3) facilitate	(4) test drive
(5) license	(6) registration	(7) commitment	(8) signature
(9) route	(10) security	(11) xenon	(12) DSC
(13) run-flat	(14) PDC	(15) airbags	

Unit 6 Derived Businesses

Exercises

I.
1-5   BACCD   6-10   CDABC

II.
1-5   EGABD   6-10   FCJHI

III.
1-5   √ × √ √ ×   6-10   √ √ × × √

IV.
1. budget

2. replaced

3. collision

4. rebuilt

5. shock absorbers

6. tailpipe

7. contract

8. losses

9. legal and court costs

10. Property damage coverage

V. 见译文。

VI.

1. used car; mileage; auto insurance; engine number; rust; leak

2. automobile exterior; paint; luggage compartment; corrosion; hood

3. headlamps; crash; tail lights

4. test drive; instrument panel; trouble light

5. third party's liability insurance; the insured; accident; insurance contract

6. length; width; height; wheelbase

7. turbocharger; EPS (Electric Power Steering); multi-function steering wheel; cruise control system; automatic air conditioning

VII.

track record; customers; public record; product recall; maintenance; research; limited service; additional information; vary; gender; accident; vehicle owners; insurance; driving record; reduce

Words

A

abbreviation [əbriːvɪ'eɪʃ(ə)n]　　*n.* 缩写；缩写词

aberration [æbə'reɪʃ(ə)n]　　*n.* 失常；离开正路，越轨

abundant [ə'bʌnd(ə)nt]　　*adj.* 丰富的；充裕的；盛产

acceleration [əkselə'reɪʃ(ə)n]　　*n.* 加速，促进；[物] 加速度

accelerator [ək'seləreɪtə(r)]　　*n.* 加速器

accent ['æks(ə)nt; -sent]　　*n.* 口音；重音；强调　*vt.* 强调；重读；带……口音讲话

access ['ækses]　　*vt.* 使用；存取；接近　*n.* 进入；使用权；通路

accommodate [ə'kɒmədeɪt]　　*vt.* 容纳；使适应

achievement [ə'tʃiːvm(ə)nt]　　*n.* 成就；完成；达到

acoustic [ə'kuːstɪk]　　*adj.* 声学的；音响的；听觉的

activate ['æktɪveɪt]　　*vt.* 刺激；使活泼；使产生放射性

adaptive [ə'dæptɪv]　　*adj.* 适应的，适合的

adjacent [ə'dʒeɪs(ə)nt]　　*adj.* 邻近的，毗连的

adjustability [ə,dʒʌstə'bɪlɪtɪ]　　*n.* 适应性；可调性

adjustment [ə'dʒʌs(t)m(ə)nt]　　*n.* 调整，调节；调节器

adversely [æd'vɜsli]　　*adv.* 不利地；逆地；反对地

agency ['eɪdʒənsi]　　*n.* 代理；机构

agile ['ædʒaɪl]　　*adj.* 敏捷的；机敏的；活泼的

agility [ə'dʒɪlətɪ]　　*n.* 敏捷；灵活

agricultural [ægrɪ'kʌltʃərəl]　　*adj.* 农业的；农艺的

airbag ['eəbæg]　　*n.* 安全气囊

alignment [ə'laɪnmənt]　　*n.* 排成直线；校直，调整

alloy ['ælɒɪ]　　*n.* 合金

aluminum [ə'luːmɪnəm]　　*n.* 铝

ambient ['æmbɪənt]　　*adj.* 周围的；外界的；环绕的

ambition [æm'bɪʃ(ə)n]　　*n.* 野心，雄心；抱负，志向

analysis [ə'nælɪsɪs]　　*n.* 分析；分解；验定 [复数 analyses]

analyze ['ænəlaɪz]　　*vt.* 对……进行分析，分解（等于 analyse）[过去式为 analyzed；过去分词为 analyzed；现在分词为 analyzing]

angular ['æŋgjʊlə]　　*adj.* 有角的

announce [ə'naʊns]　　*v.* 宣布；述说；预示；播报

annular ['ænjʊlə]　*adj.* 环形的，有环纹的
anthracite ['ænθrəsaɪt]　*n.* [矿物] 无烟煤
appeal [ə'piːl]　*vi.* 有吸引力
appearance [ə'pɪərəns]　*n.* 外貌，外观；出现
appointment [ə'pɒɪntm(ə)nt]　*n.* 任命；约定；任命的职位
appraisal [ə'preɪzl]　*n.* 评价，估量；鉴定，估价（尤指估价财产，以便征税）
approach [ə'prəʊtʃ]　*n.* 方法；接近　*vt.* 接近；着手处理　*vi.* 靠近
approximately [ə'prɒksɪmətlɪ]　*adv.* 大约，近似地；近于
architecture ['ɑːkɪtektʃə]　*n.* 建筑学；建筑风格；建筑式样
articulated [ɑː'tɪkjʊleɪtɪd]　*adj.* 铰接式的
assistance [ə'sɪst(ə)ns]　*n.* 援助，帮助；辅助设备
assistant [ə'sɪst(ə)nt]　*adj.* 辅助的，助理的；有帮助的
association [əsəʊsɪ'eɪʃ(ə)n; -ʃɪ-]　*n.* 协会，联盟
auction ['ɔːkʃn]　*n.* 拍卖；竞卖；标售　*vt.* 拍卖；竞卖
audible ['ɔːdɪb(ə)l]　*adj.* 听得见的
autolamp ['ɔːtəʊlæmp]　*n.* 汽车灯
automatic [ɔːtə'mætɪk]　*adj.* 自动的
auxiliary [ɔːg'zɪlɪərɪ]　*adj.* 辅助的；副的
available [ə'veɪləb(ə)l]　*adj.* 可获得的；可购得的；可找到的；有空的
aviation [eɪvɪ'eɪʃ(ə)n]　*n.* 航空；飞行术；飞机制造业
awkwardly ['ɔːkwɜːdlɪ]　*adv.* 笨拙地，困难地，难看地，尴尬地
axle ['æks(ə)l]　*n.* 车轴；[车辆] 轮轴

B

backlit ['bæklɪt]　*n.* 后面打光；背光式
backrest ['bækrest]　*n.* 座位靠背
badge [bædʒ]　*n.* 徽章；证章；标记
bargaining ['bɑːgɪnɪŋ]　*n.* 讨价还价；交易；交涉
batch [bætʃ]　*n.* 一批；一炉；
battery ['bætəri]　*n.* [电] 电池，蓄电池
Bavarian [bə'veərɪən]　*adj.* 巴伐利亚的
beep [biːp]　*n.* 哔哔的声音；警笛声
benchmark ['bentʃmɑːk]　*n.* 基准，参照
billboard ['bɪlbɔːd]　*n.* 广告牌；布告板
blade [bleɪd]　*n.* 叶片；刀片
blind [blaɪnd]　*adj.* 盲目的；瞎的
blister ['blɪstə(r)]　*n.* 水疱；疱；气泡；水肿　*vt. & vi.* （使）起水泡　*vi.* （使表皮等）涨破，爆裂
blower ['bləʊə]　*n.* 鼓风机

bold [bəʊld] *adj.* 大胆的，英勇的；黑体的
bolt [bəʊlt] *n.* 螺栓，螺钉
bonnet ['bɒnɪt] *vt.* 给……装上罩；给……戴上帽子 *n.* [机] 阀盖
bounce [baʊns] *vi.* 跳，反弹；急促地动；拒付，退票 *vt.* 弹跳；使弹起；（使）上下晃动 *n.* 弹跳；弹性；活力
brake [breɪk] *n.* 制动器，闸；刹车 *vt.* & *vi.* 刹（车）
brochure ['brəʊʃə] *n.* 手册，小册子
bubble ['bʌbl] *n.* 泡，水泡
buck [bʌk] *n.*（美）钱 *vt.* & *vi.* 抵制；猛然震荡
budget ['bʌdʒɪt] *n.* 预算 *vt.* & *vi.* 把……编入预算
bullet ['bʊlɪt] *n.* 子弹
bumper ['bʌmpə(r)] *n.* 保险杠

C

cabin ['kæbɪn] *n.* 车厢；客舱；船舱
capability [ˌkeɪpə'bɪləti] *n.* 才能，能力；性能
capacious [kə'peɪʃəs] *adj.* 宽敞的；广阔的；容积大的 [比较级为 more capacious；最高级为 most capacious]
capacity [kə'pæsɪtɪ] *n.* 能力；容量；资格，地位；生产力 [复数 capacities]
cargo ['kɑːgəʊ] *n.* 货物，船货
carpeting ['kɑːpɪtɪŋ] *n.* 地毯；地毯织料
centric ['sentrɪk] *adj.* 中央的，中心的
certificate [sə'tɪfɪkət] *n.* 证书；执照，文凭
characteristic [kærəktə'rɪstɪk] *adj.* 典型的；特有的；表示特性的 *n.* 特征；特性；特色
characteristics [ˌkærəktə'rɪstɪks] *n.* 特性，特征；特色
charger ['tʃɑːdʒə] *n.* 充电器
charge ['tʃɑːdʒ] *v.* 使充电
chassis ['ʃæsɪ; -iː] *n.* 底盘，底架
chime [tʃaɪm] *n.* 钟声；一套发谐音的钟
chrome [krəʊm] *n.* 铬，铬合金
circumstance ['sɜːkəmst(ə)ns] *n.* 环境，情况；事件
civilization [ˌsɪvɪlaɪ'zeɪʃən] *n.* 文明；文化
clearance ['klɪər(ə)ns] *n.* 清除；空隙
client ['klaɪənt] *n.* 客户
climate ['klaɪmət] *n.* 气候
cluttered ['klʌtəd] *v.* 杂物，零乱的东西 *vt.* (clutter 的过去式和过去分词) 堆满，塞满……
collar ['kɒlə] *n.* 衣领；颈圈
collision [kə'lɪʒn] *n.* 碰撞；冲突
column ['kɒləm] *n.* 纵队，列；专栏；圆柱，柱形物

combination [ˌkɒmbɪˈneɪʃ(ə)n]   n. 结合；组合；联合
combined [kəmˈbaɪnd]   adj. 结合的   v. (使)联合（combine 的过去式和过去分词）
combustion [kəmˈbʌstʃ(ə)n]   n. 燃烧
commemorate [kəˈmeməreɪt]   vt. 庆祝，纪念
commercial [kəˈmɜːʃ(ə)l]   adj. 商业的；营利的
commission [kəˈmɪʃ(ə)n]   n. 委员会
commitment [kəˈmɪtm(ə)nt]   n. 承诺，保证
compact [kəmˈpækt]   adj. 紧凑的，紧密的；简洁的
competitive [kəmˈpetɪtɪv]   adj. 竞争的；比赛的；求胜心切的
complimentary [ˌkɒmplɪˈment(ə)ri]   adj. 赠送的；称赞的；问候的
comprehensive [ˌkɒmprɪˈhensɪv]   adj. 综合的；广泛的
compromise [ˈkɒmprəmaɪz]   n. 妥协；折中物   vi. 折中解决；妥协，退让   vt. 损害
concentrate [ˈkɒns(ə)ntreɪt]   vi. 集中；浓缩
concerning [kənˈsɜːnɪŋ]   prep. 关于；就……而言
concert [ˈkɒnsət]   vt. 使协调   n. 一致；和谐
configuration [kənˌfɪɡəˈreɪʃ(ə)n]   n. 配置；结构；外形
confirmation [ˌkɒnfəˈmeɪʃ(ə)n]   n. 确认；证实；证明；批准
conflict [ˈkɒnflɪkt]   n. 冲突，矛盾
consideration [kənˌsɪdəˈreɪʃ(ə)n]   n. 考虑；原因；关心；报酬
console [kənˈsəʊl]   n. [计] 控制台；[电] 操纵台
consultant [kənˈsʌlt(ə)nt]   n. 顾问
consultative [kənˈsʌltətɪv]   adj. 咨询的
consumption [kənˈsʌm(p)ʃ(ə)n]   n. 消费；消耗
continuously [kənˈtɪnjʊəsli]   adv. 连续不断地，接连地
contract [ˈkɒntrækt]   n. 合同；契约；协议
convenience [kənˈviːnɪəns]   n. 便利
convertible [kənˈvɜːtɪb(ə)l]   n. 折叠敞篷汽车
coupe [kuːp]   n. 小轿车；双座四轮轿式马车
coverage [ˈkʌvərɪdʒ]   n. 范围，规模；保险项目
crack [kræk]   vt. 破裂，打开；(使……)开裂   vi. 断裂，折断
crawler [ˈkrɔːlə]   n. 爬行者；履带牵引装置
crossbar [ˈkrɒsbɑː]   n. 横梁
crossover [ˈkrɒsəʊvə]   n. 交叉；天桥；跨界车
cruise [kruːz]   vi. 巡航，巡游；漫游   vt. 巡航   n. 巡航
crusader [kruːˈseɪdə]   n. 改革者
curb [kɜːb]   n. 抑制   vt. 控制
curve [kɜːv]   n. 弧线，曲线   vt. 使弯曲，使成曲线、弧形
customize [ˈkʌstəˌmaɪz]   vt. 定制，定做，按规格改制
cylinder [ˈsɪlɪndə]   n. 圆筒；气缸

D

Danish ['deɪnɪʃ]　*adj.* 丹麦的；丹麦人的
dashboard ['dæʃbɔːd]　*n.* （汽车等的）仪表板
data ['deɪtə]　*n.* 数据（datum 的复数）；资料
dazzle ['dæz(ə)l]　*n.* 耀眼的光；灿烂　*vt.* 使……目眩；使……眼花
dealer ['diːlə(r)]　*n.* 经销商
dealership ['diːləʃɪp]　*n.* 代理商；代理权，经销权
decoration [dekə'reɪʃ(ə)n]　*n.* 装饰，装潢；装饰品
deductible [dɪ'dʌktəbl]　*adj.* 可扣除的
defect ['diːfekt]　*n.* 瑕疵，毛病；缺点　*vi.* 叛逃；背叛
demo ['deməʊ]　*n.* 演示；样本唱片；示威；民主党员
demonstration [demən'streɪʃ(ə)n]　*n.* 示范；证明
departure [dɪ'pɑːtʃə]　*n.* 离开；出发；违背
depict [dɪ'pɪkt]　*vt.* 描述；描画
deploy [dɪ'plɔɪ]　*vt. & vi.* 施展；有效地利用
deposit [dɪ'pɒzɪt]　*n.* 存款；押金；订金；保证金
descending [dɪ'sendɪŋ]　*adj.* 下降的；下行的
description [dɪ'skrɪpʃ(ə)n]　*n.* 描述，描写
deselect [diːsɪ'lekt]　*vt.* 取消选定
detailed ['diːteɪld]　*adj.* 详细的，精细的；复杂的，详尽的　*v.* 详细说明（detail 的过去分词）
detect [dɪ'tekt]　*vt.* 察觉；发现；探测
diagonal [daɪ'æg(ə)n(ə)l]　*adj.* 斜的；对角线的；斜纹的
diesel ['diːz(ə)l]　*n.* 柴油机；柴油
differential [ˌdɪfə'renʃ(ə)l]　*n.* 微分；差别；差速器
dimension [dɪ'menʃ(ə)n]　*n.* 尺寸
dimming ['dɪmɪŋ]　*n.* 调光；变暗
disarm [dɪs'ɑːm]　*vt.* 解除武装；缓和
discontinue [ˌdɪskən'tɪnjuː]　*v.* 停止；使中止
discount ['dɪskaʊnt]　*n.* 折扣
disengage [ˌdɪsɪn'geɪdʒ]　*vt.* 使脱离；解开；解除
dispersion [dɪ'spɜːʃ(ə)n]　*n.* 散布；驱散
display [dɪ'spleɪ]　*n.* 显示；炫耀；显示器
dissipation [ˌdɪsɪ'peɪʃ(ə)n]　*n.* 浪费；消散；[物] 损耗
distraction [dɪ'strækʃ(ə)n]　*n.* 注意力分散；消遣
distribution [ˌdɪstrɪ'bjuːʃ(ə)n]　*n.* 分布；分配
domestic [də'mestɪk]　*adj.* 国内的
drivability [ˌdraɪvə'bɪləti]　*n.* 驾驶性能；操纵灵活性
driveline ['draɪvlaɪn]　*n.* 动力传动系统

dynamic [daɪ'næmɪk]　*adj.* 动态的；动力的；动力学的

E

eagle ['iːg(ə)l]　*n.* 鹰；鹰状标饰
earth-shaking　*adj.* 惊天动地的
elegantly ['eləgəntlɪ]　*adv.* 优美地，雅致地，高雅地
embody [ɪm'bɒdɪ; em-]　*vt.* 体现，使具体化；具体表达
emerge [ɪ'mɜːdʒ]　*vi.* 浮现；摆脱；暴露
emergency [i'mɜːdʒənsi]　*n.* 紧急情况，突发事件，非常时刻　*adj.* 紧急的，应急的
emission [ɪ'mɪʃ(ə)n]　*n.* （光、热等的）发射，散发；喷射
emissions [ɪ'mɪʃnz]　*n.* 排放物（emission 的名词复数），散发物（尤指气体）
emphasize ['emfəsaɪz]　*vt.* 强调，着重
encompass [ɪn'kʌmpəs; en-]　*vt.* 包含；包围，环绕；完成
encounter [ɪn'kaʊntə; en-]　*vt.* 遭遇，邂逅；遇到
energetic [ˌenə'dʒetɪk]　*adj.* 精力充沛的；积极的；有力的
engine ['endʒɪn]　*n.* 引擎，发动机
entertainment [entə'teɪnm(ə)nt]　*n.* 娱乐；消遣
equity ['ekwɪtɪ]　*n.* 公平，公正
evolution [ˌiːvə'luːʃ(ə)n; 'ev-]　*n.* 演变；进化论；进展
evolve [ɪ'vɒlv]　*v.* 发展，进化
exceed [ɪk'siːd]　*vt.* 超过；胜过　*vi.* 超过其他
exclusive [ɪk'skluːsɪv; ek-]　*adj.* 独有的；排外的；专一的
executive [ig'zekjutiv]　*n.* 总经理，行政部门　*adj.* 执行的，管理的，政府部门的
explicit [ɪk'splɪsɪt; ek-]　*adj.* 明确的；清楚的；直率的；详述的
exterior [ɪk'stɪərɪə; ek-]　*adj.* 外部的；表面的　*n.* 外部；表面；外貌
extinguish [ɪk'stɪŋgwɪʃ; ek-]　*vt.* 熄灭；压制；偿清
extra ['ekstrə]　*adj.* 额外的

F

facility [fə'sɪlətɪ]　*n.* 设施；设备
factual ['fæktʃuəl]　*adj.* 事实的；真实的
fatigue [fə'tiːg]　*n.* 疲劳，疲乏　*vt.* 使疲劳，使疲乏　*vi.* 疲劳
feature ['fiːtʃə(r)]　*n.* 特征，特点；容貌，面貌　*vt.* 使有特色　*vi.* 起主要作用
fence [fens]　*n.* 围墙；栅栏，篱笆；剑术　*vt.* 用篱笆围住
fender ['fendə(r)]　*n.* （车辆的）挡泥板；防御物
filtration [fɪl'treɪʃn]　*n.* 过滤；筛选
foundation [faʊn'deɪʃ(ə)n]　*n.* 基础；地基；基金会；根据；创立
frame [freɪm]　*n.* 框架；结构
franchise ['fræntʃaɪz]　*n.* 特许权；选举权；参政权；经销权　*vt.* 赋予特权

frequently ['fri:kw(ə)ntlɪ]　*adv.* 频繁地，经常地；时常，屡次

G

gear [gɪə]　*n.* 齿轮；装置，工具；传动装置
gearshift ['gɪə,ʃɪft]　*n.* 变速杆；换挡杆
genomotive [dʒɪnəʊ'məʊtɪv]　*n.* 隐性动机
gradient ['greɪdɪənt]　*n.*［数］［物］梯度；坡度；倾斜度
gravity ['grævɪtɪ]　*n.* 重力，地心引力
grill [grɪl]　*n.* 烤架，铁格子；进气格栅
grille [grɪl]　*n.* 格栅
guise [gaɪz]　*vt.* 使化装　*vi.* 伪装
gummy ['gʌmi]　*adj.* 黏性的；胶粘的

H

hairline ['heəlaɪn]　*n.* 极细的织物
hatchback ['hætʃbæk]　*n.* 掀背式汽车
hazard ['hæzəd]　*vt.* 冒险；使遭受危险　*n.* 危险；冒险的事
headlamp ['hedlæmp]　*n.* 前照灯
heater ['hi:tə(r)]　*n.* 加热器
highlighted ['haɪlaɪtɪd]　*adj.* 突出的
hip [hɪp]　*n.* 臀部
hood [hʊd]　*n.* 机舱盖
hose [həʊz]　*n.* 软管

I

identification [aɪ,dentɪfɪ'keɪʃ(ə)n]　*n.* 鉴定，识别；认同；身份证明
identify [aɪ'dentɪfaɪ]　*vt.* 确定；鉴定；识别，辨认出
idle ['aɪd(ə)l]　*v.* 空转；怠速
illuminate [ɪ'l(j)u:mɪneɪt]　*vt.* 说明；照亮；用灯装饰　*vi.* 照亮
illustration [ɪlə'streɪʃ(ə)n]　*n.* 说明，插图；例证；图解
immobilizer [ɪ'məʊbəlaɪzə]　*n.* 防盗控制系统
implicit [ɪm'plɪsɪt]　*adj.* 含蓄的；暗示的；盲从的
impression [ɪm'preʃ(ə)n]　*n.* 印象；效果，影响；压痕，印记；感想
impressive [ɪm'presɪv]　*adj.* 给人印象深刻的，感人的，引人注目的，可观的
inadvertently [,ɪnəd'vɜ:t(ə)ntlɪ]　*adj.* 非故意地，无心地
incredibly [ɪn'kredəbl]　*adv.* 难以置信地，很，极为
independent [,ɪndɪ'pendənt]　*adj.* 独立的；单独的
indicator ['ɪndɪkeɪtə]　*n.* 指示器［计］指示符；压力计
initial [ɪ'nɪʃəl]　*adj.* 最初的；字首的

innovate ['ɪnəveɪt]　*vt.* 改变；创立；创始
innovation [ˌɪnə'veɪʃn]　*n.* 创新，革新；新方法
innovative ['ɪnəuveitiv]　*adj.* 革新的，创新的，富有革新精神的
inspect [ɪn'spekt]　*vt.* 视察；检查，检验　*vi.* 进行检查；进行视察
inspection [ɪn'spekʃn]　*n.* 检验；检查；视察；检阅
inspire [ɪn'spaɪə]　*vt.* 激发；鼓舞；启示
instantaneous [ˌɪnstən'teinjəs]　*adj.* 瞬间的，即刻的
insurance [ɪn'ʃʊər(ə)ns]　*n.* 保险；保险费
integral ['ɪntɪgrəl]　*adj.* 积分的；完整的
integrate ['ɪntɪgreɪt]　*vt.* 使……完整；使……成整体
intelligence [ɪn'telɪdʒ(ə)ns]　*n.* 智力
intelligent [ɪn'telɪdʒ(ə)nt]　*adj.* 智能的；聪明的
intense [ɪn'tens]　*adj.* 强烈的
interior [ɪn'tɪərɪə(r)]　*n.* 内部　*adj.* 内部的
interlock [ɪntə'lɒk]　*v.* [计] 互锁；连锁
intermittent [ɪntə'mɪt(ə)nt]　*adj.* 间歇的；断断续续的
interpret [ɪn'tɜːprɪt]　*vt.* 说明；口译
interurban [ˌɪntə'ɜːbən]　*n.* 市间铁路
interval ['ɪntəv(ə)l]　*n.* 间隔；间距；幕间休息
invention [ɪn'venʃ(ə)n]　*n.* 发明

J

jack [dʒæk]　*n.* 千斤顶，起重器　*vt.* 提高，增加；用千斤顶顶起；抬起
jam [dʒæm]　*vt.* 使堵塞；挤进，使塞满
joint [dʒɔɪnt]　*n.* 关节；接缝；接合处，接合点
joystick ['dʒɔɪstɪk]　*n.* 操纵杆，[机] 控制杆

K

kidney ['kɪdnɪ]　*n.* 肾，肾脏
knob [nɒb]　*n.* 把手；瘤；球形突出物

L

laminate ['læmɪneɪt]　*vt.* 将锻压成薄片；分成薄片
lane [leɪn]　*n.* 小巷；[航] [水运] 航线；车道
latch [lætʃ]　*n.* 门闩；弹簧锁　*vt. & vi.* 闩上；用碰锁锁上（门等）
lawsuit ['lɔːsuːt]　*n.* 诉讼；诉讼案件
leak [liːk]　*vi.* 漏出；透露；（指消息、秘密等）泄密；漏电，漏水　*vt.* 使泄露　*n.* 泄漏，漏洞；裂缝；漏出物
legend ['ledʒ(ə)nd]　*n.* 传奇

liability [ˌlaɪə'bɪlətɪ] *n.* 责任；债务；倾向
lid [lɪd] *n.* 盖子
liftgate ['lɪftgeɪt] *n.* 提升式门
limousine ['lɪməziːn; ˌlɪmə'ziːn] *n.* 豪华轿车；大型豪华轿车
lineup ['laɪnˌʌp] *n.* 行列，人（或物）的列队
literal ['lɪt(ə)r(ə)l] *adj.* 文字的
loading ['ləʊdɪŋ] *n.* 装载；装货；装载的货 *vt.* 装载，装填
loan [ləʊn] *n.* 贷款；借款
lumbar ['lʌmbə] *adj.* 腰部 *n.* 腰动（静）脉，腰神经，腰椎
luxury ['lʌkʃ(ə)rɪ] *n.* 奢侈，奢华；奢侈品；享受 *adj.* 奢侈的

M

magnificent [mæg'nɪfɪs(ə)nt] *adj.* 高尚的；壮丽的；华丽的；宏伟的
maintain [meɪn'teɪn] *vt.* 维持；继续；维修
maintenance ['meɪnt(ə)nəns; -tɪn-] *n.* 保养，维护，维修
management ['mænɪdʒm(ə)nt] *n.* 管理
maneuverability [məˌnuːvərə'bɪlɪtɪ] *n.* 可操作性，机动性，可控性
manual ['mænjʊ(ə)l] *adj.* 手工的；体力的 *n.* 手册，指南
manufacturer [ˌmænjʊ'fæktʃ(ə)rə(r)] *n.* 制造商
mask [mɑːsk] *n.* 面具 *vt.* 掩饰；戴面具 *vi.* 戴面具，掩饰
mechanic [mə'kænɪk] *n.* 技工，机修工
mechanical [mɪ'kænɪk(ə)l] *adj.* 机械的；力学的；手工操作的
merger ['mɜːdʒə] *n.* （企业等的）合并；并购
metallic [mɪ'tælɪk] *adj.* 金属的，含金属的
mileage ['maɪlɪdʒ] *n.* 英里数，里程；利润；（按英里计算的）运费
milestone ['maɪlstəʊn] *n.* 里程碑，划时代的事件
minimal ['mɪnɪm(ə)l] *adj.* 最低的；最小限度的
misalign ['mɪsəlaɪn] *n.* 不重合，位移
misting [mɪstɪŋ] *n.* 飞墨 *v.* 使模糊；下雾（mist 的 ing 形式）
modernity [mə'dɜːnɪtɪ] *n.* 现代性；现代的东西
moisture ['mɔɪstʃə] *n.* 水分；湿度；潮湿
monitor ['mɒnɪtə] *n.* 监视器；监听器；监控器 *vt.* 监控
motorist ['məʊtərɪst] *n.* 汽车驾驶员；乘汽车旅行的人
mudguard ['mʌdgɑːd] *n.* 挡泥板，汽车的挡泥板
multifunction [ˌmʌltɪ'fʌŋkʃən] *n.* 多功能
multipurpose [mʌltɪ'pɜːpəs] *adj.* 多目标的；多种用途的

N

nag [næg] *vt.* 不断找碴，抱怨，困扰，折磨 *vi.* 叱责，抱怨，困扰，焦虑
navigation [nævɪ'geɪʃ(ə)n] *n.* 航行；航海

negotiation [nɪgəʊʃɪ'eɪʃ(ə)n]　　n. 谈判；转让
neutral ['njuːtr(ə)l]　　adj. 中立的，中性的　　n. 空挡
nozzle ['nɒz(ə)l]　　n. 喷嘴；管口；鼻

O

occupant ['ɒkjʊp(ə)nt]　　n. 居住者；占有者
odometer [əʊ'dɒmɪtə(r)]　　n. 里程计
option ['ɒpʃ(ə)n]　　n. 选项；选择权；买卖的特权
optional ['ɒpʃ(ə)n(ə)l]　　adj. 可选择的，随意的
outlook ['aʊtlʊk]　　n. 展望；观点
output ['aʊtpʊt]　　n. 输出，输出量
oval ['əʊv(ə)l]　　adj. 椭圆的　　n. 椭圆形
overlook [ˌəʊvə'lʊkvt]　　v. 远眺；忽略；瞭望；检查　　n. 从高处眺望到的景色；忽视，忽略
override [əʊvə'raɪd]　　vt. 推翻；不顾；践踏
overspray ['əʊvəspreɪ]　　n. 不黏附喷涂物，超范围的喷涂
overtake [əʊvə'teɪk]　　vt. 赶上；压倒；突然来袭　　vi. 超车
overturn [əʊvə'tɜːn]　　v. 推翻；倾覆；破坏

P

panoramic [ˌpænə'ræmɪk]　　adj. 全景的
parallel ['pærəlel]　　n. 平行线；对比　　v. 使……与……平行　　adj. 平行的；类似的，相同的
pedal ['pedl]　　n. 踏板
pedestrian [pə'destriən]　　n. 行人；步行者　　adj. 徒步的；平淡无奇的
pelvis ['pelvɪs]　　n. 骨盆
penetration [penɪ'treɪʃ(ə)n]　　n. 渗透；突破；侵入；洞察力
performance [pə'fɔːm(ə)ns]　　n. 性能；绩效；表演；执行
permissible [pə'mɪsɪb(ə)l]　　adj. 可允许的；获得准许的
perplex [pə'pleks]　　vt. 使困惑，使为难；使复杂化
petrol ['petrəl]　　n. 汽油
phenomotive [fiːnəʊ'məʊtɪv]　　n. 显性动机
piston ['pɪst(ə)n]　　n. 活塞
platform ['plætfɔːm]　　n. 台，站台，平台
potential [pə'tenʃl]　　n. 潜能；可能性　　adj. 潜在的；可能的；势的
precise [prɪ'saɪs]　　adj. 精确的；明确的
preference ['pref(ə)r(ə)ns]　　n. 偏爱，倾向
premium ['priːmiəm]　　n. 保险费；额外费用；附加费　　adj. 优质的；高昂的
pretension [prɪ'tenʃ(ə)n]　　n. 自负；要求；主张
previously ['priːvɪəslɪ]　　adv. 以前；事先
priority [praɪ'ɒrəti]　　n. 优先，优先权；优先考虑的事

privacy ['prɪvəsɪ]　　*n.* 隐私；秘密
procedure [prə'siːdʒə]　　*n.* 程序，手续；步骤
professionalism [prə'feʃ(ə)n(ə)lɪz(ə)m]　　*n.* 专业主义；专家的地位；特性或方法
profound [prə'faʊnd]　　*adj.* 深厚的；意义深远的；渊博的
progressive [prə'gresɪv]　　*adj.* 进步的；先进的
prominent ['prɒmɪnənt]　　*adj.* 突出的，显著的
property ['prɒpətɪ]　　*n.* 特性，属性；财产，地产；所有权
prospect ['prɒspekt]　　*n.* 前途；预期
prospective [prə'spektɪv]　　*adj.* 未来的；预期的　　*n.* 预期；展望
prototype ['prəʊtətaɪp]　　*n.* 原型；标准，模范
protrude [prə'truːd]　　*vt.* 使突出，使伸出
puddle ['pʌd(ə)l]　　*n.* 水坑，泥潭；胶土（由黏土与水和成，不透水）
pullman ['pʊlmən]　　*n.* 卧车
purchase ['pɜːtʃəs]　　*n.* 购买　　*vt.* 购买
pursuit [pə'sjuːt]　　*n.* 追赶，追求

Q

quote [kwot]　　*vt.* 引用，引证

R

rack [ræk]　　*n.* ［机］齿条；行李架
radar ['reɪdɑː]　　*n.* 雷达，无线电探测器
radial ['reɪdɪəl]　　*adj.* 径向的；辐射状的；放射式的；星形的　　*n.* 子午线轮胎
radiator ['reɪdieɪtə(r)]　　*n.* 散热器；（汽车引擎的）冷却器
rancid ['rænsɪd]　　*adj.*（指含有油脂食物）因变质而有陈腐味道或气味的，（指气味或味道）如陈腐脂肪味的
rapidly ['ræpɪdlɪ]　　*adv.* 迅速地；很快地；立即
ratio ['reɪʃɪəʊ]　　*n.* 比率，比例
reap [riːp]　　*vt.* 收获，获得；收割
rear [rɪə]　　*adj.* 后方的；后面的；背面的
reception [rɪ'sepʃ(ə)n]　　*n.* 接待；接收；招待会
recline [rɪ'klaɪn]　　*vi.* 靠；依赖；斜倚　　*vt.* 使躺下；使斜倚
recommend [rekə'mend]　　*vt.* 推荐，介绍；劝告；使受欢迎；托付　　*vi.* 推荐；建议
recreation [ˌrekrɪ'eɪʃ(ə)n]　　*n.* 娱乐；消遣；休养
registration [redʒɪ'streɪʃ(ə)n]　　*n.* 登记；注册；挂号
rehabilitation [ˌriːəˌbɪlɪ'teɪʃn]　　*n.* 修复；复兴；复职；恢复名誉
reimburse [ˌriːɪm'bɜːs]　　*vt.* 偿还，付还，归还
relevant ['relɪv(ə)nt]　　*adj.* 相关的；有重大关系的；目的明确的
remarkably [rɪ'mɑːkəblɪ]　　*adv.* 引人注目地，明显地，非常地

reminder [rɪ'maɪndə]　n. 暗示；提醒的人/物；催单
rental ['rentl]　n. 租费，租金额
requirement [rɪ'kwaɪəm(ə)nt]　n. 要求；必要条件；必需品
resemble [rɪ'zemb(ə)l]　vt. 类似，像
resolution [rezə'luːʃ(ə)n]　n. ［物］分辨率；决议
resonance ['rez(ə)nəns]　n. ［力］共振；共鸣；反响
responsibility [rɪˌspɒnsɪ'bɪlɪtɪ]　n. 责任，职责；义务
responsive [rɪ'spɒnsɪv]　adj. 应答的，响应的，反应灵敏的，共鸣的，易反应的
restraint [rɪ'streɪnt]　n. 抑制，克制；约束
resume [rɪ'zjuːm]　vt. 重新开始，继续；恢复，重新占用
retail ['riːteɪl]　n. 零售　vt. 零售；零卖　adj. 零售的　adv. 以零售方式
retailer ['riːteɪlə(r)]　n. 零售商，零售店
reveal [rɪ'viːl]　vt. 显示；透露；揭露；泄露
reverse [rɪ'vɜːs]　n. 背面；相反；倒退
revolution [revə'luːʃ(ə)n]　n. 革命
rhythm ['rɪð(ə)m]　n. 节奏；韵律
rim [rɪm]　n. 轮辋
roof [ruːf]　n. 屋顶；顶部；车顶
rotation [rəʊ'teɪʃn]　n. 旋转，转动；轮流，循环
rub [rʌb]　vt. 擦；摩擦　n. 摩擦；障碍；磨损处
rust [rʌst]　n. 锈；生锈

S

saloon [sə'luːn]　n. 大厅；展览场；公共大厅；大会客室；轿车
salvage ['sælvɪdʒ]　v.（从火灾、海难等中）抢救（某物）（salvage 的过去式和过去分词）；回收利用（某物）
scale [skeɪl]　n. 规模；比例；刻度
script [skrɪpt]　n. 脚本；手迹
sedan [sɪ'dæn]　n.〈美语〉小轿车
segment ['segmənt]　n. 部分，段落，环节
sensor ['sensə]　n. 传感器
shareholder ['ʃeəhəʊldə]　n. 股东；股票持有人
showroom ['ʃəʊruːm; -rʊm]　n. 陈列室；样品间
signature ['sɪgnɪtʃə]　n. 签名，署名，识别标志
signify ['sɪgnɪfaɪ]　vt. 表示；意味；预示
simultaneously [ˌsɪml'teɪnɪəslɪ]　adv. 同时地
slack [slæk]　adj. 松弛的；疏忽的；不流畅的　vi. 松懈；减弱
slam [slæm]　vt. & vi. 砰地关上；猛力抨击
slung [slʌŋ]　v. 投掷，悬挂
socket ['sɒkɪt]　n. 插座；窝，穴

sole [səʊl]　　*adj.* 单独的，唯一的，专有的

solution [sə'luːʃ(ə)n]　　*n.* 解决方案；溶液；溶解

sonar ['səʊnɑː]　　*n.* 声呐；声波定位仪

sophisticate [sə'fɪstɪkeɪt]　　*n.* 久经世故的人；精通者

spacious ['speɪʃəs]　　*adj.* 宽敞的，广阔的

specialize ['speʃəlaɪz]　　*vi.* 专门从事；详细说明　　*vt.* 使专门化

specialized ['speʃə'laɪzd]　　*adj.* 专业的；专门的

specification [ˌspesɪfɪ'keɪʃ(ə)n]　　*n.* 规格，说明书；详述

speedometer [spiː'dɒmɪtə]　　*n.* 速度计；里程计

spherical ['sferɪk(ə)l]　　*adj.* 球形的，球面的

splash [splæʃ]　　*vt.* 使（液体）溅起　　*vi.*（指液体）溅落　　*n.*（光、色等的）斑点；溅泼声；溅上的斑点；溅泼的量

spoiler ['spɒɪlə]　　*n.* 扰流板

spoke [spəʊk]　　*n.*（车轮的）辐条；轮辐

spread [spred]　　*vt.* 传播，散布；展开；伸展；铺开

spree [spriː]　　*n.* 欢闹，狂欢　　*vi.* 狂欢，狂饮

stability [stə'bɪlɪtɪ]　　*n.* 稳定性；坚定

stain [steɪn]　　*vi.* 弄脏；污染；被玷污　　*vt.* 玷污，染污；败坏（名声）；给……染色　　*n.* 污点；瑕疵；着色剂

stall [stɔːl]　　*n.* 货摊　　*vi.* 停止，停转

stance [stɑːns; stæns]　　*n.* 立场；姿态；位置

static ['stætɪk]　　*adj.* 静止的，不变的，静电的，[物] 静力的　　*n.* 静电

stereo ['sterɪəʊ; 'stɪərɪəʊ]　　*n.* 立体声；立体声系统

sticker ['stɪkə(r)]　　*n.* 张贴物　　*vt.* 给……贴上标签价　　*adj.* 汽车价目标签

straightforward [streɪt'fɔːwəd]　　*adj.* 简单的；坦率的；明确的；径直的

stretch [stretʃ]　　*vt.* 伸展，张开；（大量地）使用，消耗（金钱、时间）

stroke [strəʊk]　　*n.* 冲程

structure ['strʌktʃə]　　*n.* 结构；构造

strut [strʌt]　　*n.* 支柱

stumbling ['stʌmblɪŋ]　　*adj.* 障碍的

stunning ['stʌnɪŋ]　　*adj.* 极好的；震耳欲聋的

submit [səb'mɪt]　　*vi.* 顺从，服从；忍受　　*vt.* 使服从，使顺从；提交，呈送

subsequent ['sʌbsɪkw(ə)nt]　　*adj.* 后来的，随后的

subsidiary [səb'sɪdɪərɪ]　　*adj.* 附属的；辅助的　　*n.* 子公司；辅助者

substantial [səb'stænʃl]　　*adj.* 大量的；结实的，牢固的；重大的　　*n.* 本质

sunroof ['sʌnruːf]　　*n.* 汽车顶上可开启的遮阳篷顶；天窗

sunshade ['sʌnʃeɪd]　　*n.* 遮阳伞；天棚

superimposition [ˌsʊpərˌɪmpə'zɪʃn]　　*n.* 添上

surround [sə'raʊnd]　　*n.* 围绕物

survive [sə'vaɪv]   *vt.* 幸存；生还；幸免
suspension [sə'spenʃ(ə)n]   *n.* 悬架
swallow ['swɒləʊ]   *vt.* 忍受；吞没
sweeper ['swiːpə]   *n.* 清扫器；清洁车
symbolize ['sɪmbəlaɪz]   *vt.* 象征；用符号表现

T

tachometer [tæ'kɒmɪtə]   *n.* 转速计；流速计
tailgate ['teɪlgeɪt]   *n.* 后挡板
tailor ['teɪlə]   *vt.* 剪裁；使合适
tailpipe ['teɪlpaɪp]   *n.* 排气管
tame [teɪm]   *adj.* 驯服的，平淡的，无精打采的 v.驯服，抑制
tamper ['tæmpə(r)]   *vt.* 窜改 *vi.* 篡改；（用不正当手段）影响，干预；瞎摆弄；贿赂 *n.* 夯，夯具；捣乱者；填塞者；反射器
telltale ['tel,teɪl]   *adj.* （机械装置）起监督作用的，能说明问题的
temporary ['temp(ə)rərɪ]   *adj.* 暂时的，临时的
tensile ['tensaɪl]   *adj.* ［力］拉力的；可伸长的
terrain [tə'reɪn]   *n.* ［地理］地形，地势；领域
tether ['teðə]   *n.* 范围；系链；拴绳
theory ['θɪərɪ]   *n.* 理论，原理；学说；推测
thorax ['θɔːræks]   *n.* ［解剖］胸，胸膛；胸腔
thrill [θril]   *vt.* 使激动，使陶醉，使颤动 *vi.* 颤动，颤动，战栗，振动
tilt [tɪlt]   *vi.* 倾斜；翘起 *vt.* 使倾斜；使翘起 *n.* 倾斜
tiptoe ['tɪptəʊ]   *n.* 脚尖；趾尖
tornado [tɔː'neɪdəʊ]   *n.* 龙卷风
torque [tɔːk]   *n.* 转矩，［力］扭矩
track [træk]   *n.* 轨道；足迹
trademark ['treɪdmɑːk]   *n.* 商标
trailer ['treɪlə]   *n.* 拖车
transceiver [træn'siːvə]   *n.* ［通信］收发器
transmission [træns'mɪʃn]   *n.* 传动装置，变速器
transmitter [trænz'mɪtə]   *n.* ［电讯］发射机，［通信］发报机
transportation [,trænspɔː'teɪʃn]   *n.* 运送，运输；运输系统；运输工具
treatment ['triːtmənt]   *n.* 处理；治疗，疗法；待遇，对待
triangle ['traɪæŋg(ə)l]   *n.* 三角（形）
triangular [traɪ'æŋgjʊlə]   *adj.* 三角的，［数］三角形的
trim [trɪm]   *vt.* 修剪；整理 *n.* 修剪；整齐
trolley ['trɒlɪ]   *n.* 手推车；（美）有轨电车（等于 trolley car）；（英）无轨电车（等于 trolleybus）；空中吊运车

trunk [trʌŋk]　　n. 树干；（汽车车尾的）行李箱
turbine ['tɜ:baɪn; -ɪn]　　n. ［动力］涡轮
turbocharger ['tɜ:bəʊtʃɑ:dʒə]　　n. 涡轮增压器
tyre ['taɪə]　　n. 轮胎

U

ultimate ['ʌltɪmɪt]　　adj. 最后的，极限的，首要的，最大的　　n. 终极，顶点，基本原理
underinsured [,ʌndərɪn'ʃʊəd]　　adj. 保险（额）不足的
uneven [ʌn'i:vn]　　adj. 不平坦的，凹凸不平的；不一律的，参差不齐的
uninsured [,ʌnɪn'ʃʊəd]　　adj. 未保险的
unladen [ʌn'leɪdən]　　adj. 未装载的；空载
unveiled [,ʌn'veɪld]　　adj. 裸露的；公布于众的
upholstery [ʌp'həʊlstərɪ]　　n. 家具装饰业；室内装饰品
urban ['ɜ:b(ə)n]　　adj. 城市的；住在都市的
utility [ju:'tɪləti]　　adj. 实用的；通用的；有多种用途的
utmost ['ʌtməʊst]　　n. 极限；最大可能　　adj. 极度的；最远的

V

valve [vælv]　　n. 阀；气门
vandalism ['vændəlɪzəm]　　n. 故意破坏，捣毁
vehicle ['vi:əkl]　　n. ［车辆］车辆；工具；交通工具
velour [və'lʊə]　　n. 丝绒；天鹅绒；毡
vent [vent]　　n. 出口；通风孔　　vt. 放出……；给……开孔
ventilation [,ventɪ'leɪʃ(ə)n]　　n. 通风设备；空气流通
versatile ['vɜ:sətaɪl]　　adj. 通用的，万能的
versatility [,vɜ:sə'tɪləti:]　　n. 多功能性；用途广泛
version ['vɜ:ʃ(ə)n]　　n. 版本；译文
vibration [vaɪ'breɪʃ(ə)n]　　n. 振动
vigorous ['vɪg(ə)rəs]　　adj. 有力的；精力充沛的
viper ['vaɪpə]　　n. 毒蛇；毒如蛇蝎的人，阴险的人
visibility [vɪzɪ'bɪlɪtɪ]　　n. 能见度，可见性
vision ['vɪʒ(ə)n]　　n. 视力；眼力；想象力
visor ['vaɪzə]　　n. 遮阳板
visual ['vɪʒjʊəl]　　adj. 视觉的，视力的；栩栩如生的
Volkswagen ['fɔ:lks,vɑ:gən]　　大众汽车

W

wagon ['wæg(ə)n]　　n. 货车，四轮马车
waistline ['weɪst,laɪn]　　n. 腰线

warranty ['wɒrənti]   *n.* 保证，担保；授权，批准
wedge [wedʒ]   *n.* 楔形物
weld [weld]   *vt. & vi.* 焊接；使紧密结合   *n.* 焊接点
wheelbase ['wiːlbeɪs]   *n.* 轴距（前后车轮轴之距离）
windshield ['wɪn(d)ʃiːld]   *n.* 挡风玻璃
wiper ['waɪpə(r)]   *n.* 雨刷

X

Xenon ['zenɒn; 'ziː-]   *n.* ［化学］氙（稀有气体元素）

Phrases

A

accelerator pedal 油门踏板
active headrest 主动头枕
air conditioner 空调
air suspension 空气悬架
anti-glare function 防炫目功能
approach angle 接近角
auto insurance 汽车保险
automatic transmission 自动变速器

B

back fender 后翼子板
backup light 倒车灯
be flush with 与……齐平，与……同高度
be nagged by 被唠叨
be selected up to 被选中了
blade set key 桨叶固定键
bodily injury liability 身体伤害责任
body panel 车身板
brake light 刹车灯
brake pedal 制动踏板
break over angle 跨越角
business card 名片

C

car insurance 汽车保险
car rental agency 汽车租赁代理
carbon dioxide 二氧化碳
cargo room 货舱
cargo volume 载运量
cast aluminum alloy wheels 铸造铝合金车轮
central locking 中控锁

child safety seat　儿童安全座椅
chrome-plated radiator grille frame　镀铬进气格栅
cigar lighter　点烟器
coil spring　螺旋弹簧
cold drink　冷饮
combined liter　综合油耗
commercial vehicle　商用车
commit to　承诺
compact car　紧凑型轿车
compact executive car　紧凑型行政汽车
compact hatchback　紧凑型掀背车
concentrate on　集中
concept car　概念车

D

departure angle　离去角
diesel engine　柴油发动机
direct frontal crash　直接的正面碰撞
disc brake　盘式制动器
door handle　门把手
door post　门柱
driver assistance system　车辆辅助驾驶系统
driver knee airbag　驾驶员膝部安全气囊
driver's license　驾驶执照
dual-clutch transmission　双离合器变速器

E

electric parking brake　电动停车制动
emission rating　排放评级
engine capacity　发动机排量
ethyl alcohol　乙醇
executive car　公务轿车
extended service plan　扩展服务计划
exterior lighting　室外照明；外部照明

F

facia ['feɪʃə]　*n.*（英）仪表板
financial loss　财物损失
financing option　融资选择

first-aid kit　急救箱
floor mat　地板垫
fog lamp　雾灯，雾天行车灯
four-point reversing radar　四点式驻车雷达
four-wheel drive　四轮驱动
front fender　前翼子板
front passenger　副驾驶
fuel capacity　燃油箱容积
fuel consumption　燃油消耗
fuel economy　燃油经济性
fuel tank　油箱
full-function key　全功能钥匙
funeral expense　丧葬费

G

gas engine　燃气发动机
gear lever　换挡杆
gear ratio　齿轮传动比
ground clearance　离地间隙
guise as　伪装成
gummy soot　树胶烟灰

H

hail damage　冰雹破坏
headlight cleaner　大灯清洗器
high beam　远光
hit-and-run driver　肇事逃逸司机
hook up　以钩勾住
hub cap　轮毂盖
hydraulic brake booster　液压制动助力器

I

iceberg theory　冰山理论
ignition system　点火系统
indicator light　指示灯
innovative comfort access system　创新舒适进入系统
instrument cluster　仪表板
instrument pack　仪表板
insurance company　保险公司

interior mirror   后视镜（内）

K

key blade   钥匙折叶
keyless go   无钥匙启动
kink to   纠结

L

leasing office   租赁办公室
lending institution   贷款机构
let alone   更不必说；听任；不打扰
license plate   车牌
load rating   额定载荷；载重率
low beam   近光
luggage compartment   行李舱

M

map light   阅读灯；航图灯
Max. permissible weight   最大载重
metallic paintwork   金属漆
minor problem   小问题
moon roof   汽车天窗
motor truck   载货汽车
multipurpose passenger car   客货两用汽车
multi-stage   多级

N

navigation system   导航系统

O

off-road   越野车
outside mirror   后视镜（外）
overall height   总高度
overall length   总长度
overall width   总宽度

P

panoramic sunroof   全景天窗
passenger car   乘用车

passive restraint 被动约束
passive safety device 被动安全装置
permitted axle load 前/后轴允许承重
permitted load 允许载量
petrol engine 汽油发动机
plane joystick 飞机操纵杆
potential customer 潜在客户
power lumbar support 腰部支撑
power source 电源
pre-owned 二手的
property damage liability 财产损害赔偿责任
pure electric power 纯电动

Q

quarter window 三角窗

R

racing car 赛车
rack-and-pinion 齿轮齿条式转向
radial ply tire 子午线轮胎
radiator fluid 散热器液
rain sensing windscreen wiper 雨点感应雨刮
rain sensor 雨量传感器
raise/lower switch 提升/下降开关
reactive grounding response 响应路面反馈
rear bumper 后保险杠
rear view mirror 后视镜
rear wheel track 后轮距
regular wage 固定工资
remote control 遥控
remote key 遥控钥匙
rental car company 出租车公司
retail owner 零售商
reverse sensor 倒车雷达
rim diameter 轮辋直径
road condition 路况
road test 道路试验
roller sunblind 卷帘遮阳帘
roof post 中柱

run flat tire　防爆轮胎

S

sales consultant　销售顾问
seat belt　安全带
seat cover　座椅套
seat-cushion airbag　坐垫安全气囊
self supporting run flat　自撑式防爆轮胎
shock absorber　减震器
shopping spree　疯狂购物
short trip　短途旅行
side airbag　侧面安全气囊
side lamp　侧灯，侧面灯
six-position demonstration　六方位绕车
skid plate　滑动保护板
spare tire　备用轮胎
special purpose vehicle　专用汽车
special vehicle　特种汽车
speed rate　速率
splash panel　飞溅板
sportback　掀背轿跑车
sports car　跑车
sports wagon　运动车
stabilizer bar　稳定杆
star safety system　星级安全系统
starter switch　启动器开关
station wagon　旅行轿车
steering column　转向柱
steering wheel　方向盘
stumbling block　绊脚石；障碍
substantial value　实质价值
sun visor　遮阳板

T

tail bumper　后保险杠
tail light　尾灯
tank capacity　油罐容量
technical data　技术参数
terrain response　全地形反馈适应系统

test drive 试驾
tire pressure monitoring system 胎压监测系统
tire width 胎宽
top off 完成
top speed 最大速度
tow hook 拖钩
trade-in service 置换服务
traffic block 交通堵塞
traffic jam 交通堵塞
transfer case 分动器，分动箱；变速箱
transmission fluid 输送流体
triangular warning symbol 三角警示标识
trunk carpeting 行李箱地毯
trunk lid 后备厢盖
turbocharged engine 涡轮增压发动机
turning circle 转弯半径

U

unladen weight 空载质量
used car 二手车

V

vehicle access 车辆通道
voice frequency 音频

W

warning indicator 报警指示器；警示器
welded seam 焊缝
wheel tread 胎面
windshield wiper 风挡雨刮器

References

[1] Lee R. Van Vechten. Understanding Feature—Advantage—Benefit [J]. Selling Power—Success Strategies for Sales Management, 2014 (5).

[2] Erik Eckermann. 从蒸汽机到汽车 [M]. 孙伟，译. 北京：电子工业出版社，2006.

[3] 段昆. 美国的无过失汽车保险 [J]. 保险研究，2001（11）.

[4] 曲金玉，任国军. 汽车文化 [M]. 北京：机械工业出版社，2014.

[5] 肖晓春. 妙语连珠：汽车销售实战情景训练 [M]. 北京：机械工业出版社，2012.

[6] 朱小燕. 汽车销售实务 [M]. 北京：机械工业出版社，2016.

[7] www. audi. com.

[8] www. bmwgroup. com.

[9] www. general monash. edu. au.

[10] www. landrover. com.

[11] www. toyota. com.

[12] 路虎揽胜用户使用手册，2008.